Rosa Luxemburg

A Life for the International

Berg Women's Series

Gertrude Bell	SUSAN GOODMAN
Mme de Staël	RENEE WINEGARTEN
Emily Dickinson	DONNA DICKENSON
Elizabeth Gaskell	TESSA BRODETSKY
Mme de Châtelet	ESTHER EHRMANN
Emily Carr	RUTH GOWERS
George Sand	DONNA DICKENSON
Simone de Beauvoir	RENEE WINEGARTEN
Elizabeth I	SUSAN BASSNETT
Sigrid Undset	MITZI BRUNSDALE
Simone Weil	J. P. LITTLE
Margaret Fuller	DAVID WATSON
Willa Cather	JAMIE AMBROSE

In preparation

Sarah Bernhardt	ELAINE ASTON
Mme de Sévigné	JEANNE A. and WILLIAM T. OJALA
Mary Wollstonecraft	JENNIFER LORCH
Dorothy Sayers	MITZI BRUNSDALE
Annette von Droste-Hülshoff	JOHN GUTHRIE
Else Lasker-Schüler	RUTH SCHWERTFEGER

Rosa Luxemburg

A Life for the International

Richard Abraham

BERG *Oxford / New York / Munich*

Distributed exclusively in the US and Canada by
St Martin's Press, New York

First published in 1989 by
Berg Publishers Limited
Editorial offices:
77 Morrell Avenue, Oxford OX4 1NQ, UK
165 Taber Avenue, Providence, RI 02906, USA
Westermühlstraße 26, 8000 München 5, FRG

British Library Cataloguing in Publication Data

Abraham, Richard, *1941–*
    Rosa Luxemburg – (Berg women's series)
    1. Germany. Marxism. Luxemburg, Rosa,
    1871–1919 – Biographies
    I. Title
    335.4′092′4

    ISBN 0–85496–182–8

Library of Congress Cataloging-in-Publication Data

Abraham, Richard, 1941–
    Rosa Luxemburg : a life for the international / Richard Abraham.
        p.   cm. — (Berg women's series)
    Bibliography: p.
    ISBN 0–85496–182–8 : $22.95 (U.S. : est.)
    1. Luxemburg, Rosa 1871–1919. 2. Women communists—Germany—
Biography. 3. International Socialist Congress—History.
I. Title. II. Series.
HX274.7.L89A63 1989
335.43′092—dc20
[B]   89–31671

Printed in Great Britain by Billing & Sons Ltd., Worcester

Contents

List of Illustrations   viii
Acknowledgements   xi
Introduction   1
1. Contexts   6
    The Murders: 'Bloody Rosa' and the Right 6
    The Unquenchable Flame: 'Luxemburgism' and the
        Left 10
    A Non-Jewish Jew: From Zamość to Zurich 16
2. A Polish Apprenticeship   25
    The Comrades 25
    The Enemies 30
    Journalism: *Sprawa Robotnicza* 38
    The Conquest of Berlin 43
3. The Eagle Soars   48
    'Nothing to do with the Women's Movement' 48
    Bernstein's 'English Spectacles' 57
    French Corruption and Belgian Chivalry 62
    Jeszcze Polska: Poland's Not Finished Yet! 68
4. The Last Two Men   79
    The Happiest Months of Her Life 79
    Kostja, Lulu, Mimi and School 83
    Kautsky's Nervous Breakdown 89
    From Mendelson to Sobelsohn 95
    'Long Live Struggle!' 104
5. Spartacus   114
    Towards the Third International 114
    Rosa's *Contemporary* 121
    The Russian Revolution 128
    'I dared to do it' 132
    Guide to Political Parties and Factions   145
    Chronology   149
    Bibliography   155
    Index   169

Illustrations

Frontispiece
Rosa Luxemburg as a student

Between pages 50 and 51
1. Marcin Kasprzak
2. Julian Marchlewski, c. 1904
3. Leo Jogiches as a student
4. Stanisław Mendelson
5. Clara Zetkin
6. Eduard Bernstein
7. Karl Kautsky
8. Luise Kautsky
9. Rosa Luxemburg, *Self-portrait*, c. 1909
10. Rosa Luxemburg and Kostja Zetkin, c. 1910
11. August Bebel, c. 1900
12. Rosa Luxemburg, prison mug shots, Warsaw, 1906
13. Teachers at the SPD Party School in Berlin in 1909. From left: E. Wurm, F. Mehring, H. Schulz, R. Luxemburg, Stadthagen, H. Cunow, unidentified
14. Rosa Luxemburg addressing workers in Deutz, 1910
15. Karl Liebknecht
16. Paul Levi

Photographs for the frontispiece and illustrations 1, 2, 3, 4, 5, 7, 10, 11, 12, 14 and 15 courtesy of the Central Archive of the Central Committee of the Polish United Workers' Party, Warsaw. Photographs for illustrations 6, 8, 9, 13 and 16 courtesy of the International Institute for Social History, Amsterdam.

Acknowledgements

I am indebted to Miriam Kochan for her encouragement, to John Biggart and Prof. Richard J. Evans (both of the University of East Anglia) for helpful suggestions, to Prof. Giovanna Fiume (University of Palermo) for reading and criticising my draft, and to Wendy Abraham for her forbearance.

Richard Abraham
Battersea, London
June 1988

To the memory of Christina Walshe and Chayana Etzioni Weintrobe, indomitable human beings who admired Rosa

Introduction

For Lenin, Rosa Luxemburg was 'an eagle', whose complete works would 'serve as useful manuals for training many generations of Communists all over the world'. Trotsky, too, was unstinting in his eulogy as he told the Petrograd Soviet of her death: 'Small in height, frail, with a noble cast of face, and beautiful eyes which shone with intelligence, she was striking for the courage of her thought. The Marxist method she mastered completely, as if it were an organ of her body. You could say that Marxism was in her blood.' Rosa Luxemburg was rarely pompous about herself, and as she informed her bosom friend, Luise Kautsky, 'I must have *someone*, who believes me [when I say] that I thresh about in the whirlpool of world history out of duty, but I was really born to herd geese.' Such an engaging combination of irony and hyperbole is not common in the great, and it is hardly surprising that no one has written as well about Rosa Luxemburg as Rosa Luxemburg herself. In her works and letters (still not published in full), she created her own myth, which is itself a serious obstacle to a detached appraisal of her achievements. Yet it was no empty myth. Throughout her life, she sought to comprehend the human condition in all its variety. As she told Sonja Liebknecht, 'Nothing human, and also nothing feminine, is foreign and indifferent to me'. For Rosa Luxemburg, as for Karl Marx, mere understanding was worthless unless it contributed to the transformation of human existence.

Rosa Luxemburg's life may also be viewed as an attempt to achieve what Bruno Bettelheim has called a 'higher integration'. She was born to multiple handicaps, but she grew up believing that to be a cripple, a woman, a Jew and a Pole would not be handicaps in the better world that was dawning and that she had a duty to be happy. Later in life, she would recognize her kinship with Vladimir Korolenko's blind musician who, as she put it, learns to 'see spiritually', 'in so far as he steps out from the egoism of his own inescapable misery, to make himself a loudspeaker for the physical and spiritual misery of all the blind'. There was a

1

darker, more driven, more neurotic aspect to this humane mission, about which Rosa Luxemburg remained for ever reticent, but which has led to the plausible assertion that she despised her own Jewish people. At the age of twelve, she shared the terror of Warsaw's Jewish community during the first major wave of 'pogroms' of the nineteenth century, an ominous portent of what awaited the human race – and all those she personally held dear – should it fail to respond to the liberating visions released by the Enlightenment.

Encouraged to think scientifically by her father and elder brothers, Rosa Luxemburg took full advantage of a Russian educational system that was beginning to offer elite women opportunities for education in mathematics and science which were denied to their counterparts in most of Europe. Growing up in a society of many languages and cultures, she imbibed Polish, Yiddish, German and Russian naturally, and with them the genius of Mickiewicz, Schiller and Tolstoy. Like so many talented Jews of her generation, who helped to interpret Russia to Western Europe and vice versa, she benefited in Western eyes from the new prestige of a Russian culture which had begun to make a contribution to the music, art and literature of the world as distinguished as that of her richer western neighbours. Western interest in Russian political ideas had followed, as the anarchist Mikhail Bakunin (1814–76) contested the leadership of the First Socialist International (the International Working-men's Association) with Karl Marx, while Marx himself praised the courage of the revolutionary Populists who assassinated Tsar Alexander II in 1881. Finally, in the mid-1880s, Georgii Plekhanov (1856–1918) established himself as the 'Father of Russian Marxism'.

Within the Russian Empire, Polish Jewry was in a state of cultural ferment, in which competing 'isms' (positivism, socialism, Zionism, Chassidism) jostled for ascendancy. Rosa Luxemburg drew sustenance from the legacies of the *Haskalah* (the Jewish Enlightenment), from the insurrectionary tradition of the Polish *szlachta* (gentry) expressed poetically by Mickiewicz, and from the proto-Marxism of the self-styled International Social Revolutionary Party *Proletariat*, the execution of whose leaders left another scar on her youthful soul. Above all, she was inspired by the uncompromising revolutionary internationalism of Ludwik Waryński (1856–89), who had the temerity to correct Marx and Engels themselves, by insisting that the progressive role of Polish patriotism was spent, and that in future, the only fatherland was the proletariat. It was in Marxist revolutionary internationalism that the young Rosa found a 'firm guarantee' of the ultimate victory of a world without pogroms.

The weakness of her physique, and the strength of her intellect, dictated that Rosa Luxemburg would not lead a Russian revolution in person but would attempt to provide a unified theory and tactics for the European-wide revolution. She went west to vie for the title of the Marx of her time; nothing pleased her more than Franz Mehring's comparisons between her and Marx. By the time she made her debut in the greatest proletarian party of her day, the Social Democratic Party of Germany (SPD), Marx and Engels were both dead. In her view, German and Polish socialists had abused the prestige of the elderly Engels to sanctify tactics which were either non-Marxist or which exalted reformist elements of Marxism to the exclusion of revolutionary ones. The intellectual vacuum at the heart of the SPD had been filled by the Austro-Czech, Karl Kautsky (1854–1938), whose journal, *Die Neue Zeit*, became the theoretical forum of the entire European socialist movement and whose synthesis of Marxism and Darwinism became the dominant ideology of the second Socialist International. Yet the more Rosa Luxemburg got to know Kautsky, the less she liked what she detected, until in the final years before the Great War, she accused him of preaching an *Offiziösentum der Theorie*, a servile rationalisation of reformist praxis. This encouraged her in the belief that she was herself the leading orthodox Marxist of her day, a confidence reflected in her willingness to 'correct' Marx himself in her major theoretical economic study, *The Accumulation of Capital* (1913).

Together with her inseparable comrade and lover, Leo Jogiches (alias Tyszka), Rosa Luxemburg united theory and practice and also practised proletarian internationalism to a degree unprecedented and unsurpassed in the history of socialism. It was as young lovers in 1892 that they founded the Social Democracy of the Kingdom of Poland (SDKP) and as old friends that in 1919 they joined Karl Liebknecht to launch the Communist Party of

3

Germany (KPD). Where the greatness of Jaurès, Bebel, Plekhanov and Lenin was rooted in a single national movement, Rosa Luxemburg intervened vigorously and often effectively in the socialist politics of Poland, Russia, Germany, France and Belgium. Her contribution to Belgian politics is often ignored as peripheral, but it demonstrates beyond doubt that her commitment to universal liberation entailed no betrayal of the interests of her sex.

Rosa Luxemburg was a brilliant agitator and political journalist; her pamphlets and speeches on such varied topics as Polish nationalism, 'democratic centralism' in Russian socialism, coalition governments in France, political strikes in Germany and women's franchise in Belgium can still be read with profit by political scientists and active politicians. In *An Introduction to National Economy*, she made a distinguished contribution to economic history, and in her introduction to V. G. Korolenko's *History of My Contemporary*, a sensitive contribution to Russian literary criticism.

Rosa confessed to Luise Kautsky that she never wanted to be an angel. She suffered from a degree of intellectual snobbery, avoiding direct contact with the daily lives of working people and entirely failing to comprehend the Eastern European peasantry. She despised organizational work, was frequently dogmatic (assuming the right to speak for 'history') and was often sectarian and unrealistic in politics. She was arguably a less consequential thinker and a less successful tactician than Lenin, though we must remember that in January 1919, she could not summon war-weariness, peasant land hunger, or rebellious national minorities to her assistance, as Lenin had in 1917.

Rosa Luxemburg's letters reveal that she entirely lacked the revolutionary asceticism that pinched the souls of Lenin and other Russian revolutionaries. She bitterly regretted Jogiches' refusal to let her bear children and compensated extravagantly in her relationship with her cat, Mimi. She loved life in all its diversity, seeking beauty and illumination insatiably in love and friendship with humans and animals, in a sensual interest in wild creatures, plants and even rocks, and in all the arts, including those domestic arts ignored or despised by male revolutionaries. She herself became a competent poet and painter. Yet she would

4

not compromise her principles to save her own life, a life she loved so well. Above all, she was the incarnation of revolutionary audacity.

1 Contexts

The Murders: 'Bloody Rosa' and the Right

On the evening of 15 January 1919, the atmosphere in the Eden Hotel in Berlin was tense but jubilant. This was the headquarters of the Guards Cavalry Rifle Division (GKSD), which had played a prominent part in smashing an apparent *coup d'état* by the Berlin Communists, still widely known by the conspiratorial title of 'Spartacists' they had adopted during the war. The moment of reckoning with their leaders, Rosa Luxemburg and Karl Liebknecht, was imminent. A well-dressed civilian approached Rifleman Otto Runge of the GKSD to offer him 50 Marks if he struck the first blow against the Communist leaders. Karl Liebknecht arrived first under an escort of the Wilmersdorf Citizens' Militia. He was taken upstairs to be identified by Captain Waldemar Pabst. Pabst informed Liebknecht that he would be taken to Moabit Prison, and a detachment of riflemen under the command of Captain Horst von Pflugk-Harttung escorted him down the stairs past jeering hotel guests through the foyer to a car waiting at a side entrance. 'Cut the swine down!' shouted Captain Petry. As Liebknecht approached the car, Runge lunged with his rifle butt at Liebknecht's head, striking a glancing blow. Liebknecht put his hand to his head to staunch the flow of blood. As the car drove off, Volunteer Edwin von Rzewuski ran after it, jumped onto the rear fender and punched Liebknecht on the head. Proudly, he showed his comrades the bloodstain on his right-hand glove.

No sooner was Liebknecht despatched than a second detachment of citizens' militia arrived with 'Bloody Rosa', as the Right affected to call Rosa Luxemburg. She was then a petite woman of nearly fifty with greying hair, who limped slightly as she was taken upstairs to Pabst's office. 'Rosy, you old whore!' someone shouted, but she looked straight ahead. 'Are you Frau Rosa Luxemburg?' Pabst asked her. 'You decide for yourself', she answered coolly. 'According to the photograph, you must be', he concluded. 'If you say so', she replied softly. Pabst summoned Lieutenant Kurt Vogel, a monocled thirty-year-old war veteran, to escort Luxemburg to Moabit. Vogel waited chivalrously for her to rearrange her clothing and then helped her on with her coat. As she left Pabst's office, hotel guests whistled and spat at her. She was closely guarded by four riflemen who marched her downstairs towards the main entrance. Runge was waiting at the swing doors, which had been locked open for the evening. He muttered, 'She's not getting away alive', and as she came through the doors, he hit her hard on the back of the head with the butt of his rifle. She collapsed, blood pouring from her nose and mouth. Rifleman Dreger broke her fall, but Runge struck her again. 'Stop, that's enough', someone shouted. The soldiers grabbed her arm and dragged her into the waiting car, throwing her hat and case in after her. Again, the zealous Rzewuski aimed a blow at the helpless prisoner, while Rifleman Kurt Becker seized one of her shoes as a trophy.

The car picked up speed with Vogel standing on the running board. After about 100 metres, he pulled his pistol out of its holster and took aim. There was a dull click. Vogel checked his safety catch and fired once more. This time there was an audible bang. The prisoner's body convulsed, and then her head sank down onto her breast. They drove along the Budapester Strasse and then turned left along the Lützow Embankment. Just before the Liechtenstein Bridge, Vogel ordered the driver to stop. As the motor idled, Riflemen Weber and Poppe were instructed to throw the body into the Landwehr Canal. 'Stop, or we shoot!' shouted the machine-gunners on the bridge. Vogel yelled back in agitation through the dusk, 'Stop, for God's sake, don't shoot. We're carrying Rosa Luxemburg.' The body flopped into the water with a dull splash and floated under the bridge. Then it disappeared from view.

While Vogel was taking care of Rosa Luxemburg, Pflugk-Harttung had returned to the Eden Hotel to report to Pabst that Liebknecht had been shot while attempting to escape when the car had broken down. Following the shooting, the car had immediately recovered, permitting the detachment to deliver the body, as an 'unknown corpse', to a first-aid station. When Vogel returned he gave Pabst a similar cock-and-bull story, informing

7

Pabst that Rosa Luxemburg's supporters had snatched her body from them. Pabst was evidently satisfied with these reports, as he made no attempt to check them until the following morning. Meanwhile, officers bought the men wine and cigarettes, while Runge shared 20 of his 50 Marks with Rifleman Dreger. The next day a photographer was summoned to record an historic meal at which Runge occupied the place of honour. Herr Ott, the director of the Eden Hotel, then assembled his staff and read out an official communiqué on the deaths, based on the stories told to Pabst. Ott demanded that his employees confirm these stories if questioned. 'Unreliable' officers and men were asked to do likewise. One or two refused. Runge was abruptly transferred to the Eighth Hussars. The military justice authorities took several days to prepare correct orders for the arrest of the putative murderers, during which they were allowed to mix freely in the Eden Hotel.

The Communists were silenced by the suppression of their paper, *Die Rote Fahne* (The Red Flag) between 16 January and 2 February, but the Independent Socialists (USPD) demanded an investigation. Chancellor Fritz Ebert's Social Democratic (SPD) government temporized, then announced its determination to leave the affair to the normal organs of military justice, contenting itself with the appointment of two 'independent' assessors to assist the military investigator and simultaneously imposing a new military investigator. The new man, Investigator Jorns, made little headway, though he conducted an amicable interrogation of Pabst in the absence of the assessors. On 12 February, *Die Rote Fahne* carried an unsigned article by Leo Jogiches, for many years the comrade and lover of Rosa Luxemburg, giving a detailed and substantially accurate account of the murders. Allegations surfaced that the son-in-law of SPD leader Philipp Scheidemann had offered 100,000 Marks for the murder of Luxemburg and Liebknecht. Ebert stubbornly refused any independent investigation. When his own 'independent' assessors finally resigned in protest at what they called 'this comedy of justice', their homes were ransacked on the orders of SPD War Minister Gustav Noske, and all papers relating to the investigation were removed. Ten days after that, Jorns finally ordered the arrest of Lieutenant Vogel. Five days later, he ordered the arrest of the remaining escorts of the two Communist leaders, yet Runge

8

remained officially untraceable until April, despite the unsolicited assistance of Jogiches, who found him without any trouble.

On 8 May, a field court-marshal of the GKSD opened in the Berlin Criminal Court. The courtroom was heavily guarded by GKSD riflemen, who searched everyone who entered for weapons. A military judge presided, flanked by four assessors (who included the future Admiral Canaris); three of them had been elected by the GKSD. The accused entered the courtroom with smiles on their faces, medals clinking on their chests and armed with excellent testimonials from their commanding officers. Pflugk-Harttung had been allowed to keep his carbine in prison, and Vogel appeared with the beard he had grown (to confuse witnesses?) since January. As Rosa Luxemburg's body had still not been found, the cause of her death could not be established, so Runge and Vogel could only be accused of attempted murder. In his concluding address for the prosecution, Jorns attacked the socialist press for 'impeding his investigation' and asked the court to bear in mind the substantial 'mitigating circumstances'.

Runge and Vogel were sentenced to two years' imprisonment and dismissed from the service, but Runge was held to have suffered enough and was immediately released. Liebknecht's escorts were acquitted on all charges. Two days after the end of the trial, Jogiches was murdered. On the following day, Vogel was illegally released from Moabit Prison using a pass bearing the 'cleverly forged' signature of Investigator Jorns, whence he departed for Holland. His 'escape' was not officially discovered for three days, so the frontier guards were not alerted to stop him. Once more, the 'normal procedures' were followed, and the GKSD was asked to investigate its own.

Rosa Luxemburg's body was dredged from the Landwehr Canal on 1 June 1919 and immediately sequestered by the military authorities. Surprisingly, her skull was still intact, so Vogel had killed her and not Runge. On 13 June her corpse was escorted to its final resting place (pending Adolf Hitler) in Friedrichsfelde by tens of thousands of Berlin workers. On 23 December her assassin, Kurt Vogel, was amnestied.

The following month, Otto Runge, the sole 'proletarian' among Rosa Luxemburg's killers, became so exasperated at the failure of his bourgeois protectors to honour their promise of a trouble-free future, that he set down an account of the events in the Eden Hotel that completely contradicted his earlier versions. This time, he confirmed the allegations made by the Communists and Independent Socialists that Jorns' investigation had been a 'comedy'. Jorns did nothing to clear his name until eight years later when he was promoted to the rank of *Reichsanwalt* (something like QC or State's Attorney). When the newspaper *Das Tagebuch* queried Jorns' suitability for promotion, he sued for libel. In court he faced Paul Levi, once Rosa Luxemburg's comrade, defence attorney and intimate friend. Jorns lost. As for Otto Runge, Communist workers repeatedly exposed his aliases and regularly beat him up. Germany only became safe for Runge with the rise of the Nazis. But by then, there were few Communists with a good word for Rosa Luxemburg either.

The Unquenchable Flame: 'Luxemburgism' and the Left

Why did this innocuous-looking little woman 'disappear' from public discourse for so long? And why is she still regarded with ambivalence by so many of the people who profess her values? A large part of the answer must be sought in her differences with Lenin. Rosa Luxemburg had criticized Lenin in 1903 and had feuded with him in 1912–14. Lenin sharply disagreed with her on the 'national question' and had doubts about her economic theories. Yet at critical moments, in their reactions to the 1905 Russian Revolution and the First World War, they stood shoulder to shoulder against a hurricane of reformist funk and patriotic hysteria. Her doubts about Lenin were revived in 1918 when he dissolved Russia's only freely-elected parliament, the Constituent Assembly, and when he accepted the infamous Treaty of Brest-Litovsk with the German imperialists. From her prison cell, she wrote angry letters of protest to her comrades, which they refused to publish. To convince them, she drafted a critique, *The Russian Revolution*, which Paul Levi smuggled out for her. Still her comrades refused to publish it. Then came the few heady weeks of freedom and foreboding and the apotheosis of martyrdom, or as she had once called it, 'the highest honour which a Social Democrat can be granted'. Her niche in the Communist pantheon was

10

now secure, and whenever Western Social Democrats criticized Bolshevik 'terror', they replied with taunts of 'Where are Rosa Luxemburg and Karl Liebknecht?'

Even then, there were Communists who demurred. The fate of Marxism or 'scientific socialism' was indissolubly tied to the success of the socialist revolution not just in largely rural Russia, but in the major industrialized countries of Western Europe. Until 1914, millions had hoped (and other millions had feared) that Germany, with its huge, disciplined Social Democratic Party, inspired by Marxist ideas, would lead the world revolution. Yet the predicted German revolution fizzled out in a series of hiccups. The January 1919 'Spartacist Rising' was followed by the ephemeral 'Bavarian Soviet Republic', the unsuccessful 'March Action' of 1921 and the final botched Hamburg insurrection of October 1923. Competing factions within the fractious Communist Party of Germany (KPD) blamed one another for these debacles, magnifying the demoralization. Ruth Fischer, a leading member of the KPD, went so far as to blame 'the syphilis of Luxemburgism', the KPD's libertarian tradition, for the party's failure to realize the predictions of Marx and Engels.

Yet this interpretation was not representative, and Fischer was denounced in turn. Many Communists still revered Rosa Luxemburg and echoed the feelings expressed by the 65-year-old Clara Zetkin, her old bosom friend and comrade, at the Third Congress of the Communist International (Comintern) in Moscow: 'All that I was and achieved, it was a collective effort with Rosa Luxemburg. And I can't hold back the pain that she no longer stands beside me . . .' Rank-and-file socialists were able to share more of her pain, when Rosa's dearest woman friend, Luise Kautsky, published some of Rosa's letters, which showed that behind the public face of the committed revolutionary was a human personality of unsuspected vulnerability and great warmth, of discriminating tastes, illuminating aesthetic opinions and encyclopaedic interests.

In 1921, Paul Levi was expelled from the Communist movement for criticizing the Comintern for its heavy-handed intervention in the affairs of the Italian Socialist Party. Released from the constraints of party discipline, and with a powerful urge to pre-empt the inevitable campaign of defamation against him, he

11

published Rosa's *The Russian Revolution*. This brought a sharp retort from Lenin, who called Levi 'a hen rather than an eagle'. Lenin's comments on Rosa Luxemburg herself were magisterial, but not lacking in magnanimity:

> Rosa Luxemburg was mistaken on the question of the independence of Poland; she was mistaken in 1903 in her appraisal of Menshevism; she was mistaken on the theory of the accumulation of capital; she was mistaken in July 1914 when . . . she advocated unity between the Bolsheviks and Mensheviks; she was mistaken in what she wrote in prison in 1918 (she corrected most of these mistakes at the end of 1918 . . . after she was released). But in spite of these mistakes she was – and remains for us – an eagle. And not only will Communists all over the world cherish her memory, but her biography and her *complete* works (the publication of which the German Communists are inordinately delaying . . .) will serve as useful manuals for training many generations of Communists all over the world.

At the Fourth Comintern Congress in 1922, Clara Zetkin was obliged to distance herself from Rosa Luxemburg's *The Russian Revolution*, but the leader of the German Communists, August Thalheimer, still extolled the economic theories of the woman he called 'our incomparable predecessor in struggle' (*Vorkämpferin*). Rosa's Polish comrade, Maria Koszutska (Kostrzewa) also praised her, while Clara Zetkin boasted that women workers demonstrating in Turin had recently carried banners inscribed with her name. At the Fifth Comintern Congress in 1924, there were extensive and comradely debates on Rosa Luxemburg's views on capital accumulation and the national question, though it was perhaps significant that the Comintern boss, Manuilsky, used the pejorative term, 'national nihilism', to describe her views on Polish independence. The remarks of the Soviet party historian, David Ryazanov, testified to her continuing influence, but also betrayed a certain irritation:

> The debates on the programme and the interesting debate on the accumulation theory of Rosa Luxemburg in the German commission have shown how necessary a thorough study of Marxism is for the younger generation of Communists. We are in danger of getting people who know Luxemburgism and

Leninism from A to Z, but not the ABC of Marxism.

This same year, 1924, was also the year of Lenin's death, the year in which he ceased to be a mere mortal, permitting Stalin to begin his campaign to proclaim the dead leader's infallibility. Trotsky's self-serving *Lessons of October* provoked a stiffening resolve among his rivals to defend a synthetic 'Leninism' against any other ideology. By 1928, when the Comintern Congress finally reconvened, no one found it advisable to mention Rosa Luxemburg. The academic study of her work recommended by Lenin limped on for another two years, allowing the Soviet historian, I. V. Gerchikov, to publish the first instalment of what promised to be a sympathetic and comprehensive study of her life.

In 1928, Stalin overturned Lenin's New Economic Policy, opting instead for rapid industrialization financed by the forced expropriation of peasant surpluses through 'collective farms'. Simultaneously, a 'cultural revolution' was unleashed on surviving 'bourgeois' experts in the universities, in cultural organizations and in the economic administration. Many Communists were delighted. This was the kind of Communist 'voluntarism', heedless of alleged 'objective' constraints to socialism, which Lenin had several times denounced. Perhaps the time had come to ask whether Lenin himself had been as consistently Bolshevik as he might have been. In an article published by the historical journal of the Communist Party, A. G. Slutsky suggested that Lenin had been inconsistent, in failing to support Rosa Luxemburg's criticisms of the German socialist leadership before the First World War. This was precisely the pretext Stalin needed to close the debate. No papal bull was ever more magisterial than his rebuttal: 'the question as to whether Lenin *was* or *was not* a real Bolshevik cannot be converted into a subject of discussion'. The message was clear: the serious study of the life and times of Rosa Luxemburg was out.

In his pamphlet *Hands off Rosa Luxemburg*, Trotsky enlisted her in his support, thereby making matters far worse for her Soviet admirers. The rest of Gerchikov's study never appeared, and we know nothing of his subsequent fate. In 1938, Stalin reported that the Polish Communist Party had become an agency of the 'bourgeois Pilsudskyite regime' in Poland and suppressed it. Dozens of Rosa Luxemburg's comrades and old friends disappeared into Soviet prisons and concentration camps, among them Adolf Warski, her senior surviving comrade.

Yet, the darker the sky, the brighter the stars. It was in a Europe dominated and intimidated by the 'technocratic conquistadors' that the rehabilitation of Rosa Luxemburg was now begun by her younger comrade, Paul Frölich. To write a positive account of the life and work of a woman regarded with hatred by Hitler and Stalin in 1939 required enormous moral courage. Frölich's status as an exile in Switzerland provided flimsy protection against dictators who had abrogated the rights of their own citizens and extinguished the independence of smaller neighbours. It was not unknown for them to send assassins to terrorize their critics abroad. Frölich and his wife, Rosi Wolfstein, had known Rosa well in Germany, and his vivid account of her impact on the radical wing of German socialism before 1914 has never been bettered.

The next step towards Rosa Luxemburg's rehabilitation was unintentionally facilitated by Stalin himself. As he tried to create friendly governments in Poland and East Germany after the Second World War, he had to use the few Communists at his disposal; many of them were admirers of Rosa Luxemburg or her closest comrades. The Polish Communist President Bierut was particularly assiduous in asking Stalin what had happened to Warski and other Polish Communists. For a while Stalin played along with him, suggesting that they had simply got lost somewhere and telling his police chief, Beria, to find them. Eventually, the dictator tired of the game, and as Bierut was escorted off, Beria said to him, 'Why are you fucking around with Iosif Vissarionovich? You fuck off and leave him alone. That's my advice to you, or you'll regret it.'

The first major Communist to take up the cudgels publicly on Rosa's behalf was Wilhelm Pieck, President of the (East) German Democratic Republic. As a young carpenter and Communist, Pieck had also been taken to the Eden Hotel on that terrible January evening in 1919. Pieck remembered a premonition which had prompted him to turn to face Otto Runge just as he prepared to knock Pieck unconscious in turn. Eventually, Pieck had man-

14

aged to escape. In 1951, he prefaced a short anthology of Rosa Luxemburg's works with an introduction that now sounds churlish unless we consider the risks Pieck was taking. An East German biographical sketch followed. Pieck and his comrades felt that it was vital to demonstrate to the citizens of the new 'workers' and peasants' state' that Communism was no alien Muscovite importation, but a political philosophy deeply rooted in the traditions of the German working class.

The Poles did nothing until they regained a measure of independence following Khrushchev's denunciation of Stalin in 1956. Their first move was to rehabilitate Warski and the rest of the purged Polish Communists. Soon, Feliks Tych began that indefatigable burrowing in the archives in Warsaw, Berlin and Moscow that has immeasurably enriched our knowledge of Rosa Luxemburg's life and milieu. In 1970, the East Germans began the publication of an impressive edition of her works; her letters followed (though neither edition is *complete* as Lenin had recommended). A pleiade of fine East European historians has since emerged; yet Gerchikov's work remains unfinished, one of so many reproaches to the alleged unity of theory and practice in Marxism. Just why Rosa Luxemburg is still such a hot potato for Communist historians was illustrated in 1988, when the Soviet dramatist Mikhail Shatrov revived her arguments for free elections in the context of the debate on the limits of reform in the USSR.

Ironically, it was in non-revolutionary England in the 'swinging Sixties' that the first 'scientific' biography of Rosa Luxemburg appeared. (It was surely no accident that both Rosa and her revolutionary peer, Leon Trotsky, featured in biographies by non-academics published by Oxford University Press at that time.) Rosa's biographer, Peter Nettl, was a businessman with radical libertarian sympathies. He was also a tireless researcher who began to restore Rosa's Polish background and to cast light on some little-known episodes in her career. Nettl's book now seems a little pious. It has attracted niggling criticism but no serious rival. It was in the sixties, too, that Lelio Basso reintroduced a new generation to the vitality of Luxemburg's Marxism in his efforts to rekindle the revolutionary spirit of Italian socialism. A generation of radical West German students adopted her as their inspiration, and in 1968 their banners bore her name, like those of the women workers of Turin forty-five years earlier. The ebbing tide of student radicalism left behind a more diffuse but longer-lasting women's movement or movements. Interest in Rosa Luxemburg's serious works waned as readers focused on her letters, which demonstrate the great variety of her achievements and the predicaments she faced as a woman. Yet her own sharply-worded hostility to the bourgeois feminism of her day makes her a problematic figure for contemporary feminists. Her arguably less distinguished but more feminist comrade, Alexandra Kollontai, has attracted three western feminist biographies. Rosa's women biographers, Raya Dunayevskaya and Elżbieta Ettinger, are the products of an East European formation. Dunayevskaya, still a Marxist, argues unconvincingly that Rosa Luxemburg was a contemporary radical feminist before her time. Ettinger's revulsion against Marxism leads her to refrain from any serious examination of Rosa Luxemburg's theoretical work. Instead, she concentrates on Rosa's personal life. The moving portrait of Rosa by Barbara Sukowa in Margarethe von Trotta's film, *Rosa Luxemburg*, takes us close to the essence of Rosa Luxemburg in her prime, but ignores her differences with Lenin and has little to say about her origins. Yet, as Ettinger has convincingly demonstrated, it is to these origins that we must return if we want to understand one of the most attractive and controversial figures in the history of socialism.

A Non-Jewish Jew: From Zamość to Zurich

On 5 March 1870 Lina née Loewenstein gave birth to her fifth and last child, a second daughter. She and her husband Eljasz Luxemburg called the baby Rozalia, but the shorter pet-name Róża (pronounced *Roozha*) soon caught on. They lived in the city of Zamość in an area of Eastern Europe that had once belonged to independent Poland and was now subject to the Russian tsar, the reforming Alexander II. It was seven years since Russian forces had suppressed the last great Polish revolt, restoring an uneasy peace to the area. Yet events were afoot that would shatter this peace. Four months after Róża's birth, war broke out between France and Prussia. The Luxenburgs were as distraught as most Poles at the unexpected rout of Poland's traditional friend by Poland's mortal foe.

What followed was even more shocking. The French bourgeois government of Adolphe Louis Thiers abandoned Paris, the centre of humane civilization, to the mercy of the Prussians. The Parisians refused to accept Thiers' orders to lay down their arms, and in the early morning of 18 March 1871, a woman teacher called Louise la Canaque led a group of working women from Montmartre to defend the city's artillery. The city council or 'Commune' supported them. 'Once more', it proclaimed, 'Paris works and suffers for the whole of France', as it prepared its defences and embarked on the reconstruction of Parisian society on egalitarian, socialist lines. Two months later, the Commune was overwhelmed. On 23 May, General Jarosław Dąbrowski, a veteran of the 1863 January Rising in Poland, was killed commanding the forces of the Commune in the Neuilly sector. The bloody repression that followed could not efface the memory of this epic struggle. For socialists, it assumed the stature of a struggle for humanity, in which men and women of many nationalities besides the French had fought, administered, experimented and suffered martyrdom together. It was to this ideal that Rosa Luxemburg would dedicate her life.

Two years later, Eljasz and Lina Luxenburg abandoned their failing timber yard in Zamość and moved to Warsaw. We can only guess at what Rosa retained from these infant years in Zamość. Even the date of her birth was only finally established by Peter Nettl, and only the barest facts about her childhood and youth are verifiable. From her parents' apartment, Róża had glimpsed the magnificent Renaissance Town Hall, an assertive gesture of identification with the Latin and Catholic culture of Italy (and of Poland's self-imposed mission to extend it further east), which had been built by Chancellor Jan Zamoyski three-hundred years earlier. In the market square, she must have seen Polish peasants in lace and bright costumes trading in patois with Jewish artisans in sober black. She must often have passed the grim fortress, home of the Russian garrison, which held Zamość for the distant tsar in St Petersburg. The Jews of Zamość were a self-confident lot, not afraid to let the world glimpse the violent

17

disputes that set liberal *Maskalim* against fundamentalist *Chassi-dim*. From this vibrant culture would come Isaac Loeb Peretz, a major figure in Yiddish literature, Alexander Tsederbaum, the founder of Russo-Jewish journalism, and his son, Julius Martov, a future Menshevik opponent of Rosa Luxemburg. Perhaps the one legacy of Zamość that never left her was her love of running through the woods and fields in all weathers, a love that survived the dislocated hip that doctors failed to cure, causing her periodic pain and a permanent limp.

Perhaps, too, Rosa Luxemburg's feelings about capitalism might have developed differently had her father conducted his business in Warsaw, Łódź, Dąbrowa or Żyrardów. While Zamość had stagnated with Austro-Russian trade, they had prospered behind Russian tariffs. Their capitalists had grown fat on the demand for Polish textiles, iron and coal from Petersburg and Moscow, Tashkent and Vladivostok. Piously averting their eyes from the unsavoury living conditions of their Polish, Jewish and German workers, they affected to despise the quixotic insurrectionary traditions of the Polish *szlachta* (gentry), embracing instead an optimistic Positivist philosophy. Eljasz Luxenburg arrived in Warsaw as a victim, not a beneficiary of market forces, but he, too, hoped for a better future. Assuming the Christian name Edward, he and his wife invested in the future of their children by buying them the best, most modern, education they could find. Bilingual in Polish and German, they introduced their children to Mickiewicz and Schiller, poets whose assertive and humorous revolutionary liberalism was quite distinct from the quietism of the contemporary Warsaw Positivists. The family enjoyed the theatres, art galleries and concert halls of a city which still felt and looked like a capital.

Shortly before Róża's eleventh birthday, Warsaw was shaken by the news of the assassination by Russian revolutionaries of Tsar Alexander II. One of the assassins was the young Jewish girl, Hessia Helfman, and as Russian peasants began to mutter about gentry children killing their tsar–liberator, cynical figures in the administration saw an opportunity to focus popular resentments on the Jewish minority. In May 1881, anti-Jewish riots and massacres began in Elizavetgrad, Kiev and Odessa. They were soon nicknamed 'pogroms'. In December, the pogroms reached

18

Warsaw. As elsewhere, the Russian army and gendarmerie waited until 1,500 Jewish homes, shops and synagogues had been destroyed by Polish Catholic artisans, before intervening to restore order. Like the other Jewish bourgeois families, the Luxenburgs were forced to cower impotently in their apartments hoping that the angel of death would pass them by.

The Russian government set up a commission to investigate not the rioters but 'the injurious economic activity' of the Jews and to find ways to 'protect the Christian population' from them. During the years that followed, a series of measures were enacted to restrict Jewish rights of residence, economic activities and access to educational and professional opportunities. This was a chilling demonstration of the barbaric potential of inter-ethnic violence, which cast a long shadow over the Luxenburgs' hopes for the careers of their children. The adult Rosa Luxemburg *never* referred to these events, a reticence that may be compared with Lenin's reticence about the execution of his elder brother. It is one of the main virtues of Elżbieta Ettinger's book that she argues the importance of the 1881 pogroms in Rosa's development.

The pogroms of 1881 enormously accelerated emigration to America, and they also sowed the seeds of organized Zionism. Yet more of Russia's Jews, inured to unpopularity, stayed at home than left, and many more Jewish intellectuals turned to socialism than to Zionism. Many years later, Rosa Luxemburg reproved a German–Jewish friend for her particular concern with Jewish grievances: 'For me the poor victims of the rubber plantations in Putamayo, the Negroes in Africa, with whose bodies the Europeans play catchball, are just as close.' Although Jews had now moved into liberal professions in numbers, many were still involved in the kind of huckstering and arguably exploitative economic activities socialists wished to abolish. She could not accept that these were 'her people'. With Karl Marx she believed that 'The *social* emancipation of the Jew is the *emancipation of society from Jewry* [i.e. from capitalism]'. But Rosa had also learnt from the 1881 pogroms that racial stereotypes could be dangerous, and unlike Marx and Engels, she never accepted the Jewish racial stereotype at face value. Religion was also a serious obstacle to Rosa Luxemburg's identification with the Jewish people. For

19

someone who, as she put it, 'simply cannot take a religious *Weltanschauung* seriously', a return to the ghetto was unthinkable. As Isaac Deutscher said of her, and of those other 'non-Jewish Jews', Spinoza, Marx, Trotsky and Freud, 'the conditions in which they lived and worked did not allow them to reconcile themselves to ideas which were nationally or religiously limited'.

In time, the young Róża had to grapple personally with the uniformed agents of the anti-Semitic autocracy. Since the 1863 January Rising, Polish schools had become instruments of ruthless Russification, and young Poles were regularly beaten or expelled for speaking Polish together during school breaks. To gain admission to the Second Women's Gymnasium (grammar school) in Warsaw in 1884, Róża had both to overcome the Jewish quota and to become fluent in the language of the masters. She identified indignantly with Polish victims of linguistic oppression far more easily than with her fellow Jews, as is evident from an article she wrote attacking Prussian oppression of Polish schoolchildren a few years later: 'So it is a crime to speak one's own language, which one has sucked up with mother's milk, it is a mistake to belong to a people with whom one has come into the world.' Yet her Jewish detachment probably protected her from that unthinking hatred of everything Russian that many of her Polish contemporaries developed. In time she came to love the language of *War and Peace* and *Anna Karenina*, and to love Leo Tolstoy as she loved Mozart. The Gymnasium gave her an excellent grounding in mathematics and added Latin and French to her existing four languages. Subsequently, she taught herself to read in Italian, English and Dutch.

In November 1885, the whole of Warsaw was rivetted by the trial by a Russian military court of 29 members of the first quasi-Marxist party in the Russian Empire, the International Social Revolutionary Party *Proletariat*, as it styled itself. On 28 January 1886, four young revolutionaries were hanged, the first Poles to be executed since the 1863 Rising; *Proletariat*'s chief ideologist, Ludwik Waryński, was entombed in the Schlüsselberg Fortress near Petersburg. Before his death, he left his comrades an unforgettable message: 'Don't let the cause die, and if your strength permits, don't forgive the hangman. Let the enemy know that working people, once aroused, do not tire of the struggle until they conquer.'

The indignation aroused by the sentences was intense, and this was probably when Róża first met Waryński's comrade, Marcin Kasprzak, a fateful meeting for them both. It was Kasprzak, ten years her senior, who inducted her into the shadowy organization known subsequently as *Proletariat II*, in which she found at last a 'scientific' doctrine that promised an end to all national hatreds. Yet, almost from the beginning, Róża felt that Marx and Engels themselves had been inconsistent in the application of their own principles.

Kasprzak was a disciple of Marx and Engels, before Marxism had crystallized into a doctrine. Marx himself died in 1883, leaving Engels to edit and publish the second volume of *Capital* (in 1885) and the third volume (in 1894) before his own death in 1895. Their views on Poland had been formed in the first half of the century, when the Polish Risings of 1830 and 1863 had reduced the power and prestige of the Russian 'gendarme of Europe'. Their respect was enhanced when they met such Polish exiles as Dąbrowski in the front ranks of revolutionary and progressive struggles everywhere. It seemed only fitting for them to send a congratulatory message to Polish socialists meeting in Geneva to commemorate the fiftieth anniversary of the 1830 Rising. Their message ended with the rousing words 'Long Live Poland!'

At this meeting, Waryński had scandalized his compatriots by invoking Marxist principles against Marx and Engels themselves. Waryński denounced the insurrectionary tradition of the Polish *szlachta* for its class egoism, and with it, the very idea of Polish independence. To the fury of his listeners, he announced, 'We are compatriots, members of one great nationality more unhappy than Poland: the nation of the proletarians'. The result of Waryński's challenge was a schism in Polish socialism that would curse it for three generations. When Waryński returned to Poland to found *Proletariat* and to conclude an alliance with the Russian revolutionaries, Bolesław Limanowski and the nationally orientated Polish socialists created a rival *Lud Polski* (Polish People) organization.

When Róża graduated in 1888, she failed to receive the gold medal to which her final results should have entitled her, perhaps

21

in reprisal for disloyal conversations. Peter Nettl describes her as then 'working openly for her revolutionary group', but in the Russian police state all political activity was illegal. In practice, Róża could only participate in clandestine discussions, secret woodland meetings and occasional adventures leafleting workers' barracks. Legend has her hiding in the country and then going abroad to evade arrest (even getting the assistance of a Catholic priest to assist her alleged conversion to Christianity). As Nettl disingenuously puts it, 'this story is substantiated by almost all sources and presumably originates from Rosa Luxemburg herself'. The paucity of verifiable details about her early life enabled her and her comrades to make it fit mythic stereotypes.

The truth was probably less heroic but not at all discreditable. Marcin Kasprzak was a self-educated working man well aware of his intellectual limitations. He saw in Róża Luxenburg Waryński's successor as the theoretician of Polish revolutionary internationalism. To fulfil this vocation, she needed a university education and contact with the leading Marxist thinkers abroad. The institution most likely to welcome a radical Russian citizen, and to offer a woman an elite education, was the University of Zurich. In January 1889, just a few months before the formation of the Second Socialist and Workers' International, Róża Luxemburg was smuggled across the frontier to Austrian Galicia. It was as Rosa Luxemburg, the name by which she is known to the world, that she enrolled in the university.

The adult Rosa Luxemburg was just over five feet tall, with strikingly 'Jewish' features and glossy long black hair. (In the self-portrait she painted many years later [see illus. 9], she straightened the Semitic contours of her nose, though without reducing its prominence.) 'My nose always advances ahead of everything else', she once joked. She also mocked her physical disability, and when Luise Kautsky broke a leg, Rosa told her friend that she enjoyed Luise's competition in all things, 'but in limping I tolerate no competition'. She never complained about her bad hip; indeed, an early intimation of Karl Kautsky's moral weakness came when she found she could easily outwalk him. As a young woman, she was well aware that she was no classical beauty, and she always admired beautiful women. 'I am for luxury of every kind', she wrote. She had the sense to understand

22

while still young that 'Venus de Milo only preserved her reputation as the most beautiful of women for thousands of years because she kept silent'. Keeping her mouth shut was not part of Rosa's plans. Her beauty was of a different kind, as Irena Izvolskaya, a younger comrade, remembered: 'You had to see her in movement during a conversation, in speech, to observe how she listened. Everything [in her face] then assumed a rather special expression; her open forehead fringed with hair, and her pretty, straight mouth, as expressive as the eyes, lively, observant, penetrating, wise, and at the same time, thoughtfully gentle.'

As a young woman, Rosa Luxemburg was competitive and industrious. She did not suffer fools gladly, coining cutting epithets for those she met, even close friends. She treasured the privacy she used to indulge her tastes in reading and the hobbies that grew more absorbing as she grew older. Her tastes were uncompromisingly high-brow and 'classical'. She loved plants and animals and was not happy for long away from the open air. Since childhood, she had loved to watch the sky. Later on, her prison skylights and a book of Turner's paintings would comfort her darkest hours. In some unfathomable way, this was connected with the soaring ambition of this youngest child. 'In those days I firmly believed that 'life', 'real' life, had gone somewhere far away over the rooftops; since then I have been travelling after it'.

The major influences in young Róża's life were her father and three elder brothers. Toward her elder sister, the less intelligent Anna, she later confessed, 'I was always irritated, impatient, insufferable'. Many hard knocks later, she would develop a sense of remorse about her neglect of her mother and seek a rapprochement with Anna, but it was only quite late in life that she began to appreciate that her mother's religiosity and naïveté had not lacked wisdom.

Radical women in the Russian Empire were inhibited from developing a specifically feminist ideology for a variety of reasons. Their legal dependence on father or husband and the total absence of free expression or association played a part. More important was the fact that in a country where men also lacked political rights, the differences between the aspirations of male and female revolutionaries were less apparent. All revolutionaries

23

demanded legal equality for both sexes and offered women an alternative route to immediate equality, the equality of sacrifice. Many women accepted this offer with enthusiasm.

The aristocratic wives of the 'Decembrist' rebels of 1825 followed their menfolk to Siberia. Katerina Breshkovskaya accepted hard labour in Siberia with equanimity. Sofia Perovskaya, Hessia Helfman's fellow conspirator, shared the gallows with the male assassins of Alexander II. Within the feuding ranks of Polish socialism, Rosa Luxemburg would befriend or confront Maria Jankowska, Zofia Daszyńska, Cezaryna Wojnarowska, Estera Golde-Stróżecka and Maria Koszutska (Kostrzewa). As she travelled to Western Europe, she became more aware of the contradictory attitudes within the mass socialist parties on the 'woman question', but her own exceptional qualities helped persuade her that they would gradually be resolved. She believed in correcting the failings of her male comrades, not in conceding to demands that might fragment the movement, bringing pogroms to all. Rosa Luxemburg would become the archetypal Athena-figure of socialism, aspiring to be the most authoritative exponent of the ideas of Karl Marx (if not always of Friedrich Engels). Therein lay her colossal political strength, and the seeds of her tragedies, both personal and political.

2 A Polish Apprenticeship

The Comrades

In our time, the good name of Switzerland has been besmirched as the country has grown fat on money deposited by Nazis, Mafiosi, Third World dictators and Wall Street swindlers, while whistle-blowers on Swiss scandals are pursued vindictively in the name of commercial secrecy. It was not always so. Less than fifty years ago, victims of Nazi tyranny cried with emotion at the first sight of the Swiss Alps with their promise of liberty. Fifty years before that, Swiss democracy enjoyed even higher esteem, its exclusion of women notwithstanding. Switzerland's medieval 'democratic' heroes, William Tell and Ulrich von Hutten, belonged to the pantheon of all European democrats, including Rosa Luxemburg. Conrad Meyer's poem, 'Hutten's Confession' was probably her favourite political poem.

The University of Zurich occupied a special place in the hearts of the Russian and Polish democratic intelligentsia, since it admitted them without regard (as we would now say) to ethnic background, religion or gender. It was for many years almost the *only* place where Russian women could qualify as doctors. Radical exiles from Russian autocracy were also given a warm welcome by the German socialists who had put down roots in Zurich during their own period of exile from persecution under Bismarck's 'Anti-Socialist Laws' (1878–90). Their *Eintracht* (Unity) Club contained a fine library on the history of socialism and also arranged lectures by such luminaries of German Social Democracy as August Bebel, Wilhelm Liebknecht and Eduard Bernstein, who often took their holidays in Switzerland. Typical of this Russo-German comity was the Lübeck family, with whom Rosa first took lodgings. Carl Lübeck was a socialist journalist, a Prussian exile who had lost the taste for home. His dynamic Polish wife, Olympia Łada, offered Rosa her motherly protection when she felt homesick.

As the Poles were subject to both political and national oppres-

25

sion, the Zurich colony included young people of every conceivable view, studying the full range of subjects. Rosa Luxemburg's peer group included the Barent brothers, novelist and scientist, the philosopher and psychologist Władysław Heinrich, and Feliks Wiślicki, an inventor of artificial fibres.

Rosa spent two years studying natural sciences and mathematics, from which she acquired the life-long hobby of botany and the mathematical understanding which gave her the confidence to tackle the more intimidatingly abstract aspects of Marxist economic theory. Her scientific studies reinforced her conviction that Marxism was indeed 'scientific socialism'. She then transferred to economics, becoming a pupil of Professor Julius Wolf. The liberal Wolf was one of a number of professors in Zurich who regularly examined Marxist ideas in their lectures. His mockery of Marxist neophytes, ignorant of Marxism, drove some of them to seek more congenial professors elsewhere. Rosa Luxemburg and her friend Julian ('Julek') Marchlewski responded more positively to this challenge, luring Wolf into expressions of opinion on aspects of Marxism with which *he* was unfamiliar and then ambushing him with their superior knowledge. Despite these moments of discomfiture, Wolf evidently enjoyed the stimulation of these brilliant young Poles. Rosa played the academic game, treating Wolf's ideas with as much respect as Marx's, though without concealing her enthusiasm for the latter.

By 1893, Rosa Luxemburg had gathered around herself that group with which her name will always be linked. In addition to their real names, they all used pseudonyms to confuse the tsar's courts. They were a brilliant bunch. In addition to Luxemburg herself ('Kruszyńska', etc), there were Leo Jogiches ('Grozovsky', 'Jan Tyszka'), Julian Marchlewski ('Karski') and Adolf Warszawski ('Warski'). Rosa Luxemburg's distinctions were so many and so striking that it was her alter ego, Leo Jogiches, who became the 'unknown revolutionary', a reversal of the normal fate of female consorts, which astonished some of their surviving comrades. Few now remember Jadwiga Warszawska or Bronisława Marchlewska, Rosa's less brilliant schoolfriends, whose family burdens ensured that they would not compete with their husbands. Yet the three women helped to bond the three monog-

26

amous couples, Rosa and Leo, Adolf and Jadzia, and Julek and Bronisława. The peer group was completed by the tragic figures of Bronisław Weselowski and Kazimierz Ratyński, who returned to Poland to work illegally, only to be arrested and exiled to Siberia, from which 'Kazik' never returned. Weselowski would be murdered by Józef Piłsudski's police in 1919.

An even more dramatic nemesis awaited the mentor and 'elder brother' of the group, Marcin Kasprzak, an infrequent visitor who never lost touch with his apprentices in Marxist internationalism. An 'elder brother' of a different kind was Alexander Helphand (whose pseudonym 'Parvus' was an ironic reference to his obesity). In many ways Parvus was the ideological and practical trail-blazer for the whole group, arriving in Zurich in 1886 and moving on to Germany in 1891. All these young comrades were products of a highly competitive educational system, and there was a clear intellectual pecking order within the group, but they also gave one another great mutual support, foreseeing no doubt the trials ahead.

The Marchlewskis, Warszawskis and Rosa Luxemburg had known one another in Poland. Julian Marchlewski, born in 1867, was the grandson of an impoverished *szlachta* family from Grudziądz (Graudenz) in West Prussia. His father, a grain merchant, was ruined by the market, like Rosa Luxemburg's. His German mother was abandoned by her father (who fought and died for the Union in the American Civil War), but she kept the family together after her husband's bankruptcy. Augusta von Rückersfeldt ensured that all seven children were competently bilingual, cultured, decent and ambitious. Like Rosa, the young Julek Marchlewski had to endure compulsory Russification and military discipline to obtain a formal education at the *Realgymnasium* or technical school in Włocławek. This assumed farcical forms when the school tried to teach him his mother's language in Russian. Julek left school early, took up the proletarian occupation of dyer, and supported his brother (a future Rector of Kraków University) through his studies in Zurich. Marchlewski was one of the leading organizers of the Union of Polish Workers, the first mass trade union on Marxist lines in Poland. He personally established its branch in Łódż, rapidly emerging as the 'Manchester' of Poland, whose population increased tenfold between 1860 and 1890. Marchlewski also worked in factories in Germany, where he got to know the grassroots of the German Social Democratic movement. He prepared the May 1892 general strike and uprising in Łódź, which became the subject of Rosa Luxemburg's first articles, though Julek himself was arrested in November 1891. Marchlewski arrived in Zurich in 1893.

Bronisława Guttman was a friend of Marchlewski's socialist sister, Marta. She became his comrade in *Proletariat II* and in the Union of Polish Workers, and she distributed Marxist literature to the workers. In 1893, she followed Marchlewski to Zurich, where she qualified as a biologist at the Polytechnic. Julian and Bronisława were married in 1897 in the romantic setting of the Island of Heligoland, which Queen Victoria had recently presented to her grandson, Kaiser Wilhelm II.

'Warski' was born Adolf Warszawski in Warsaw in 1868. The son of a commercial clerk, he took to journalism, writing for the Positivist *Prawda* (Truth), the socialistic *Głos* (Voice) and the *Tygodnik Powszechny* (Universal Daily), the paper closest to the Union of Polish Workers, on themes relating to the lives of working people. He met Marchlewski in 1886, becoming his comrade in *Proletariat II* and the Union of Polish Workers. It was Rosa Luxemburg who introduced him to her school-friend Jadwiga ('Jadzia') Chrzanowska, whose lifetime partner he became. Warski followed Marchlewski to Łódź and was arrested with him in 1891. In 1893, he and Jadzia arrived in Paris. A straightforward, hard-working couple, the 'Jadzios', as Rosa nicknamed them, devoted their entire lives to the painstaking organizational work required for the creation of a Polish Marxist party.

The outsider was Leo Jogiches. Lyov Yankelevich Jogiches, to give him his Russian name, was born on 17 June 1867. A member of a wealthy industrial and commercial family, 'Leo' was brought up in an environment strongly influenced by German culture. In 1885, he left the *gymnasium* in Wilna (Vil'no, Vilnius) without graduating to 'go to the People'; in his case, 'the People' was not the Russian peasantry, but the mostly Jewish metal-workers of his home town. He also began to associate with members of the secret Russian Populist group that included Lenin's elder brother, Alexander Ulyanov, and Józef Piłsudski's elder brother, Bronisław.

His talents as a conspirator and organizer aroused admiration, though his comrades were also repelled by his isolation, sarcastic denigration of comrades and strong personal antipathies. Still, his talents were indispensable, and in 1887, it was Jogiches who smuggled the leading Wilna Populists to safety across the nearby Prussian border after the discovery of the plot to assassinate Tsar Alexander III and the arrest of its leaders.

In 1887, Jogiches, Lev Kopelzon and Wacław Sielicki formed a 'radical Marxist' group in Wilna, each of them agitating in the circles they knew best in the multi-national Lithuanian capital. Jogiches worked among the Jewish working class and the Russian garrison. He managed the group's library of illegal publications, at one point hiding it with a Polish mistress, with whom he was improving his grasp of the Polish language. He also conducted classes in the natural sciences and in basic Marxism for the workers and helped to organize strike funds. In 1888, their efforts resulted in a strike of 30 to 40 men in a Wilna printing works. His arrest that year was the accidental result of the interrogation of a comrade by the Russian political police or *Okhrana*. Forced to release him for lack of evidence, the Russian authorities then decided to conscript him into the army. In 1890, he slipped across the Prussian border, arriving in Zurich a year after Rosa Luxemburg.

The 1880s were years of reorientation for the radical Russian intelligentsia. Confidence in the insurrectionary potential of the Russian peasantry was replaced by a growing hope that the rapidly expanding industrial proletariat would complete the destruction of tsarist autocracy, a hope fostered by the writings of Georgii Plekhanov in Geneva. The Marxist journalist Ryazanov met Jogiches in 1890 and later remembered him as a 'supporter of [the Populist] People's Will, closely linked with the *Proletariat*-people . . . already to a considerable extent inspired by Marxism'.

At twenty-three, Jogiches was a handsome devil, his debonair looks offset by a grave demeanour; his perpetual furled umbrella gave him the air of a knight-errant. Rosa appreciated his fine appearance, but it probably made little difference to her choice. What she found in him was a total dedication to her own ideals, combined with talents that neatly complemented her own. Devoted to revolutionary Marxism, unusually intelligent and ex-

29

tremely ambitious, Leo was also totally self-confident in practical matters and at twenty, as Rosa admitted later, she was a 'goose' looking for a mentor.

At first, Rosa was amused by Leo's biting sarcasm and his pejorative comments on all and sundry. Plekhanov came to see him as a Lithuanian, perhaps even as a Jew, but for Rosa, he was an ascetic Russian 'Nazarene', who badly needed the urbanity and civilization that only an emotionally warm and intellectually sophisticated West European, or 'Hellene', could provide. She still possessed the hubris of the young woman who believes she can save a man from himself. Within their relationship, as in their joint relations with the Russian Marxist movement, there was an echo of that Polish Messianism which has often seen Russia as an object for civilization. Jogiches recognized Rosa's genius from the start, saving every one of her intimate letters even though they contained many bruising references to himself. He rarely doubted his will power and organizational gifts. With Rosa's talents as a writer and debater, he foresaw that they might become the most influential partnership in European socialism.

The Enemies

German newspapers picked up every one of Rosa Luxemburg's provocative remarks, and the European Right came to regard her with a malicious, spiteful and highly personal hatred. She was that ultimately threatening combination in Hohenzollern Prussia, a crippled, Polish-Jewish woman intellectual. She regarded this hostility with humorous condescension, solemnly cutting their caricatures and slanders of the 'eternal feminine', as she ironically put it, from the papers and filing them away for the amusement of her friends. The detached tone she used with Captain Pabst, in ironic echo of Christ before Pilate, was typical of her attitude towards representatives of the exploiting classes. In 1904, she was sent to prison for publicly mocking the ignorance of Wilhelm II about the lives of working people, but her hostility towards even that histrionic imperialist was political rather than personal. She never doubted his capacity for destructive violence; on that she was much clearer than most of her contemporaries. She also knew that there were still more than enough misguided working men in uniform eager to end her life for a crust. Though she never begged for mercy, she was prudent in avoiding unnecessary danger. She also believed that martyrdom was an honourable consummation of a revolutionary career that would itself fuel the class struggle. Emperors, popes, capitalists and *Junkers* could not deflect her from her chosen course.

The same cannot be said for her enemies within the Socialist International. They inflicted traumatic humiliations on Rosa Luxemburg which substantially determined many key episodes in her life, including her disgraceful treatment of Karl Radek, which so many of her admirers have found inexplicable. The first of these comradely enemies was Georgii Plekhanov, the autocratic 'Pope' of Russian Marxism. In this, she was entirely innocent, the victim of guilt by association with Jogiches.

Georgii Plekhanov was already 45 years old when Jogiches first met him in Geneva. He was already a living legend. Plekhanov had been a founder of the revolutionary Populist *Zemlia i Volia* (Land and Liberty) organization. On 6 December 1876, Plekhanov had been the main speaker at the first working-class demonstration ever held in Russia, at the Kazan Cathedral in St Petersburg. He also conducted Populist agitation among the Saratov peasantry, but at the 1879 Voronezh congress, he broke with the supporters of terrorism to form his own *Chernyi Peredyel* (Black Repartition) group, attempting unsuccessfully to create a mass political movement. In 1880, he settled in Geneva, where, for the next thirty-seven years, he devoted himself to the study of Marxism and its application to Russian conditions. There he was joined by his old comrades, Axelrod and Deutsch, and by Vera Zasulich, who gained the admiration of Russian 'Society' by assassinating the venal Governor of St Petersburg. (Her acquittal by the jury, which was in no doubt as to the facts, was a milestone in the growing alienation of educated Russians from the autocracy.)

In 1883, Plekhanov and his comrades formed the Emancipation of Labour Group, the first Russian Marxist organization. Plekhanov's pamphlets, *Socialism and the Political Struggle* (1883) and *Our Differences* (1885) declared war on the Populist tradition and established their author as the 'Father of Russian Marxism'.

This status was accepted by Engels and the Second International. As the repressive reign of Alexander III ground on, there was little to show for these efforts. Yet Plekhanov's granite faith in Marxist *science* allowed him to accept every political setback with equanimity. Alexander III's enthusiasm for the industrialization of Russia would, he believed, inevitably lead Russia along the path previously trodden by the countries of Western Europe. As a Marxist, he added a crucial rider: in the future bourgeois democratic revolution in Russia, the proletariat must maintain its leadership, or hegemony, or at a minimum, its organizational integrity to ensure that it did not merely bleed for bourgeois demands as the French workers had in 1789 and 1848.

Jogiches offered his family's wealth and his priceless contacts on the Prussian-Russian border to a group whose increasing detachment from Russian society threatened to undermine its influence. Plekhanov's initial impression of Jogiches was condescending but positive. He seemed to be 'a most interesting, intelligent and apparently very efficient young man', someone who could devote himself to 'practical questions so that we are not obliged to forsake theoretical work'. Plekhanov offered Jogiches full membership in his Group, an extraordinary honour denied many seasoned revolutionaries. The largely unknown 24-year-old was invited to become virtual 'Crown Prince' of Russian Marxism. Yet within three years, Plekhanov was defaming Jogiches to Engels as a revolutionary careerist, intriguer and 'a miniature edition of Nechaev'. Jogiches certainly shared Sergei Nechaev's obsessive revolutionary asceticism, but Nechaev had become a pejorative byword for unhinged paranoid violence, his brilliant career terminating in the murder of an innocent comrade. So what went wrong?

Plekhanov's widow remembered that it had something to do with 'a lack of respect for the authorities'. Plekhanov was angry when Jogiches refused to return to Russia as his Group's representative, perhaps to secure the formal subordination of Marxist circles inside Russia to the Geneva group. Jogiches also had the effrontery to bargain with Plekhanov over a contract whereby Jogiches subsidized their publications, while stipulating that they must include pamphlets addressed to Russian workers. Plekhanov took the money, treated the agreement with contempt, and accused Jogiches of 'greed' when he objected.

Perhaps Jogiches' most heinous offence, in Plekhanov's eyes, was that Jogiches caught Plekhanov out in an act of ideological heterodoxy. Nothing could be more calculated to damage the reputation of the pillar of Marxist orthodoxy than 'stuffing the red flag into his pockets'. The occasion for this lapse was the 1892 Russian famine. Surprisingly for a Marxist of his generation, Plekhanov responded positively to Leo Tolstoy's appeals for famine relief, urging all Russian opposition groups abroad to collaborate, while using the opportunity to explain the Russian government's responsibility for the famine. For once, Plekhanov omitted the usual Marxist demands for proletarian hegemony and ideological clarity, and Jogiches had the temerity to point this out. Like many a crown prince before him, Jogiches had shown a disturbing capacity for disloyalty, and Plekhanov determined to annihilate him. When Jogiches accepted defeat by abandoning Russian work to help Rosa Luxemburg in her work on Poland, Plekhanov made common cause with Rosa Luxemburg's patriotic-socialist enemies, the Mendelsons.

Stanisław Mendelson and Maria Jankowska were the most distinguished couple in Polish socialism before Rosa Luxemburg and Leo Jogiches. In 1878, Mendelson had drafted the first Polish socialist programme with Waryński's encouragement. Mendelson escaped from Russia and was then expelled from Austria, arriving in Geneva (where he met Jankowska) in the same year as Plekhanov. Plekhanov's comrade, Deutsch, described Mendelson as 'very ambitious and thirsty for power . . . he wanted to play a dominant role in the Polish movement'. Hostility towards younger rivals was a recurring feature of the Russian revolutionary movement. Mendelson became editor of the socialist journals *Równość* (Equality) and *Przedświt* (Dawn), while Jankowska edited *Walki Klas* (Class Struggles). In the mid-1880s, the Mendelsons moved to Paris, where Jankowska's salon became a magnet for socialist luminaries including Jean Jaurès and Wilhelm Liebknecht. The Mendelsons continued to visit Russian Poland and wrote the programme of *Proletariat II*, the group Rosa joined as a schoolgirl. In the following year, they took part in the founding Congress of the Socialist International in Paris.

In 1891, the Mendelsons moved to London, quickly becoming

33

close friends with Friedrich Engels just at the moment when socialists in Poland and in exile were agreed on the need for the foundation of a united Polish Socialist Party. Rosa Luxemburg and Leo Jogiches shared so much with the Mendelsons, but one major issue divided them. Disillusioned by the slow progress of the Russian revolutionary movement, the Mendelsons had come to the conclusion that the Polish working class must strike out on its own for emancipation. They were determined to ensure that any socialist party that emerged in Poland was irrevocably committed to fighting for Polish independence, even though they knew that Waryński's hostility to nationalism was widely shared by working-class militants at home.

The Mendelsons' first move was to appeal to the loyalty of the elderly Engels. The time had come, they suggested, for Polish workers to read *The Communist Manifesto*. They offered to translate it, if Engels would only write a new introduction endorsing the independence of Poland. The old man did them proud, insisting that 'the workers of the whole of the rest of Europe need Poland's independence just as much as the Polish workers themselves'.

The next step was to have this and other documents printed in Warsaw, but then the tsarist gendarmerie intervened by capturing their presses. The Mendelsons convinced themselves that the *Okhrana* had been tipped off by the internationalist, Marcin Kasprzak, Rosa Luxemburg's friend and mentor. The Mendelsons' charges against Kasprzak were heard in the Westminster Palace Hotel, London, in August 1892, by a revolutionary court of honour, which included the English Marxist, Hyndman, and the Irish revolutionary, Michael Davitt. The charges were circumstantial, confused and mutually contradictory, and Davitt was in little doubt that they resulted from a conviction that the tsarist authorities were deliberately favouring socialist internationalism at the expense of Polish nationalism. The court dismissed the charges, but Mendelson refused to accept this verdict and continued to smear Kasprzak as a police spy.

The Mendelsons next created a Union of Polish Socialists Abroad, tightly governed by a 'Central' which they controlled. The Union then summoned Polish socialists of all factions to a congress in Paris in November 1892, but the balance was decisively in favour of the 'patriots', as was evident when the veteran patriot, Limanowski, was asked to take the chair. The eighteen participants approved a *Draft Programme of the Polish Socialist Party* prepared by the Mendelsons. In January of the following year, Mendelson visited socialist groups in Warsaw, Wiłna, Riga and St Petersburg to test their reactions. No one objected to the creation of a Polish Socialist Party under that name, and the party, called by its initials, PPS (*Polska Partia Socjalistyczna*), became a permanent feature of Polish politics. The internationalists awaited the opportunity to eliminate the demand for an independent Poland from the *Draft Programme* at a founding Congress of the PPS. Mendelson had no intention of conceding such an opportunity, and in Wiłna he found what he was looking for. The Polish socialists there were led by a skilled conspirator with the self-confidence Mendelson's scheme required. This was Józef Piłsudski, the younger brother of Alexander Ulyanov's comrade, Bronisław. While Mendelson returned to London to assist Engels and Hyndman in 'taking the salute' at the May Day demonstration in Hyde Park, Piłsudski chose his moment. At the end of June 1893, he and four comrades met in a wood outside Wiłna, declared themselves the founding Congress of the PPS and adopted Mendelson's *Draft Programme* without amendment. Mendelson now construed his agreement with the Warsaw socialists as authorizing his Union of Polish Socialists Abroad to represent the PPS at the imminent Third Congress of the Socialist International.

The success of Mendelson's *coup de main* depended on surprise: the internationalists were given the minimum possible time to react before the International Congress convened in Zurich on 6 August. Perhaps they got wind of what was afoot, for when Marchlewski, still suffering from pneumonia contracted in the Warsaw Citadel, arrived in Zurich in May, he brought with him an impeccable mandate from workers in Warsaw. In Paris, Warski rushed out the first number of a paper entitled *Sprawa Robotnicza* (The Workers' Cause) with funds supplied by Jogiches. In Zurich, Paris and Warsaw, the young internationalists announced the formation of a rival to the PPS, which they called the Social Democracy of the Kingdom of Poland (*Socjaldemokracja Królestwa Polskiego* or SDKP). Rosa Luxemburg drafted its *Report* to the Socialist International. Carefully avoiding all mention of the PPS, she argued that, 'Our patriotic "intelligentsia" also, which unwittingly represents petit-bourgeois ideals in the social sphere, is trying to drag the workers' movement in its patriotic wake.' This attempt would fail, she insisted: 'The patriotic tendency, the ideal of an independent Polish state, has no prospects of winning over the social-democratic working class. The economic-social history of the three parts of the former Kingdom of Poland has *organically incorporated them* into the three annexing states and created distinct aspirations and political interests in each of them.' The phrase 'organic incorporation' was never forgiven by Polish patriots, who felt that Rosa Luxemburg was suggesting that the rape of Mother Poland had been consummated as a happy marriage. Plekhanov had some justification for denouncing the *Report* as 'Jesuitical'.

On 6 August 1893, the sunlit streets of Zurich were alive with 10,000 Swiss workers, many of them pouring from special trains, who greeted the hundreds of socialists and trade unionists gathering for the Congress. A cheerful procession of bands and banners, gymnasts and tableaux, wound its way up to the *Kantonschule* for speeches by Hobson, Bebel, Turati and others. When the 400 delegates pushed their way past the pamphlet sellers at the Concert Hall, they found it decorated with a portrait of Karl Marx flanked by red flags. The motto 'Workers of the World, Unite!' hung in sixteen languages from the walls. The flat workers' caps of the British trade unionists were offset by the feathered Alpine hats of the Swiss, but the most striking contrast was between the flamboyant Latins from France and Italy, representing a medley of ideologies, organizations and regions, and the hundred-strong delegation of ideologically homogeneous and strictly disciplined German Social Democrats. In the first big test of the Congress, over the admission of anarchists, the German veto was decisive. Rosa Luxemburg was present to see a demonstration of the power of the German SPD (*Sozialdemokratische Partei Deutschlands*), which she would never forget.

Her own ordeal came on 8 August, when Bebel and Vandervelde reported back from the Mandate Commission. Ignacy Daszyński, the suave and handsome founder of the socialist party of Austrian Poland, the PPSD (*Polska Partia Socjaldemokratyczna Galicji i Śląska Górniego*), opposed both SDKP mandates. Finding

36

himself unable to cite any acceptable grounds for rejecting March-lewski's mandate, he concentrated his fire on Rosa Luxemburg's, which had been supplied by *Sprawa Robotnicza*. Daszyński pointed out that the paper had only appeared once and hinted darkly at sinister reasons for the absence of a signature on Luxemburg's mandate: 'no one knows who is the editor of the paper who is sending a delegate here'. Rosa knew that Daszyński was insinuating that she had been sent by the alleged police-spy, Marcin Kasprzak. The 23-year-old Marxist apprentice was forced to defend her integrity before the established patriarchs of the International, against the dictates of prudence and personal preference. The bitter discussion lasted for an hour and was finally resolved by a ballot, in which Plekhanov voted against her. Marchlewski would find words of consolation: the affair had attracted massive interest in the SDKP; copies of her report had gone like hot cakes, while he himself had been invited to tea with Engels and Bebel. This was cold comfort for Rosa. She would never forget that she had been expelled from the Congress of the international proletariat as a possible police-spy.

The SDKP fought back. Marchlewski denounced the behaviour of Daszyński and Mendelson to the Warsaw workers. Jan Strożecki successfully demanded Mendelson's resignation from the PPS and the Union of Polish Socialists Abroad, yet when the Second Congress of the PPS met in Warsaw in February 1894, Strożecki, like most other Polish socialists, threw in his lot with the one Polish party acknowledged by the International, by the vast majority of Polish socialist exiles, and by the fraternal parties, the PPSD in Austria and the PPS of Prussia. Piłsudski's unparalleled success as editor, printer and distributor of the illegal PPS paper, *Robotnik* (The Worker), convinced many Polish workers that this was the correct choice. The Mendelsons' career as leaders of Polish socialism was over, but their chicanery had defeated Rosa Luxemburg's polemics. They had been actively assisted by Piłsudski, Daszyński and his sister-in-law, Zofia Daszyńska, by the Austrian socialist leader, Victor Adler, by Plekhanov and, last but by no means least, by Friedrich Engels.

Today's radical women would see this chicanery as typical of patriarchal behaviour; even then, commentators were struck by the patriarchal portrait of Marx that dominated the hall and the

37

slogan 'The strivings of the fathers will be our blessing'. Yet this was not Rosa's reaction, and not just because women had also opposed her. On the contrary, this experience reinforced her devotion to Karl Marx, whose one true daughter she was resolved to be; her subsequent correspondence was peppered with denigration of the 'false sons'. She rarely laid traps for these enemies, waiting instead for the class war to expose their feet of clay, but when it came she shared her delight at the sight with her friends. In the meantime, as she explained several years later, the ideas of Karl Marx provided her with what she called, in paraphrase of the Battle Hymn of the Reformation, 'a firm guarantee (*eine feste Bürgschaft*) of the ultimate victory'. She believed she had found in Marxism a 'calm insight into the conformity with laws of objective historical evolution'. It was this certainty, variously described as religious or 'scientist' by her critics, that gave her the characteristic Marxist virtues of 'patience, strength for deeds and courage for endurance'.

Rosa Luxemburg's fiasco at the Zurich Congress had mortgaged her future. There were immediate practical tasks to be addressed if Daszyński's taunts about the ephemeral nature of *Sprawa Robotnicza* and the SDKP were to be rebutted. In her *Report*, Rosa Luxemburg had also hinted at a controversial interpretation of Marxist economics. Unless she could prove this proposition sound, she herself would be exposed as the bad Marxist. This presented her with a scholarly challenge of many years' duration. In some ways, the whole of her future political and intellectual life was an extended recapitulation of this heroic moment when she and her young peers first found themselves a harassed internationalist minority within the Socialist International.

Journalism: Sprawa Robotnicza

Rosa Luxemburg's *Works* are famous for their Marxist rigour and their biting sarcasm. They provide only half the explanation for her ability to retain her poise, optimism and humanity in the most distressing circumstances. For the other half, we have to read her letters; and what a pleasure that is. For beyond the

38

obsessive world of factional feuding, we find in them an enchanted garden of pets and landscapes, geology and dress making, archaeology and music, painting, plants and literature. The letters allow us to meet Rosa as few of her contemporaries could, walking in Rousseau's haunts above Lake Geneva in 1893:

Today: for the first time it's been quite grey since the morning. No sign of rain. The whole sky is covered with clouds of varying sizes and shadings; it looks like a deep, stormy sea. The lake glitters with a smooth, steely-coloured surface. The mountains, shrouded in mist, are sad, the Dent du Midi can be glimpsed through a cloud. The air is mild, fresh and filled with the scent of apple trees and grasses. Around me it is quiet; the birds twitter dreamily, softly and evenly. I am sitting near the house on the grass at the little path that passes the well. The grass is pushing up wildly; flowers, especially the big yellow ones, in masses. Over them the bees flutter in such masses that there is a constant hum. There is a scent of honey. Now and then a big bumble-bee flies off with a loud buzz. I am in a sad mood, and yet my soul feels well, because I particularly like such quiet, meditative weather.

This all sounds rather dreamy and sentimental, chiefly remarkable for coming from the pen of one of Lenin's rivals. On other occasions, Rosa Luxemburg's relations with 'nature' were strenuous and intense. She had an unusual empathy with living creatures of all sizes and orders (fleas and bedbugs excepted), and she was fascinated by geology. As a scientist she sought out the underlying order and symmetry which lay behind the random scenes that met the eye. As she got older, and particularly in periods of depression and imprisonment, she studied botany, geography and geology systematically, yet her 'science' had little in common with the procedures of white-coated specialists in antiseptic laboratories. She was more like an artist, whose eyes and hands edited and reconstructed 'nature' after a painstaking study of the laws of perspective, anatomy and light.

She continued to find her formal 'scientific' work challenging and absorbing. As we have seen, this derived from a controversial interpretation of Marxist economics. In explaining the anti-patriotic devotion of the Polish grande bourgeoisie for the Russian tsar, Rosa's *Report* had asserted that, 'The Russian export market, which allows it [the Polish bourgeoisie] to realize the surplus value expropriated from the Polish workers, has made it a loyal support of "Throne and Altar".' This might be paraphrased as follows: Polish capitalists would be unable to realize surplus value within the limited markets available within an independent Poland; only the Russian Empire, with its pre-capitalist Eurasian markets, guaranteed their economic viability. Zofia Daszyńska, already a doctor of economics from Zurich University, was not the most eminent of the experts certain to try to disprove this contention. Rosa Luxemburg had to marshal impressive evidence in its support. The result was her doctoral dissertation, *The Development of Industry in Poland* (1897). As Polish economic literature was scarce in Switzerland, she decided to visit the major Polish library in Paris.

Rosa Luxemburg set off for Paris in March 1894. As she did so, Weselowski and Ratyński read to the ten delegates at the founding Congress of the SDKP in Warsaw the resolutions she had drafted for them; they were enthusiastically approved. Paris was a city in a grander mould than Warsaw or Zurich, the centre of world fashion, both intellectual and material. For Rosa it was also the city of Revolution, the city of the Commune. As a plain and far from wealthy young woman with a tendency to depression and neurasthenia, she found it rather overwhelming, as she confided to Jogiches:

> I have such a noise in my head . . . that I'm fit for nothing. Ah, my golden one, if only I had you with me! Well, later we rode with the tram to the Bois de Boulogne and back. I saw the Trocadero, the Arc de Triomphe, the Eiffel Tower and the Grand Opera. I am deafened by the noise. And there are so many beautiful women here! Actually, they're all beautiful, or at least they seem to be. No, you mustn't come here on any account! You stay in Zurich!

Cezaryna Wojnarowska, an old comrade of Waryński, took Rosa under her wing and introduced her to the leaders of French socialism. Rosa was charmed, finding 'Cezarynko' 'pretty, warm and intelligent'. She lodged with the Warskis, who were everlastingly kind, but their limitations created problems which demanded tact and self-discipline on her part. As she informed Leo,

'Adolf and Jadzia are real children, people of a different calibre than us . . . It's enough to see how they approach people to see whether they are capable of exercising influence as representatives of the Party. Naïveté, Arcadian homeliness!'

Rosa tried to correct Jadzia's contributions to *Sprawa Robotnicza* without her noticing, but Jadzia and Adolf must have known that the paper had been taken out of their hands. It was Rosa who now wrote the leaders (and recast them to fit odd column sizes), who prodded the Warskis, Marchlewski and Jogiches himself for their contributions, who hassled the printer and read the proofs. And when the copies were ready, it was Rosa who distributed them to Polish exiles throughout Europe and to Kasprzak in Poznań, so that they could be smuggled into Poland.

It is not every 24-year-old journalist who works her ticket as an editor. This was both a marvellous challenge and a huge problem. The Polish schools taught Russian, and many of her prospective readers were barely literate in their own language. There was no existing school of Polish socialist journalism, and Rosa's own contacts with Polish working men and women had been extremely limited. She had neither circulation figures nor election returns to tell her whether *Sprawa Robotnicza* was better received than Piłsudski's *Robotnik*.

Some of her articles were standard socialist *agitprop*, hammering away the message that the capitalists were hand in glove with the Russian tsar: 'When our worker demands a bit of a better life from his exploiter, the Polish manufacturer asks just as meekly for cossacks and gendarmes for his Polish 'brothers', as do the German [manufacturers] Scheibler or Geyer.' Other articles, such as her descriptions of the heroic May Day Rising in Łódż in 1892, were more gripping. She began with a description of the peaceful, even cheerful, May Day demonstrations permitted in London, Hamburg and Zurich. She then contrasted them with the scenes in Warsaw, where gendarmes had arrested demonstrating workers on their way home; 'And in Łódż . . . in Łódż instead of red flags, red blood glistens on the streets. Instead of songs, there is the crack of whips and a salvo of carbines . . .'

Then there were moments when all of this excitement and incessant activity could not hold back her desperate nostalgia for Leo's familiar form, propped up in bed wreathed in smoke as he

41

read. He reproved her for bothering him with her emotions, criticized her work relentlessly and used her guilt at taking his money as a whip for her back.

At home in Poland, the SDKP militants capitalized on working-class resentment of the intelligentsia, most of which rallied to the PPS. The SDKP's internationalism went down well with the German minority, but it had to compete with the PPS and the General Jewish Workers' League (the *Bund*) for Polish and Jewish support. Then in 1895, nearly 400 members were arrested, and in January 1896, the Central Executive of the SDKP disbanded itself, advising its remaining supporters to join the PPS. This was an appalling blow for Rosa, who had hoped to turn the tables on the PPS at the Fourth Congress of the Socialist International in London that summer.

The resourceful Wojnarowska rapidly organized an Association of Polish Social Democratic Workers Abroad to assure the internationalists at least one valid mandate. Rosa also gained the sympathy of Karl Kautsky, editor of the German socialist review *Die Neue Zeit* (The New Era), the socialist world's most prestigious journal, who allowed her to attack Polish 'social patriotism' on the eve of the Congress. Under pressure from Daszyński, Victor Adler protested apoplectically to Kautsky, demanding a preview of any future article by Luxemburg, so that he could 'save what the doctrinaire goose has ruined'. Allemane, Vaillant and Bernstein were more sympathetic, while Plekhanov, who had given up trying to blackball her, now tried to co-opt her to the Russian delegation; an offer she indignantly declined.

In London, Piłsudski and Jodko-Narkiewicz of the PPS glowered furiously as Rosa Luxemburg urged the International to reject the demand for the independence of Poland; for, as she explained, 'The adoption of the Polish demand into the Programme of the International Proletariat would logically trigger a whole series of analogous natural questions, like the independence of Bohemia, of Ireland, the annexation of Alsace-Lorraine.' This would lead to, 'the dissolution of the compact political struggle of all proletarians in each state into a series of fruitless national struggles.'

The International was not convinced. A composite resolution was adopted which omitted the demand for the recreation of a

Polish state, but asserted 'the right to complete self- determination of all nations', while summoning the oppressed nationalities to join the socialist movement in abolishing all forms of oppression. Rosa pretended to be jubilant about her victory over the PPS. In reality, her campaign had been counter-productive, committing the socialist movement to supporting 'fruitless national struggles' everywhere. Thereafter, the Russian and Austrian Social Democrats, and the British labour movement, became increasingly sympathetic towards demands for 'autonomy' and 'self-determination'. Only the German SPD interpreted the resolution in the sense desired by Rosa Luxemburg. She remained adamant and always remembered her labours for the SDKP as 'earnest and respectable work'.

The Conquest of Berlin

Once Rosa Luxemburg received her doctorate in 1897, her residence in Switzerland served little purpose. She might have waited for Leo Jogiches to finish his doctorate, but his plans for a dissertation on the economic-political ideas of Russian Populism, or on ground rent, came to nothing. As Rosa remembered later, 'Despite his extraordinary gifts and sharpness of intellect, Leo is simply incapable of writing. That was the curse of his existence . . . after he had to leave practical, organizational activity in Russia. He felt quite deracinated, vegetated in permanent bitterness, [and] finally he lost the habit of reading, because it was pointless.' Blackballed by Plekhanov from the Russian revolutionary movement and discouraged by the collapse of the SDKP, Jogiches was well on the way to becoming yet another 'superfluous' man.

Their relations had changed considerably since the days in 1893, when she had complained to Jogiches that she was 'totally alone' in his absence. Her work in Paris had opened her eyes to what she felt were weaknesses in his character, some of them masquerading as strengths. She came to resent his carping criticisms and his demands that she account to him on the smallest particular (even on her clothing), while he said little about his work and evaded any discussion of their personal life. Her com-

43

plaints could be echoed by so many women: 'When I, fit to drop from the endless cause, sit down for a moment's rest, I let my thoughts wander, and I realize that I have never had my own personal corner, that I never exist and live as my own *I*.'

The experience of making decisions on her own in Paris enhanced her self-confidence, though it was a long time before she ceased to rail at Leo for leaving her alone. 'If you were with me, I would fear no work', she implored. Gradually, she began to assert herself and to urge him to reform himself:

> I have a right to do so, for I am ten times better than you and decisively condemn this strongest side of your character. I will now terrorize you without any sympathy, until you become soft to me and begin to feel and behave towards people like an ordinary good human being. At the same time, I have unlimited love for you and a remorseless strictness towards your character weaknesses.

She entirely failed to comprehend that her growing strength was bound to exacerbate his incorrigible tendency to reticence. She was nearer the mark when she located this reticence in his fear of her competition: •

> My *success and public appearances can poison our relationship*, the more the longer they continue – because of your pride and suspicion . . . If, after mature consideration I come to the conclusion that I have the alternative [either] to withdraw from the movement and to live with you in some nest in harmony, or to work in a wider arena in enmity with you – I choose the former.

Mature consideration must surely have persuaded her that this was not a real choice for so gifted and ambitious a person.

In 1897, when Rosa tried to discuss her feelings with Leo, he mockingly replied that he needed no 'medicine'. As she wrote him a long letter of protest, she could already see his eyes darting impatiently as if to say, 'What is she driving at?' She just wanted to love him: 'I want that soft, trusting, ideal atmosphere to reign, as it did in those other times'. She closed with a long, sad poem about the silences that had begun to engulf their lives. Looking back, it seemed to her that 'for eight long years, we made appointments, but didn't live a single month'. But there were still times when they dreamed together about their future work:

Do you remember, how musicians came into the garden once on Sunday there and woke us up, we went on foot to Maroggia and came back on foot, and then the moon went up over San Salvatore, and we discussed whether I should go to Germany; we stood tightly embracing on the path in the dark and watched the sickle moon over the mountain.

Rosa's mother died just as she completed her dissertation, but a return to Poland was virtually ruled out for someone of her notoriety. Later, this would plague her with remorse. None of her Marxist rivals had any doubt that they owed it to the movement to keep their brains in Europe rather than their bodies in Siberia, and Rosa shared with the Warsaw Positivists a contempt for romantic self-sacrifice. In fact, she and her comrades frequently dissuaded one another from unnecessary risks. A far more welcoming alternative was offered by the great Social Democratic Party of Germany.

The abrogation of Bismarck's anti-socialist legislation still left dozens of petty restrictions on SPD activities. No member of the party could expect state employment (which included virtually all employment in education). To qualify as a lawyer, Karl Liebknecht had to avoid the slightest suspicion of political activity until his late twenties. Party newspapers were subject to petty censorship, party meetings broken up without reason and party militants imprisoned for incitement. In Prussia, women and young people were forbidden to attend political meetings. The annual report of the SPD contained an appendix proudly listing the party's persecutions for the year in question.

The SPD throve under this relatively mild harassment. Its share of the vote for the Reichstag, the German parliament, elected on universal male suffrage, rose from 10 per cent in 1887, to 20 per cent in 1890, to 23 per cent in 1893 and to 27 per cent in 1898. By 1895, the SPD boasted thirty-nine daily papers, twenty-eight bi-weeklies and nine weeklies. (In its entire history, the British labour movement has *never* supported more than *two* dailies for any length of time!) The pinnacle of the edifice was the Reichstag fraction, which appointed a *Vorstand* or Executive, led by August Bebel, which kept a close eye on the SPD organ,

Vorwärts (Forwards), in Berlin. Karl Kautsky, since Engels' death the most influential Marxist, edited *Die Neue Zeit*, published in Stuttgart, which had established itself as *the* theoretical journal of the entire Socialist International. Equally striking was the special position within the International won by Clara Zetkin, leader of the German proletarian women's movement and editor of its paper, *Die Gleichheit* (Equality). Yet such was the alienation of the SPD from educated German society that the socialist press was chronically short of decent journalists and always happy to pay a generous fee for good articles from foreign comrades.

The first of Rosa's comrades to respond to these opportunities was Parvus, who moved to Stuttgart in 1891 to work with Kautsky and Clara Zetkin. Later, he followed Kautsky to Berlin, but the Prussian police expelled him to Saxony. So began his obsessive quest for Prussian citizenship, that would ultimately lead him into a Faustian bargain with the German Foreign Ministry. In 1896, Marchlewski followed, but despite his Prussian maternal pedigree the Prussian police denied his application for citizenship, forcing him to remain in Munich and to avoid any public part in SPD affairs.

Not for the last time, Rosa Luxemburg was able to turn patriarchal institutions against themselves. What Parvus and Marchlewski could not, as men, achieve was quite simple for a woman. She simply had to find a Prussian and persuade him to marry her. In Russia, young men frequently lent themselves to fictional marriages to rescue young women from authoritarian fathers. Marrying into Prussian citizenship was less conventional, but this did not deter Rosa Luxemburg. Her old landlady, Olympia Lübeck, finally conscripted her son, Gustav, a rather aimless Bohemian painter, who reluctantly agreed. In 1898, Gustav and Rosa were married. Rosa Luxemburg was now a Prussian.

In May 1898, Rosa left Zurich by rail for Munich and then on to Berlin. It struck her as a vast, cold parade ground: 'I feel as though I had arrived quite alone and foreign 'to conquer' Berlin, and when I look it in the eye, I am anxious in the face of its cold power, indifferent to me.' Her train had run over a peasant herdsman in the night; 'no good omen', as she noted. She thought over her life and, for a moment, yearned once more for a quiet existence with Leo in Switzerland. She wept, but realized that he would only say, 'Now stop crying, you'll look like the devil knows what!' And stop crying she did.

3 The Eagle Soars

'Nothing to do with the Women's Movement'

Just eight days after her arrival in Berlin, Rosa Luxemburg rang the bell at No. 9 Katzbachstrasse, the home of the Executive of the Social Democratic Party of Germany. A blond, Bavarian giant opened the door, a magnanimous twinkle in his eye. At 52, Ignatz Auer looked much younger than his years. In his prime now, he was one of the most powerful men in German Socialism. As SPD Secretary, he was a member of the five-man Executive that included August Bebel, Paul Singer, Wilhelm Pfannkuch and Albin Gerisch. Auer was absolutely amazed at the news that Rosa Luxemburg had already acquired Prussian citizenship but far from displeased, for they were allies already. Auer had fought his own battles with Rosa's enemies in the PPS. The most portentous had occurred during the 1892 Vienna Congress of the Austrian socialists, at which Daszyński had declined to join the Austrian Germans in a single party, while offering them a federal link with his Galician PPSD, pending the merger of the three Polish nationalist socialist parties. Auer had strongly urged the Austrian socialist leader, Adler, to reject this offer and insist on a single socialist party for the Austrian Empire. It was in ignoring this advice that Adler had won Daszyński's friendship.

Auer lost no time in confirming that the SPD entirely shared Rosa Luxemburg's view of Polish patriotism. 'All five of us in the Party Executive regard the independence of Poland as a folly, a fantasy', he told her. Indeed, in Auer's opinion, 'One can do the Polish workers no greater favour than to Germanize them, but one mustn't say so to them'. Wilhelm Liebknecht's outdated attachment to Polish patriotism was simply an old man's conceit with no political significance. Rosa Luxemburg then gave Auer a short lecture on Polish politics, not so much to demonstrate her superior knowledge as to suggest that she might be useful to the SPD during the imminent Reichstag elections. Auer was delighted and, waving aside her offer of assistance among the Polish

48

migrant workers in the Ruhr, he urged her to set to work in the predominantly Polish areas of Upper Silesia, where the pedestrian figure of August Winter, one of the few internationalists in the Prussian PPS, badly needed reinforcement. It was, therefore, as a 'token' Pole that Rosa Luxemburg was first welcomed into the SPD, and this was one of the roles that she continued to perform right up to 1914.

The SPD needed a talented Polish representative if it was to stand any chance of rallying the Polish working class. Prussia itself had once been carved out of Polish territory by the Teutonic Knights and their *Junker* successors. By 1815, Silesia, West Prussia and the Principality of Poznań (Posen) had also been annexed. By the end of the nineteenth century, there were Polish communities numbering over three million people along the long border with Russia's Polish domains. They were increasingly threatened by ruthless colonizing activities by the German authorities, themselves under pressure from the so-called 'Hakatists', a vigilante group of protagonists of German superiority. In addition, tens of thousands of Poles had flocked to the booming economies of western Germany, to the mines and steel works of the Ruhr and to the shipyards and docks of Hamburg and Bremen. Relations betwen Poles and Germans were analogous to those between the Irish and English. Some Poles assimilated to the 'superior' German culture, while others found their nationalism reinforced by German condescension.

The Poles had many reasons to be receptive to the anti-government rhetoric of the socialists, yet most Poles in the borderlands still looked to the bourgeois and clerical Polish People's Party, while the migrant workers looked for protection from their fellow Catholics in the *Zentrum* (Centre Party), based on the German Catholic areas of South and West Germany. This tendency was reinforced during the so-called '*Kulturkampf*' of the 1870s, when Catholics had shared in the persecution Bismarck had inflicted on the socialists. The Catholics had responded by developing an ideology of Thomist community values which successfully insulated most Catholic workers from Marxism. In 1892, Stanisław Mendelson had persuaded the SPD to permit the PPS to organize an affiliate in Prussia. As time went on, it became increasingly obvious that the majority of PPS activists in

49

Prussia were taking SPD money, while attempting to wean Polish workers away from allegiance to the SPD and into supporting the demand for Polish independence.

Jogiches was horrified by Rosa's immersion in electoral agitation, which he regarded as a demeaning distraction. She was more percipient: 'This work alone creates respect for me in the eyes of . . . the Executive, and in all their eyes it can only create a good reputation, for the single reason that I am emerging as a *first rate speaker* . . .' The Reichstag candidates in Silesia were soon quarrelling for her services, and for two weeks, she travelled from one end of the province to the other, earning cheers and bouquets from packed meetings wherever she went. For the first time, she was part of a real mass movement; even the police were, as Rosa put it, 'correct'. Despite all the turmoil, there was time for nostalgia, for this was the first time she had visited any part of Poland since 1889. 'The . . . strongest impression was made on me by the countryside here: cornfields, meadows, woods, wide expanses, and the Polish language, Polish peasants all around. You have no conception how happy all that makes me.'

Polish politics made her much less happy. To begin with, she accepted that she had no choice but to work with the Prussian PPS, and for a while, a truce obtained between them. Her defence of the rights of Polish-speaking schoolchildren even won their grudging approval. Then, one morning in 1900, she was dragged from her bed by Stanisław Trusiewicz with the news that he and Feliks Dzierżyński were well on the way to refounding the SDKP (though they called the party, the SDKP*iL*: Social Democracy of the Kingdom of Poland *and Lithuania*, thereby blurring a distinction she and Jogiches had insisted on).

To begin with, Rosa Luxemburg was charmed by Trusiewicz and enthusiastic about the venture of reviving the party she had helped to found, but to her disgust, its new leaders looked not to her, but to Cezaryna Wojnarowska for ideological mentorship. They showed every intention of compromising with 'social-patriotism' by opting for Polish autonomy. Rosa preferred no party at all to one that compromised its Marxist principles and confided her misery to Jogiches:

The [re]creation of Social Democracy in the Kingdom [of

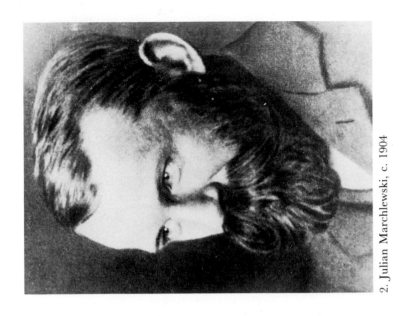

2. Julian Marchlewski, c. 1904

1. Marcin Kasprzak

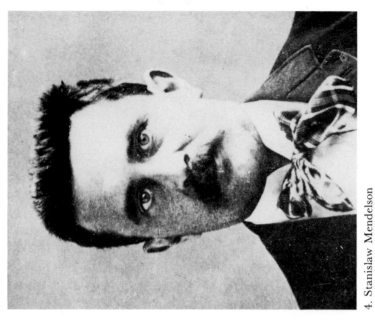

4. Stanislaw Mendelson

3. Leo Jogiches as a student

6. Eduard Bernstein

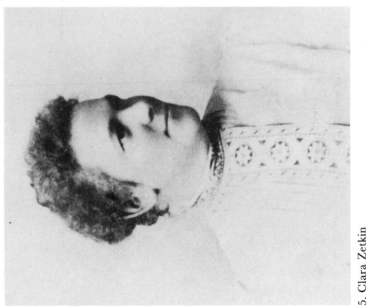

5. Clara Zetkin

7. Karl Kautsky

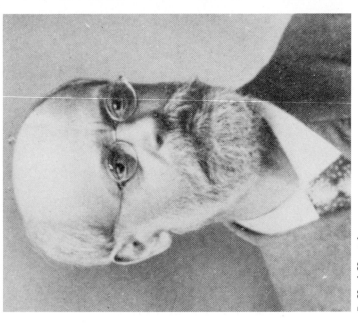

8. Luise Kautsky

10. Rosa Luxemburg and Kostja Zetkin, c. 1910

9. Rosa Luxemburg, *Self-portrait*, c. 1909

11. August Bebel, c. 1900

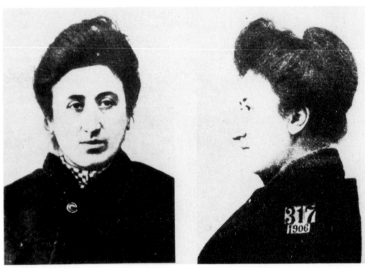

12. Rosa Luxemburg, prison mug shots, Warsaw, 1906

13. Teachers at the SPD Party School in Berlin in 1909. From left:
E. Wurm, F. Mehring, H. Schulz, R. Luxemburg, Stadthagen,
H. Cunow, unidentified

14. Rosa Luxemburg addressing workers in Deutz, 1910

16. Paul Levi

15. Karl Liebknecht

Poland] is a veritable misery for us. So long as *nothing* followed us, a certain memory remained of a serious and respectable undertaking. That which has now emerged destroys this respect rapidly, curses and befouls the name and will certainly disappear by itself in the end leaving only a . . . rotten smell. That pains me terribly, the more so, as I neither can nor will involve myself in this morass to alter the course of events.

In fact, she simply could not escape Polish politics. At the International Socialist Congress in Paris in the summer of 1900, Rosa Luxemburg's eyes moistened at the sight of an SDKPiL mandate addressed to her by inmates of the Warsaw Citadel. With a heavy heart, she declined it. On the other hand, she could not permit the PPS to deny the SDKPiL delegates their seats, and she had the bittersweet satisfaction of seeing her friend and rival Wojnarowska become the first woman member of the newly-established International Socialist Bureau. The PPS struck back at Rosa with a campaign denouncing her as unfit to represent Polish socialism. That hurt.

Another important strand in Rosa Luxemburg's first interview with Ignatz Auer concerned the women's movement. Jogiches had originally suggested to her that she approach the SPD Executive via Emma Ihrer, the doyenne of the Berlin working women's movement. Rosa Luxemburg had ignored this suggestion: 'What an unhappy idea you had, Dziodzio, that I should go to Auer with Ihrer; I could only laugh at it. Not just that. I told him at the first opportunity with an unmistakeable gesture: *I have nothing to do with the women's movement*, which certainly met with his approbation.' In other words, she was offering her services not just as a 'token' Pole, but as a 'token' woman as well. Not all elite-educated East European women behaved this way in the West. This was the period when Maria Zakrzewska joined Emily Blackwell in battering at the doors of the male medical establishment on behalf of all women doctors in New York, while Maria Skłodowska (Curie) and Sophia Balakhovskaya opened the doors of academic science and the legal profession to their French sisters in Paris. By comparison, Rosa Luxemburg's eruption into German Social Democracy was notably deficient in a sense of

51

sisterhood. It was, however, based on a realistic assessment of the current anxieties of the party fathers of the SPD.

As elsewhere, the German women's movement was divided in Prussia (and Germany) almost from the start. Even to obtain a minimum degree of toleration for the bourgeois women's movement, its founder, Luise Otto-Peters, had to assure the crowned heads of Germany that 'the only emancipation to which we aspire for our women is the emancipation of our work'. Unhampered by the egalitarian constitutions of France and the United States and, in contrast to the Russian Empire, suffering no shortage of qualified personnel, the Prussian State was almost uniquely resistant to the idea of women's emancipation. When, in 1898, thirty years after the opening of the first *gymnasium* for women in Russia, the city of Breslau tried to follow suit, Culture Minister Brosse hastened to extinguish this 'spark before it became a devastating flame'. In the following year the Russian government founded a Pharmaceutical School for girls, while the German Chemists' Association refused to admit women as members. There were even practising women doctors in Ethiopia and Afghanistan before there were any in Prussia. The obduracy of German ruling-class men ensured a following for the Federation of German Women's Unions, which by 1894 boasted 131 affiliates and an impressive array of publications. Meanwhile, several attempts to form a socialist women's movement had foundered, culminating in the collapse in 1896 of the Central Union of Women and Girls of Germany. As radical feminists, such as Lina Morgenstern, began to highlight the problems facing working women, there was a real fear among the SPD leadership that they might be more successful in mobilizing working women than the SPD.

Socialist women's organizations in Germany were sometimes broken up by internal disputes, more often by police persecution, but most often frustrated by the sheer objective difficulties of organizing the most oppressed category of the working class, whose absorption in child-care denied them leisure, and whose material resources were meagre. Of the five million working women in 1882, one-and-a-half million only were industrial workers, disproportionately concentrated in the poorly-paid textile, clothing and service sectors. A further reason for the difficulties of the German socialist women's movement arose from differences over the desirability of paid work outside the home for wives and mothers.

When the bourgeois feminist, Countess Gertrud Guillaume-Schack, made contact with the working-class women of Berlin in the 1870s, it was to warn them of the dangers of 'immorality'. Emma Ihrer told her that this was nonsense: what they needed was greater material security. Guillaume-Schack accepted the reproof, becoming notorious as the 'red countess', editing a socialist women's paper and founding a sick-benefit fund. Ihrer's Union for the Representation of the Interests of Working Women defeated a government plan for a yarn tax that would have ruined seamstresses and secured a Reichstag enquiry into conditions in the laundry and confectionary trades, which led to an extension of the Truck Acts, but also, unfortunately, to the suppression of women's labour unions. The SPD supported *all* women's demands, whether they came from the bourgeois or socialist women's organizations, demanding full freedom of association for women, women's property rights *and* the protection of working women.

August Bebel, the SPD leader, committed his own immense prestige to the resolution of 'the woman question' in his authoritative *Woman, in the Past, Present and Future*, which went through numerous editions after its first appearance in 1878/9. Bebel's plausible description of a socialist utopia ensured his book a much wider readership than Engels study of *The Origins of the Family, Private Property and the State* that appeared five years later. Bebel, who never concealed his sympathies for the radical feminists, appeared to concede that patriarchy is a distinct category of domination by stating that 'woman was the first human existence to taste servitude. Woman was a slave before the slave existed'. Paradoxically, he then attempted to sell equal rights for women to working class men on the grounds that this would improve their sexual gratification and the mental health of their wives.

As Alys Russell noted in the 1890s, 'Bebel's is the psychology of the proletariat, and when he insists on the necessity of the satisfaction of natural wants, he has in mind the man of few pleasures and little imagination.' And that was part of the problem. While the entirely male SPD leadership accepted equal rights for women at the 1890 Party Congress, the trade union rank and file remained at best patronizing towards their female comrades. In the year Rosa Luxemburg first met Auer, the SPD gained 27 per cent of the (male) vote for the Reichstag, but a pitiful 13,000 women belonged to the socialist trade unions. It was Clara Zetkin who brought order and even rigidity into this ideological confusion by legitimizing women's work in the eyes of the German working class.

Clara Eissner, born in 1857, was a Stuttgart schoolteacher, whose cohabitation with Ossip Zetkin, a refugee from Russia, left her with a permanent sympathy for East European revolutionaries. It was Clara Zetkin who provided the keynote speech on 'the woman question' at the founding Congress of the Socialist International in 1889 and who converted her paper, *Die Gleichheit* (Equality), into the directing organ of the avowedly Marxist Proletarian Women's Movement she set out to build. Clara Zetkin argued that capitalism was engaged in liberating women from men, and that women's work was capable of enriching all, once capitalism ceased setting worker against worker. It followed that the liberation of women required their immersion in the world of work and in the class struggle. Zetkin's initial toleration of radical feminists turned to unrelenting hostility towards the 'bourgeois women's righters' when she felt that they threatened to undermine the unity of the proletariat and to incorporate proletarian women into the existing order by reforming some of the outstanding abuses to which they were subjected.

Rosa Luxemburg's initial impressions of women were frequently less favourable than her considered judgments, and in a first *positive reassessment* of Clara Zetkin, her future patroness, after some months of acquaintanceship, Rosa commented, 'Clara alone is an upright and honourable women's room, but to a certain extent also *an empty tube*, filled up by every last conversation.' (After a few meetings, she also concluded that Luise Kautsky lacked magnanimity; at least she didn't damn Luise in the men's room jargon she used on Clara Zetkin.)

Rosa's condescending reference to the women's movement was no mere ploy to ingratiate herself with Auer. When Emmy Stock invited her to speak to the 'females' (Rosa almost invariably used the pejorative terms *baba/Weib* rather than the neutral *kobieta/ Frau* to describe political women), Rosa excused herself on the grounds that this would lead to the closure of their meetings by the police. Shortly afterwards, Bebel himself upbraided her for her indifference to the 'females' movement'. 'When I said that in this matter I can do nothing and I understand nothing, he looked astonished', she reported to Jogiches.

Rosa Luxemburg even complained to Jogiches of Clara Zetkin's absorption in the women's movement: 'Clara is good as always, but somehow mad [*meschugge*]; she has ensnared herself in female questions and doesn't get through to general questions. I am therefore *quite alone.*' When hostility broke out between Lily Braun and Clara Zetkin, ostensibly over future tactics for the Proletarian Women's Movement, but partly over Lily Braun's attempt to write Zetkin out of the history of the German women's movement, Rosa gravitated slowly to Clara's side, but only because of their common hostility to reformism and the 'Revisionists'. Raya Dunayevskaya attempts to reconcile Rosa's well-documented indifference to feminism with her claim that Rosa was a feminist by putting it all down to a fear of marginalization. The price Rosa Luxemburg paid was to accept the views of her male comrades as to what really mattered.

A further sub-text to Rosa's first conversation with Ignatz Auer was more personal. She liked the man, and she carried on liking him, even though he frequently tried to belittle her as a foreigner. This was typical of her relations with the SPD leaders she cultivated. Her *infrequent* barbs at the expense of Bebel and Kautsky reverberated through the party, causing intense resentment; few stopped to consider how often she had to massage their brittle egos. Fewer still can have guessed that she was the discreet recipient of an amorous declaration from SPD co-Chairman Paul Singer. She had to tolerate Bruno Schoenlank's flirting to ensure that her articles reached the columns of the *Leipziger Volkszeitung*, while she first found her way to Franz Mehring's heart via her excellent cuisine. (It is difficult to imagine Lenin cooking *blinys* to win over Plekhanov!) Of course, she knew it was a man's world and that this was unjust.

The principal men in her personal life were still her father and Leo. Edward Luxemburg remained a haunting figure, the devoted father who hoped that his children would avenge his failures. She tried to repay him the guilt she had incurred by neglecting her mother. After Lina Luxenburg's death, Edward suffered a series of psychosomatic complaints, and Rosa felt obliged to help. Her need to earn money to send home gave her journalism an added urgency. In 1899, she took time off to take her father on holiday in Silesia. Things did not go well. The hotels in Breslau (Wrocław) were full, and they had to travel around like nomads until they found somewhere tolerable to stay. The 'holiday' became an ordeal, a duty to be accomplished. As she confided to Leo:

> From old habits, Papa wakes up every two hours and coughs so badly that neither of us can sleep. As early as five, or five-thirty, he is already up, so I must get up too, for I must give him a cold rub-down (doctor's orders), and make his tea. After the tea, when he has rested a while, I must make him eggs, then coffee. When he has eaten, I must wash and tidy up, get dressed myself and go for a walk with him, which is a torture for me, for Father crawls along like a snake (no exaggeration), so I can't stand it . . .

Duty accomplished, she turned her back on him once more. He died during the Paris International Socialist Congress the following summer. Remorse caught up with her during her long, final imprisonment.

In Rosa's eyes, Leo was her partner, more a husband than a lover. Through all their frequent separations, she continued to dream of their future life together

> . . . Our own little home, a few pieces of our furniture, our own library, calm and regular work, walks together, now and then an opera, a small, a *very* small circle of friends, whom we invite for an occasional supper, every year a month in the country, that *quite* without work however! . . . (And perhaps, too, a little, a very little baby? Will it never be permitted? Never? Dziodziuś, do you know what happened to me unexpectedly during a walk in the Tiergarten yesterday? Suddenly, a little baby of three or four in a charming little dress with fine blond hair tumbled before my feet and began to stare at me. Something struck me, as though I should pick up this baby, fly home quickly with the child and keep it for myself. Ah, Dziodziu, will I never have a baby?!)

All they needed, she wheedled, was for Leo to obtain his doctorate and permission to live in Germany. 'No pair on earth has so many capabilities for being happy as *we* do.'

This dream (and Jogiches) continued to elude her overwhelming embrace. He could not bring himself to finish his doctorate, and when he arrived in Berlin in 1901, he stayed for just four months before taking his invalid brother off to Italy and Algeria. Perhaps to avert a scandal over the fictitious marriage of convenience, their brief periods of cohabitation were conducted in strictest secrecy.

Gradually, Rosa ceased to idealize Leo, accusing him instead of wasting and abusing his talents, and of only responding to 'trumpet calls' from the battlefield of class war. She preferred a calmer, more ordered existence and warned him: 'I have thought over our whole way of life here, and you will have to *fit in* humbly with the ways of the household and of life'.

Bernstein's 'English Spectacles'

Rosa Luxemburg could only retain her distance from the persecution of her fellow Jews and on the oppression of her fellow Poles and women, by aiming for what Bruno Bettelheim calls a 'higher integration'. In her view, the partial demands of particular categories of the oppressed were based on a 'lack of understanding for the fact that the liberation from socio-economic slavery is simultaneously an emancipation of individuals and of all groups from every form of material and moral oppression'. On the other hand, her intense awareness of these specific forms of oppression made her extremely intolerant towards any challenge to the revolutionary Marxist frame of reference which might involve the prioritization of different forms of oppression. One of her motives for coming to Germany was precisely to excise the cancer (as she considered it) of 'Revisionism' from the SPD.

When Rosa Luxemburg arrived in Berlin in 1898, she found the SPD engulfed in a crisis of conscience provoked by Eduard Bernstein, another companion of Engels' declining years and Engels' literary executor. Bernstein had spent long years in exile in Switzerland and England as a result of the anti-socialist laws.

But while German workers continued to see Bernstein as a victim of bourgeois class (in)justice, Bernstein himself had begun to enjoy his London exile. More to the point, he had come to envy the relative gentility which marked relations between the social classes in late-Victorian Britain. Between 1896 and 1898, he wrote a series of articles for *Die Neue Zeit*, which were eventually republished as *The Preconditions for Socialism and the Task of Social Democracy*, which set Marxist orthodoxy by the ears. Embarking from the empirical observations that no major economic crisis had occurred for some decades and that the intermediate social classes, so far from suffering the immiseration foretold by Marx, seemed to be getting more numerous and more prosperous, Bernstein attacked the very idea of revolutionary upheaval, the dialectical method, the materialist basis of Marxist philosophy and the labour theory of value. He argued that, if only it abandoned these 'dogmas', the SPD would facilitate peaceful social and political reform in Germany of the kind that had already occurred in England.

Plekhanov and Parvus lashed out at the heretic, or 'Opportunist', as Bernstein was labelled. But Plekhanov's philosophizing went over the heads of the German rank and file, while the vitriolic tone adopted by Parvus alienated SPD activists, who had come to value the warmth of instinctive loyalties and group solidarity. They waited anxiously for reassuring words from August Bebel and for a civilized refutation of Bernstein's errors, of the kind they had come to expect from Karl Kautsky. Instead, there was an embarassed silence. Bernstein was probably right when he suggested that Adler was 'blushing' at mere indiscretions, while Kautsky seemed uncertain over the line to take.

Sensing her opportunity, Rosa Luxemburg prepared for battle. With total professionalism and considerable tactical acumen, she exploited Bruno Schoenlank's devotion by placing a series of articles in the *Leipziger Volkszeitung* on the very eve of the 1898 SPD Party Congress in Stuttgart. Thus began *Social Reform or Revolution*, one of Rosa Luxemburg's most dynamic and enduring contributions to socialist thought. It left no one, least of all Bernstein, in any doubt about the identity of his most formidable ideological adversary within the SPD. She was more comprehensible than Plekhanov and less pedagogical than Parvus. To begin with, she queried the antithesis contained in her own title:

Can Social Democracy be *against* social reforms? Can it oppose social revolution, the transformation of the existing order, its final goal, to social reforms? Certainly not. The practical daily struggle for reforms, for the amelioration of the condition of the workers within the framework of the existing social order, and for democratic institutions, offers Social Democracy the only means of engaging in the proletarian class struggle and working in the direction of the final goal: the conquest of political power and the suppression of wage labour.

It was apparent to Rosa Luxemburg that 'Revisionism' was not merely opposed to revolutionary Marxism, but to socialism itself. If there was no tendency to anarchy in capitalism, no progressive socialization of production and no inevitability in the growth of proletarian class consciousness, 'socialism ceases to be an historical necessity. . . . Either revisionism is correct concerning the course of capitalist development, and therefore the socialist transformation of society becomes a utopia', or socialism is no impractical utopia, and capitalism is incapable of saving itself.

The first half of *Social Reform or Revolution* examines the aspects of recent economic and social development which Bernstein had cited in support of his view that revolutionary Marxism was outdated. On the contrary, she argued, it was Bernstein's theory which, by mistaking a particular moment in capitalist development for its whole history, was prone to obsolescence. Thus, the extension of credit might lengthen the gaps between crises, but it would intensify them once they occurred. Tariff policy would reinforce the development of militarism, which was bound to lead to fatal results for capitalism now that the possibility of relatively painless expansion into new worlds was exhausted. The revisionist theory was therefore 'a theory of socialist standstill justified through a vulgar economic theory of capitalist standstill'. In the second half of her argument, Rosa Luxemburg restates Marxist orthodoxy, asserting, for example, the literal scientific truth of the labour theory of value (in her view the only theory that satisfactorily explained money). Why, Marx had even foreseen opportunist theory! And what does such theory contain? 'Not a single idea that was not refuted, crushed, ridiculed, and reduced to dust

59

by Marxism decades ago!' The most provocative phrase in the whole argument came in her refutation of the view that trade unions could modify relations between capital and labour. While she agreed with the necessity of their work, she described it as a 'labour of Sisyphus'. For the leaders of German trade unionism, this was an insult they would neither forgive nor forget.

The kernel of Rosa Luxemburg's argument consisted in her insistence on the necessity and imminence of social revolution. 'Only the hammer blow of revolution, that is, the conquest of political power by the proletariat', could break down the barriers to socialism created by the political and juridical relations of capitalist society. Bernstein was guilty of a false antithesis. The struggle for reform educated the masses on the need for socialism, but only the threat of revolution ever extorted real reforms from the ruling classes.

The SPD Party Congress that met in Stuttgart, 3–8 October 1898, was something of an anti-climax. Bernstein himself was still in England, a circumstance that aroused considerable personal sympathy. Many delegates were also irritated by the 'presumption', as Gustav Noske put it, 'with which a group of foreigners coming from Poland and Russia set themselves up as schoolmasters for the German workers'. Even Schoenlank could do little more than echo the sentiment that, while nine-tenths of the German workers were opposed to Bernstein's 'Revisionism', there should be no 'Vatican expulsions'. Bebel's soothing oratory easily persuaded the Congress to license a period of debate in the party press.

In this cloying atmosphere, all Rosa Luxemburg could do was to remind the SPD of its Marxist principles. Most of her scorn was directed at Konrad Heine, who had argued that socialists should support the German government's military programme, provided they were compensated with democratic reforms. She also retaliated when the leader of the Bavarian socialists, the ex-officer Georg von Vollmar ungallantly mocked her youth. 'I know', she declared, 'that I must still earn my epaulettes in the German movement; but I want to do it on the left wing, where people are struggling against the enemy, and not on the right wing, where people are seeking out compromises with the enemy'. Finally, she inverted one of Bernstein's pithy phrases in a memorable declaration of her own: 'The movement as an end in itself is nothing to me; the final goal is everything'.

During the following year, Bernstein and Luxemburg developed their positions, while Kautsky reaffirmed the party orthodoxy, as he explained apologetically to Bernstein, 'so that Luxemburg doesn't get another opportunity to go off'. On the eve of the 1899 Hannover Party Congress, she raised the possibility of 'organizational consequences', presumably the expulsion of Bernstein from the party, but though the party faithful did their best, in the words of George Lichtheim, 'to stone revisionism to death with cream puffs', the Revisionists were left within the party to fight another day.

This was not Luxemburg's fault. She gave them no respite, vigorously rejecting the widely-canvassed excuse that Bernstein had merely been misled by his 'English spectacles'. Bernstein had also misunderstood English social history, she countered. The English trade unionists had been successful for two reasons: in the early nineteenth century they had fought by revolutionary means for trade union rights, while in the mid-nineteenth century, worldwide commercial hegemony had permitted the English bourgeoisie to bargain with the craft unions. From a socialist point of view, the results were deplorable: 'From a school of class solidarity and socialist ethics, the trade union movement became a business, a commerce, the trade union became a highly complex work of art, a comfortable home erected for permanence, and in the whole working class world of that period a *spirit of prudent*, if somewhat *restricted* statesmanship reigned.' But this period was over. With the disappearance of English commercial hegemony, social tensions were sharpening and larger, and more politically-minded industrial unions were emerging. The end result would be trade unions of the German type, committed, she believed, to fighting the class struggle and fully subordinated to a single Marxist party. Once more, she dismissed Bernstein's discoveries: '. . . what he takes to be the future of German Social Democracy is the rapidly disappearing past of the English movement in its development to Social Democracy.'

Rosa Luxemburg had made her mark, and in a moment of euphoria, she wrote to Jogiches that 'in a year or two, no intrigue, anxieties or obstacles will help them, and I shall occupy one of the foremost positions in the party'. Vanity apart, she affirmed her vocation to revive the cutting edge of German socialism:

> The Party is only now moving . . . into the whirlpool of more and more difficult tasks, more and more dangerous phenomena; there will be thousands and thousands more opportunities to demonstrate one's strength and indispensability. I certainly haven't any intention of limiting myself to criticism; on the contrary, I intend to enjoy positively *pushing* not individuals but the movement in its totality, to revise the whole of our positive work, agitation, praxis, . . .

Nor was her activity limited to Germany. Events in Western Europe provoked her equally vigorous intervention in French and Belgian politics.

French Corruption and Belgian Chivalry

When in the 1970s, the prestige of the capitalist world's most prestigious and powerful institution of state, the US Presidency, was threatened by 'Watergate', the Communist leaderships in Moscow and Beijing reacted with bewilderment and confusion. How was it possible to deal with a system that destabilized itself over a petty burglary? And what did it have to do with the class struggle? This was exactly the reaction of orthodox Marxists, such as Rosa Luxemburg, to the Dreyfus affair that shattered the prestige of the French Army at the turn of the twentieth century. Yet the framing of a bourgeois Jewish officer on false charges of espionage in 1894 led by a tortuous route to the formation in 1905 of a unified French socialist party with a Marxist programme. Rosa Luxemburg herself played a notable auxiliary role in a process of whose successful outcome she often despaired.

Rosa Luxemburg had little time for Alfred Dreyfus. He epitomized the kind of Jewish bourgeois on whom she had forever turned her back. When it began to appear that the French Army and Catholic Church had committed themselves to a whitewash of those who had framed Dreyfus, she had some sympathy with her French Marxist comrade, Jules Guesde, whose attitude to the affair was, 'What has this got to do with the working class?' A very different answer was given by the 'independent' parliamentary leaders of French socialism, Alexandre Millerand and Jean Jaurès, for whom the defence of Dreyfus was vital for the sake of the Republic and the sake of humanity.

Millerand was a combative radical lawyer, a defender of countless persecuted socialists and trade unionists, who had in 1896 drawn Marxists and reformists, Blanquists and parliamentarians, behind a 'minimum programme' for French socialism. The Saint Mandé Programme demanded the substitution of private by social ownership and the renunciation of violence. When in July 1899, René Waldeck-Rousseau formed a cabinet dedicated to the liquidation of the conspiracy against Dreyfus and the defence of the Republic, Millerand accepted the post of Minister of Labour, alongside a Minister of Defence, General the Marquis de Gallifet, who had personally butchered the Communards of 1871. Jaurès, the charismatic leader of French socialism, justified Millerand and defended the Waldeck-Rousseau cabinet and its equally bourgeois successor under the anti-clerical Emile Combes. As Sir Denis Brogan (no Marxist militant) put it, 'for years to come, it was Jaurès . . . who held a large section of the French workers to an alliance with the bourgeoisie which produced no very striking benefits for the proletariat and seemed to deny the premises of the class war'. This practical version of 'Revisionism' was even more threatening than Bernstein's essays. For Rosa Luxemburg, Millerand was a renegade, while Jaurès was the 'great corrupter' of the French working class.

It speaks volumes for Rosa Luxemburg's international stature that Jaurès canvassed her opinion, as one of only eleven leading 'German' socialists, on Millerand's entry into a 'bourgeois' government. (Only Vollmar supported Millerand and Jaurès.) Luxemburg's articles on 'The Socialist Crisis in France' and 'The Conclusion of the Socialist Crisis in France' appeared in *Die Neue Zeit* between 1900 and 1902. Rosa Luxemburg denied that the French Republic had ever been in danger and accused the Waldeck-Rousseau government of failing to honour its pledge to clear up the Dreyfus affair. The promised social reforms had also been emasculated, while the new system of conciliation in labour relations threatened to replace the class struggle by civil litigation: 'The experiences with the Waldeck-Millerand ministry are calculated to spoil the taste for opportunistic experiments of the whole international Social Democracy. So we wish them a long life!'

A year later, she returned to the theme:

> Since Newton was brought to his theory of gravity by the fall of an apple, it seems to be a law that people don't become clear about the simplest things until rotten apples rain on their noses . . . The three-year period of Millerandism is, in our opinion, an equally significant milestone in the history of the international workers' movement, as – in another sense – were the ten weeks of the Paris Commune of 1871.

These articles won her the enthusiastic praise of Karl Kautsky, Edouard Vaillant and even Georgii Plekhanov, while Franz Mehring presented her with the bouquet she most convetted: 'Only one person ever wrote like that: Karl Marx'. Even more usefully, the Franco-Russian journalist, Charles Rappoport, summarized her arguments in his articles for the French workers in *Le Petit Sou*.

By 1902, the six feuding currents of French socialism of the 1890s had crystallized into the reformist *Parti Socialiste Français* and the revolutionary Marxist *Parti Socialiste de France*. Rosa was active in diplomacy designed to consolidate the latter. Then in 1903, the SPD Executive decided to impose a solution. At the Dresden Party Congress, they kept Rosa's mouth firmly shut on Revisionism, while giving her free rein to attack the PPS. (She nicknamed the Congress 'Bebel's bedroom'!) The 'Dresden Resolution' condemned Revisionism, declined all responsibility for the current social order and prohibited all participation by socialists in bourgeois governments. The resolution was put to the 1904 Amsterdam Congress of the Socialist International, together with a resolution declaring that, 'It is indispensable that, in every country, in face of the bourgeois parties, there is only one Socialist Party, as there is only one proletariat.'

The centrepiece of the Amsterdam Congress was an odiously chauvinistic confrontation between Bebel and Jaurès. Bebel admitted the superiority of the French republican form of government over the Hohenzollern monarchy, but added, 'We are not going to break our heads for it: it isn't worth it'. If the Germans had a democratic republic, he boasted, 'We'd show you something else'. To Jaurès' taunt that the SPD had received universal suffrage for the Reichstag elections from Bismarck, Bebel replied that it was Bismarck who had restored the French republic also. Rosa Luxemburg, speaking with her usual 'vehemence' and 'incisive gestures', declared her faith in the International: 'They ask us what is the sanction of a decision of the International Congress. It is moral, but it is immense! It is a matter of the future of the International, of socialist solidarity itself!' It caused some mirth when Rosa then translated Jaurès' response into German, particularly when he demonstrated the fallibility of some of her own past prophecies. The Dresden Resolution was then passed: Jaurès bowed to its authority, while Millerand made an acrimonious exit from French socialism. From 1905, Jaurès led a team, which included Guesde and Vaillant, at the head of a new French Section of the Workers' International (*Section Française de l'Internationale Ouvrière*: SFIO).

Despite her distaste for 'rotten apples', Rosa Luxemburg and Leo Jogiches believed right up to 1914 that 'the amputation of members of the party showing symptoms of illness' was the wrong way to handle the problem of Revisionism. After all, if Marx's theory of immiseration were true, petty-bourgeois elements were bound to join the proletariat, bringing their ideas with them. The Marxist response to Revisionism must be to 'overcome it in every single manifestation and subordinate it to the entirety of the revolutionary movement'. For Rosa, the Congress was a triumph, and in one of her warmest letters ever to Karl Kautsky, she referred to 'our victory in Amsterdam'. At the Congress, she herself had held solid mandates from both the SPD and the SDKPiL*, whose representative on the International Socialist Bureau she now became. She also made a good friend in Henriette Roland-Holst, one of the Dutch Congress organizers.

Rosa shared with Henriette her hopes for the invigoration of the International. There must be more international activity and greater militancy to combat parochialism and opportunism:

I am not at all enamoured of the role which the so-called

---

* For the circumstances of Rosa's reconsiliation with the SDKPiL, see below, pp. 69–70.

orthodox 'Radicalism' has played so far. Running after individual Opportunist idiocies and critical nagging is not satisfying work for me; on the contrary I am so heartily sick of that task that I would rather stay silent in such cases. I am also amazed at the certainty with which many of our radical friends always feel it necessary merely to bring the errant sheep – the party – back into the safe homely staff of a 'firmness of principles' and do not feel that in this purely negative way we fail to take a single step forwards. And for a revolutionary movement, not going forwards means going backwards.

Henriette was Rosa's first good woman friend in the socialist movements of the Low Countries. (Rosa instantly admired this 'Madonna' as she had admired the 'pretty' Wojnarowska on their first meeting). But it was the men of neighbouring Belgium who would succeed, where Bebel, Lily Braun and even Clara Zetkin had so far failed, in making Rosa Luxemburg aware of her responsibilities towards her fellow women.

Belgium was famous within the socialist movement as the country where mass political strikes in 1891 and 1893 had secured a revision of the constitution, a ministry responsible to the Chamber of Deputies, and universal male suffrage, albeit with multiple voting for the wealthy, which confirmed the domination of the Catholic clergy. For many of the 'fathers' of the International, this reappearance of the mass political strike was uncomfortably close to the Anarchist demand for a 'General Strike', which they had denounced as 'general nonsense'. When Czech workers tried to imitate the 'Belgian method' in 1894, Adler, with Engels' encouragement, vigorously discouraged their Viennese brothers and sisters from following suite.

Rosa Luxemburg saw in mass political strikes a possibility for converting 'quantity into quality', of transforming the radicalism of the socialist movement into something truly revolutionary. She was therefore deeply dismayed when Emile Vandervelde, the Belgian socialist leader, announced in March 1902 that he had concluded a deal with the Belgian Liberals for parliamentary action in favour of *equal* suffrage, *but only for men*. Foreseeing that the Catholic Clerical Party would try to disrupt the socialist–liberal alliance by proposing votes for women, Vandervelde promised that the socialists would 'spoil this manoeuvre and uphold the alliance of supporters of universal suffrage', or, as Rosa Luxemburg decoded it, 'in good German: vote *against* women's suffrage!'

Rosa had taken weeks to reply to Jaurès in 1899; it took her less than a week to *publish* her indignant commentary on this Belgian betrayal. She was particularly irked by male socialists who muttered, like the emperors of Russia and Germany, that women were not yet 'ready' for the vote:

> On the contrary, every clearly thinking person must expect from the involvement of proletarian women in political life, in the short or long term, a mighty upsurge of the workers' movement. This perspective does not merely open an enormous field for the agitational work of Social Democracy. In its political and spiritual life, too, a strong, fresh wind would blow in with the political emancipation of women, which would dissipate the stagnant air of the present Philistine family life, that so unmistakably colours our party members, workers and leaders alike.

For someone who found the 'woman question' alien, there is a sureness of touch and a profundity of sociological observation in this instantaneous reaction that reminds us that, whatever their shortcomings in the eyes of the radical feminists of the late twentieth century, Rosa Luxemburg and Clara Zetkin were making demands for *women* more radical than the major organizations of bourgeois feminism in their time, and tolerating no backsliding from proletarian men or their leaders. Lalie Vandervelde's defence of her husband's conduct aroused Rosa's scorn, and she dismissed her as just another bourgeois prima donna like Lily Braun.

On 14 April 1902, Vandervelde presented the Socialist–Liberal demands to the Belgian Chamber. The Socialist Party simultaneously called for a mass strike; 300,000 workers downed tools and prepared for a confrontation. Four days later, the Belgian conservatives rejected the demands. Two days after that, Vandervelde told the workers to go back to work. When they asked him what would happen next, he told them he was appealing to the king, and following the Biblical injunction, 'Thou Shalt Not Kill!'

67

Rosa Luxemburg's bitter commentary on this fiasco won the approval of Bebel and Kautsky, leading to some sharp exchanges between the leaders of the SPD and Adler. The essence of her case was that the proletarian cause *cannot* be defeated by its enemies:

> Should the cause of Social Democracy submit, even for a moment, to the superior force of its enemy, then it rises up even more powerfully in the next moment . . . and that which the triumphant bourgeois world considers . . . as our *defeat*, soon reveals itself as our *victory*. It was so with the butchery of the Commune, it was so with the [Anti-]Socialist Laws.

On the other hand, it could suffer temporary defeats if its leaders demonstrated their own lack of self-confidence by making deals with liberal 'allies' less powerful than the party of the proletariat. She noted that the general strikes of 1891 and 1893, which had been substantially spontaneous, were more successful than the organized one of 1902. This was one of the first occasions on which she showed an interest in the concept of 'spontaneity', with which her name has become, somewhat misleadingly, associated by some of her admirers. She contrasted this earlier spontaneity with the advance guarantees of legality given by Vandervelde: 'A general strike welded to legality *in advance* is like a military demonstration with cannons, whose magazines have previously been thrown into the water in the eyes of the enemy.'

Many Belgian socialists never forgave the pasting Rosa Luxemburg gave them. One of them was Camille Huyssmans, Secretary of the International Socialist Bureau, who glared at this self-confident woman antagonistically for ten years, until one day in July 1914, when Rosa confessed to him her 'incompetence' at organizing her return from Brussels to Berlin. A decade's hostility thawed into instant cordiality, as Huyssmans persuaded himself that his chivalry was not, after all, redundant.

Jeszcze Polska: Poland's not finished yet!

Rosa Luxemburg did not like to be reminded that Polish working men and women sang both the proletarian anthem *Warszawjanka*

68

and the national *Jeszcze Polska nie zginęła* (Poland's not finished yet) on their demonstrations. This did not deter her from acting and speaking in an incongruously patriotic way about Polish Social Democracy. The revival of the SDKP as the SDKPiL at the beginning of the twentieth century, its adoption of an impeccably 'German' mode of organization, its heroic actions in 1905–6 and its growing influence within the All-Russian Social Democracy all enhanced Rosa Luxemburg's status within the SPD and throughout the International. This led to a readjustment in her working relations with Jogiches, her first public quarrel with Lenin and an amity with Bebel through which she briefly attained that position of influence within the SPD to which she had long aspired.

As so often, it was the tsar's gendarmes who changed the course of Polish socialist history. In November 1901 they arrested Trusiewicz and Dzierżyński, virtually decapitating the SDKPiL. An emergency conference met under Warski's chairmanship in Munich, which initiated a process of consolidation of power within the party in a new Foreign Committee (*Komitet Zagraniczny*) and later in a Chief Executive (*Zarząd Główny*) based in Berlin and led by Jogiches and (after his escape from Siberia) Dzierżyński. Wojnarowska's influence was radically curtailed. Rosa Luxemburg refused 'on principle' to accept any elected office in the SDKPiL, apart from representing it within the International. This did not prevent her from acting as *de facto* editor of its theoretical journal *Przegląd Socjaldemokratyczny* (Social Democratic Review) and contributing regularly to its popular paper *Czerwony Sztandar* (Red Flag). She also joined Marchlewski and Warski in a sub-committee to work on a party programme for which she herself provided the theoretical introduction.

Many commentators see Jogiches' emergence as SDKPiL 'dictator' as the inevitable result of his iron will power and organizational talents. It is hard to reconcile this assessment with two known facts. The first is that Jogiches spoke and wrote poor Polish. The second is that his position within the SDKPiL was, in practice, only secure so long as he was fully supported by Rosa Luxemburg's peer group. He might think that Marchlewski and Warski were impressed by his brusque orders, but there are many hints in Rosa Luxemburg's correspondence that they were often brought back from the brink of revolt by Rosa's appeals to their shared past and ideals. It is worth noting that the younger generation of leading Polish Social Democrats (i.e. not Rosa Luxemburg's peers) all eventually rebelled against Jogiches' 'dictatorship'.

What kind of 'principle' could have dissuaded such an uncompromising internationalist as Rosa to decline office in the party which claimed her as one of its founders? The only reasonable supposition is that she deliberately turned over all Polish organizational work to Leo to save him from superfluity, while presenting this decision in the way most likely to shore up his increasingly brittle self-esteem. Though their relations had cooled, this was little enough for Rosa to do for the man she still loved. Why should an international celebrity deny her partner a little local success? Anyway, organizational work bored her. If Leo did it, he would maintain the course they had set since the early 1890s, while she concentrated on theory and agitation.

Now that they had captured the SDKPiL, Rosa Luxemburg and Leo Jogiches were determined to ensure that the party became a model of Marxist orthodoxy in its programme, organizational structure and tactics. Furthermore, they hoped that it would be the vehicle for the dissemination of the best West European practice throughout the Russian Empire. The SDKPiL would continue to strive to be the only socialist party in Poland. As in France, this would require, at a minimum, the acceptance by members of the PPS and the *Bund* of a fully Marxist programme. To counter the damage caused by repeated arrests, the SDKPiL adopted the system of *Vertrauensmänner* (later *Vertrauenspersonen*) or 'trusted persons' developed by the SPD under the Anti-Socialist laws. These were officials appointed by the Chief Executive to manage the affairs of local groups and committees. The trade unions fostered by the party were to conform to the ideal 'German' rather than the obsolete 'English' model, fully subordinated to the party and committed to its Marxist programme. There could be no compromise with 'social patriotism' and no attempt to follow Vollmar's 'Opportunistic' Bavarian path of concessions to the peasantry, which offered the prospect of short-term, petty-bourgeois support but at the price of encouraging reactionary illusions about a return to a natural agrarian economy.

Rosa personally ensured that the party's 'Minimum Programme' did not neglect women. Point Ten of the Programme
demanded, 'The abolition of all state laws, both civil and criminal, which have been issued to the detriment of woman, or which
in any way restrict her personal freedom, her right to dispose of
her wealth or the right to exercise parental care over children on
equal terms with the father of those children.' It also demanded
full political freedom and equality for women. The Programme
also provided for legislation for the protection of women working
in industry.

No sooner had Jogiches and Luxemburg re-established their
authority within the SDKPiL, than the party was faced by a new
challenge in the shape of an invitation from Plekhanov, Lenin
and Martov to join in the reconstruction of Russian Social
Democracy, from which they had been blackballed a decade
earlier. In principle, this was a welcome challenge. The internationalism, even Russophilia, of the SDKPiL positively demanded
the amalgamation of Polish and Russian Social Democracy. But,
as Rosa Luxemburg reminded her comrades in an article comme-
morating *Proletariat I*, past precedents were not encouraging. The
alliance between the Marxist, western-influenced *Proletariat*
and the Russian Populist *Narodnaia Volia* had also seemed the
logical step for Waryński, but it had led to the adoption by the
Poles of the outmoded elitist and terrorist methods of the (back-
ward?) Russians. The implication could not be shirked: 'The
development of Social Democracy in the Kingdom [of Poland]
will only be guaranteed in the long term, when Russian socialism
also places itself on the terrain of Social Democracy.'

Unfortunately, Point Seven of the draft Programme of the
Russian Social Democratic Labour Party (*Rossiiskaia Sotsial-
Demokraticheskaia Rabochaia Partiia*: RSDRP), written by Lenin
and published in *Iskra* (The Spark) in 1902, provided for the right
of all nations in the Russian Empire to self- determination, not
'Social Democratic terrain' in Rosa Luxemburg's eyes. What
made this seem suspiciously reminiscent of Mendelson's tactics in
1892–3 was the insistence of the *Iskra* group that the forthcoming
Congress of the RSDRP would not be the founding congress of a
new party, but the Second Congress of an existing organization.

(A poorly attended Russian Congress had taken place in Minsk in 1898, leaving little but an impressive manifesto behind.)

In view of the seriousness of the issues raised by the Russians, the Fourth Congress of the SDKPiL met in Berlin on 25 July 1903. After a long wrangle between the Luxemburg and Wojnarowska camps, the Congress agreed to demand that the RSDRP respect the complete internal autonomy of the SDKPiL and recognize it as its sole partner in Poland. In effect, they demanded the exclusion of the PPS and a federal relationship between the RSDRP and the SDKPiL. Warski and Jakub Hanecki were sent as delegates to Brussels to state terms and not negotiate, and they were nonplussed when Lenin replied with organizational counter-proposals, including the demand that the RSDRP determine the method by which the SDKPiL elect its representatives to RSDRP organs. It was just at this point that Rosa Luxemburg read Lenin's latest defence of the contentious Point Seven in the July 1903 number of *Iskra*. 'Self-determination', argued Lenin, 'does not exclude in any way the advocacy by the Polish proletariat of the slogan of a free and independent Polish republic'. This was grist for the PPS propaganda mill and the last straw for Rosa Luxemburg.

Rosa Luxemburg now telegraphed Jogiches and Dzierżyński to obtain their support for demanding that the Russians postpone the adoption of Point Seven: '. . . in this cardinal question for us, there would not be that basic ideological and moral unity, without which we would consider organizational unity to be pointless'. The negotiations then collapsed. Cezaryna Wojnarowska raged: the revision of Point Seven had not been one of the conditions imposed by the SDKPiL Congress. Marchlewski sympathized with Wojnarowska, but when she persisted in making a fuss, he acquiesced in her elimination from all her leading positions in the party. Rosa Luxemburg did her best to treat her vanquished rival, whom she often addressed as 'My Dear Cezarynko', with dignity and cordiality. Her own position was acutely embarassing. She had overturned a decision of a Party Congress of a party in which she held no elective post 'on principle', and had stymied the unification of Social Democracy within the Russian Empire, a goal to which she had always aspired.

To demonstrate that organizational questions *had* been as important to her as Point Seven, Rosa Luxemburg now attacked Lenin's conception of the RSDRP, the view which had carried the 'Majority' (in Russian: *bol'shinstvo*, hence 'Bolsheviks') at the Brussels–London Congress. This famous essay, *Organizational Questions of Russian Social Democracy* (1903), and her later pamphlet on *The Russian Revolution* (written in 1918) were later employed by Paul Levi to create the myth that Rosa Luxemburg had successfully charted a third road to socialism between Leninist authoritarianism and Kautskyan reformism.

It was not, Rosa Luxemburg suggested, Lenin's insistence on a compact proletarian class party to which she objected, but his demand for the 'blind subordination of all party organizations in the smallest detail of their activity' to a central committee. She objected to Lenin's 'Jacobin' distinction between the 'organized kernel' and the masses. 'Social Democracy', she countered, 'is not bound up with the organization of the working classes; rather it is the very movement of the working class'. Lenin was guilty of confusing industrial discipline with revolutionary discipline. 'There is nothing in common between the corpselike obedience of a dominated class and the organized rebellion of a class struggling for its liberation'.

Once more, she was drawn to reflections on the importance of spontaneity. To Lenin's cogent empirical arguments for conspiratorial centralism in *What is to be Done?* (1902), she opposed the even more cogent empirical observation that the qualitative steps in Russian militancy – strikes, street demonstrations and mass strikes – had all been spontaneous. Indeed, German experience suggested that centralized leadership had 'an essentially conservative character' and that this would also be true of Lenin's 'sterile and domineering' central committee.

Like Lenin an arch-intellectual, Rosa Luxemburg affected to despise the category to which she belonged, vying with his hatred for 'the West European literati' and his contempt for 'the Russian socialist intellectuals'. She felt that institutional countermeasures to infiltration by the literati would not work, and she warned that the arrival of bourgeois parliamentary government would convert the Russian intelligentsia to bourgeois ideals, as it had the German. The intelligentsia would then attempt to capture the proletarian movement, a task that would be easier if it were rigidly centralized. Finally, she parodied Freudian psychology, identifying the Russian revolutionary intellectual (Lenin) as the 'ego' and Tsarism as the 'object' (or *id*?): 'But now the 'ego' of the Russian revolutionary . . . declares itself once again as the all-powerful director of history – this time as his majesty the central committee of the Social Democratic labour movement.'

On 7 January 1905, the coal-miners of the Ruhr shrugged off the timidity of their trade union leaders and began a bitter unofficial strike. As many German workers went on strike in 1905 as during the five preceding years put together. Two weeks later, on 22 January (by the Western calendar), Russian cossacks and gendarmes gunned down a peaceful and ostensibly monarchist attempt by tens of thousands of Petersburg workers to present a petition requesting democratic elections to the Tsar. The proletariat of the entire Russian Empire erupted in protest strikes. The Polish workers ignored Daszyński's appeal not to submerge their activities in those of the All-Russian movement, preferring instead to follow Bebel's advice to support 'Social Democracy'.

Rosa Luxemburg's ecstatic reaction to these longed-for events was not devoid of patriotism:

> The Russian Party fractions (I am speaking only of the Social Democracy) are so little equal to the moment, and the party in *Poland* shows incomparably more political energy and foresight . . . Just think, in Poland in January–February alone 350,000 workers struck – more than in the *whole* of the rest of Russia. And now – look at May Day with *us* and the silence in Petersburg.

Predicting that the Russian Revolution would last for years 'like the Great French Revolution', Rosa Luxemburg belittled the contribution of the intelligentsia. It was not the work of intellectuals, however great their courage, but of 'the enormous sum of political enlightenment, which has been invisibly disseminated by the social-democratic agitation of women and men among the Russian working class milieux in recent years'. As one of the few SPD 'experts' on Russia, she was even invited to contribute to that citadel of 'Opportunism', *Vorwärts*, where she defined the role of the party in the revolution as,

To conquer for itself the leading role *in the course of the revolution*, to skilfully exploit the first victories and defeats of the elemental upheavals, so as to take hold of the current in the current itself; . . . To master and direct not the *beginning* but the *end*, the result of the revolutionary outburst, this is the only goal which a political party can rationally set itself, if it does not wish to give itself over to fantastic illusions of conceit or an indolent pessimism.

Still smarting from Rosa Luxemburg's reference to their work as 'a labour of Sisyphus', the leaders of the General Commission of the German Trade Unions panicked at the sight of industrial militancy. At their Congress in Cologne in March 1905, they decreed that mass strikes must not even be discussed (quite literally, they were labelled '*indiskutabel*') in the German unions. This ban on free speech contrasted comically with their earlier demand for freedom of enquiry for Bernstein. It was an implicit rejection of Rosa Luxemburg's conception of their proper role *vis-à-vis* the party. The tone of this discussion (which sometimes verged on the racist) was captured by the trade unionist Bömelburg's plea that 'to develop our organizations further, we need peace in the labour movement'.

Rosa traded blow for blow, mocking the vaunted 'experience' of trade union leaders in 'a country, that has *never yet* even been in a position to conduct an experiment with a political general strike'. She pressed home her attack at the Jena Party Congress of the SPD in September 1905, suggesting that the trade union bosses only worried about the spilling of their members' blood, when the workers were prepared to shed it in their own interests. The masses were with her, she insisted: 'Despite all the pettiness, we must remind ourselves that for us the final words of the *Communist Manifesto* are not merely fine phrases for mass meetings but that we are in bloody earnest when we appeal to the masses [saying]: the workers have nothing to lose but their chains – but a whole world to gain.' For the German Right, she was now forever 'Bloody Rosa'.

Rosa Luxemburg had become a powerful force within the SPD, the most prominent and influential of the party's 'radicals', yet she had failed to achieve 'one of the foremost positions in the party', as she had once hoped. As a woman, she could not stand for the Reichstag, while she had no taste for bureaucratic work in the party or trade unions. Kautsky was still an ally and could not in any case be deprived of the editorship of the theoretical journal he had founded. Clara Zetkin was now an intimate friend and comrade, but Rosa never coveted her role in the mobilization of the 'females'. Rosa Luxemburg was briefly editor of the *Sächsische Arbeiterzeitung* in 1898 and of the *Leipziger Volkszeitung* in 1901–2. Both experiences ended in her rapid ejection amid accusations of censorship and power-grabbing. In 1905, for the first and last time, she enjoyed a real victory within the SPD, thanks to August Bebel.

Rosa Luxemburg always revered Bebel for the uncompromising courage he had shown in opposing the Franco-Prussian War in 1870. She knew very well that he was now a changed man, 'already old and not in a position to lead in the more important questions'. Still, she was pleased when he adopted some of her criticisms of Bernstein and Millerand. Goaded by the PPS and the German trade union bosses, Bebel supported Rosa Luxemburg throughout 1905, though when the euphoria of her moral victory had worn off, she had to admit privately that the mass strike resolution adopted at the Jena Party Congress in 1905 stipulated that the trade unions would only ever support mass strikes as a *defensive* weapon. But the old man did not let her down entirely. He now purged the board of *Vorwärts*, replacing six revisionists by five radicals, including (unofficially) Rosa Luxemburg.

The limits to Bebel's radicalism were clearly illustrated by his decision to go off for the usual long family holidays in Switzerland, even though the Russian Revolution was in full swing and France and Germany close to war over Morocco. In a prophetic moment in the autumn of 1905, he even warned Rosa: 'Watch out, if revolution comes to Germany, then Rosa will stand on the left side and I on the right . . . But we shall hang you; we won't let you oversalt our soup . . .' To which she replied dryly, 'You don't know who will hang whom'.

In an attempt to furnish Rosa Luxemburg with a heroic feminist curriculum vitae, Raya Dunayevskaya suggests that

Rosa was only restrained from returning to Poland by the chauvinism of her male comrades and that once in Poland, she personally took part in pistol-packing activities. After her death, when the legend-building had begun, Hanecki did indeed make such a claim. It must be treated with some reservation. Her own letters suggest a more complicated situation.

In March 1905, Rosa claimed that she was devoting all her attention to the revolutionary events in the Russian Empire: 'I am now, by God, completely Russian Revolution', yet the aftermath of pleurisy and recurrent liver infections were not the only reasons for not returning to Poland. *None* of the leaders of the revolutionary parties save Trotsky, Parvus and the Socialist Revolutionary, Avksentiev, made any attempt to return to Russia before Nicholas II was forced to grant civic freedoms as a result of the October 1905 general strike. (Plekhanov never returned at all.) As late as the day before the Tsar's October Manifesto, Rosa herself dissuaded male comrades from returning to Poland. The eight weeks that followed were taken up with her vital work on the board of *Vorwärts*. Meanwhile, a *real* chauvinist in the person of Otto Hué, the miners' union boss, had suggested that it was 'high time for all those with such an excess of revolutionary zeal to take a practical part in the Russian battles for freedom, instead of carrying on mass strike discussions from summer holiday resorts'.

Despite her physical remoteness from events in Russia, Rosa worked relentlessly for the Russian (and Polish) revolution throughout 1905, doing what she was best at, writing, fundraising and lobbying for victims of Tsarist repression. She corrected Jogiches' Polish articles and got Marchlewski to find space for women's demands in the SDKPiL Programme. In September, she was deeply shaken by the execution, despite intensive lobbying of the German Foreign Ministry by the SPD leaders, of her old mentor Marcin Kasprzak. Kasprzak had been surprised by Tsarist gendarmes at an SDKPiL press in Warsaw in April 1904. In view of past PPS allegations that he was a police spy, he chose to fight – not normal Social Democrat practice – killing four officers. Kasprzak's execution gave his former protégée nightmares and induced a brief mood of deep depression and nostalgia, in which she cried over her dead parents' letters and felt like giving up 'this whole *goddamned politics*'. Yet some days later, and after some time in the sunshine, her spirits began to lift a little. On 28 December 1905, a short, Jewish-looking woman bearing a passport issued to Anna Matschke boarded a train from Berlin bound for East Prussia. The next day she crossed the frontier into revolutionary Russia.

4 The Last Two Men

The Happiest Months of Her Life

Rosa Luxemburg arrived in Warsaw on 29 December 1905. The city was ice-bound and under martial law, yet her comrades were able to force printers to publish *Czerwony Sztandar* regularly. There was a political hiatus following the suppression of the December Uprisings in Moscow and the Baltic provinces and the sympathy strikes in Warsaw. Casting aside her former reservations about premature insurrections, Rosa Luxemburg fully supported the December risings. The insurrections were justified, she explained, solely because 'the *general strike alone* has played its part.' 'Now', she told the Kautskys, 'only a direct, general street battle can bring a conclusion, but for that the moment must be better prepared.' Rosa Luxemburg now conceded that technical preparations were 'important and essential', but still could not bring herself to agree with those, such as Lenin, who believed that the party should itself prepare an uprising.

For Rosa Luxemburg, 'the task of the leadership of Social Democracy consists solely in infusing the consciousness of its own class movement into the masses of the Proletariat and to assemble and consolidate the leading circles, which are enlightened in the course of the Revolution and [by] social democratic agitation into a permanent class organization'. She asserted once more that the revolution could not fail if it remained true to itself. In previous revolutions, the working class had lost out because it had let itself be led by the bourgeoisie. This would not happen again, from which it 'followed logically that the exhaustion of the revolutionary ranks, and the violent strangling of the whole movement [had been] possible and inevitable in certain moments of bourgeois revolutions, but are impossible today'.

The time had come to mend fences with the RSDRP. Rosa Luxemburg was horrified by the pusillanimity of the Mensheviks and gloated over Plekhanov's willingness to accept bourgeois leadership. She and Jogiches now decided to throw the full weight

79

of the SDKPiL (and if possible, the SPD) behind the Bolsheviks, while maintaining the integrity of their own party. Then, on 4 March 1906, they were summarily arrested in a routine police operation. When her true identity was established, Rosa was moved from a crowded women's cell to the cold 'luxury' of the Tenth Pavilion of the Warsaw Citadel, until Bebel stumped up the money for her bail. As usual, she bore her imprisonment with exemplary dignity. In reporting on a botched hunger-strike to mark the opening of the first Russian *Duma*, or elected parliament, in St Petersburg, a prison official noted laconically: 'Altogether 21 persons fasted, of whom only one prisoner, Rosa Luxemburg, took no food at all'. Yet, on her return to Germany, she protested strenuously at attempts to portray her as a martyr: 'I can assure you without exaggeration . . . that the months I spent in Russia were the happiest of my life'.

With Luxemburg and Jogiches in prison, it was left to Warski and Dzierżyński to represent the SDKPiL at the 'Unification Congress' of the RSDRP in Stockholm in April 1906. At the congress, the Mensheviks (now in a majority) and Bolsheviks buried the hatchet, while permitting the *Bund* and the Latvian Social Democrats to join the All-Russian Party. The SDKPiL gained an even more favoured status, with two seats on the joint Central Committee, while still preserving its internal autonomy. Although young Marxist intellectuals had now taken over the PPS, Polish socialists could still only join the All-Russian party as members of the SDKPiL. To avert public wrangling over the contentious 'national question', each of the parties simply pretended that the other had changed its views.

In May 1907, Rosa Luxemburg was finally able to speak at a Russian Marxist congress, the 5th RSDRP Congress in London. She arrived with a mandate from the SPD, as well as the SDKPiL, so she spoke with the overwhelming authority of the German party, subjecting the Russians to a lecture on Marxist principles which left Plekhanov 'raging' and the Bolsheviks and centre ecstatic. She warmly endorsed Lenin's preference for the rebellious Russian peasantry over the politically bankrupt Russian bourgeoisie as allies in the revolutionary struggle. She was fortified by the January 1907 Reichstag election campaign, in which the German liberals had fully endorsed the imperialist ambitions of the conservative Bülow government. In Russia, as in Germany, she argued, there must be no deals with liberals, since 'the proletariat is necessarily the sole fighter and defender of the democratic forms of the bourgeois state'. When Plekhanov reproached her with a willingness to sacrifice Russian workers to unnecessary defeats, she countered with a ringing defence of revolutionary audacity: 'I find, on the contrary, that the leader is poor, and the army pathetic, which only commit themselves to battle, when victory is already in their pockets'.

If Rosa spoke with 'German' authority to the Russians, she also had 'Russian' lessons for the Germans. She had returned in the autumn of 1906 from heroism and sacrifice in Russia to the 'spinelessness and pettiness' of the SPD. For all her boasts to the Russians, she knew quite well that the radicalization of the SPD was proceeding at snail's pace, if at all. The German socialists had shown their solidarity with the Russians by dipping into their pockets, but only in Hamburg had there been a brief (and unofficial) political strike. Her brilliant pamphlet, *Mass Strike, Party and Trade Unions* (1906) was an attempt to share the experiences of Russian and Polish trade unionists with their German brothers and sisters. Triumphantly, Rosa Luxemburg contrasted 'The Two Methods of Trade Union Policy' (the title of an article), comparing the pitiful experience of the German printers' union, which had tried to emulate peaceful 'English' practice, with the Russian Printers' Union, which had leap-frogged the achievements of its German counterpart in 'a single year of revolutionary storm'.

The SPD 'fathers' turned a deaf ear to Rosa's pedagogy, instead conceding the Trade Union General Commission a veto over any future mass strikes and gradually conceding to the demands of the trade union leaders that the May Day strike be abandoned also. In effect, the 'German' model had now been stood on its head: it was now the party that was subordinate to the unions.

Rosa confided her growing sense of frustration in Clara Zetkin: 'At any turn which exceeds the limits of parliamentarianism, they abdicate totally, or worse still, they try to screw everything back on parliamentary lines, and so [they] will bitterly fight as an "enemy of the people" anyone who wants to go further.' Still, it simply never occurred to her that there could be any alternative to Social Democracy. Her task was to remind it of its historical vocation: 'Social Democracy is the most enlightened and class-conscious vanguard of the proletariat. It cannot and must not wait fatalistically for the arrival of a "revolutionary situation" [or] wait until such time as that spontaneous popular movement falls from Heaven. On the contrary, it must, as always, *hurry ahead* of the development of things, [and] try to *accelerate* them.'

In affiliating to the RSDRP, Luxemburg and Jogiches hoped to overcome its 'inconsistency, [and] disorganization, but above all [its] conceptual and tactical confusion'. At the 1907 London Congress, they had worked with Lenin to create a new majority in the RSDRP. Rosa Luxemburg assessed the situation as follows: 'The majority, in the sense of the politics of principle, was formed by half of the Russians (the so-called Bolsheviks), the Poles and the Latvians'. Opposed to them were what she called the 'shabby chess-players' of the *Bund*, who supported Plekhanov's 'opportunism'. She felt that Plekhanov himself was 'finished and now only fit to tell jokes, and indeed very old jokes'. For their part, the Mensheviks assumed that Jogiches was now paying them back for the way Plekhanov had treated Jogiches fifteen years earlier.

When Lenin's insistence on taking part in electoral politics in Russia isolated him within the Bolshevik faction, Jogiches and Luxemburg were careful not to help Lenin's opponents. To some extent this was a matter of principle: Jogiches did not want to 'break the neck of Social Democracy', but tactical considerations were not lacking. If they interfered in Bolshevik affairs, Lenin might intervene in theirs. In the summer of 1909, Luxemburg still advised Jogiches against breaking the alliance with Lenin despite what she termed Lenin's 'Tatar Marxism'. It was better to use the SDKPiL's casting vote in the RSDRP Central Committee than risk polemics with the well-funded and articulate Bolsheviks. For Rosa, however, the old PPS trauma was again decisive:

> ... the most important [thing] is ... that our breach with the Bolsheviks would fundamentally increase and drive to extremes the chaos in the party and bring the greatest benefit to the Mensheviks, who are the most dangerous plague for the party,

and especially for us, for they are protectors of the PPS and our bitterest enemies from the depths of their souls.

This was a confession of the weakness of the SDKPiL within the Russian party, though Rosa persisted in believing that Jogiches had won not only 'the position of the leader in the Polish movement, but also in the Russian'.

Kostja, Lulu, Mimi and School

Plekhanov was not alone in his fury at Rosa Luxemburg during the 1907 London Congress. Jogiches' fury was more personal. He already suspected Rosa of infidelity, and in a fit of jealousy, he grabbed a letter addressed to her, tore it open and walked off with it. The letter confirmed his worst fears: Rosa was conducting an affair with Clara Zetkin's son, Konstantin, a medical student fifteen years her junior. Jogiches was not prepared to tolerate what he regarded as a ridiculous mésalliance, and it was years before he ceased to abuse their necessary political relations by subjecting Rosa to unpleasant harassment in her personal life.

Following her arrival in Berlin in 1898, Rosa had done everything in her power to speed up her divorce from Gustav Lübeck, and had besieged Leo with pleas to join her in a 'normal' family life, in which she would bear their children. Appalled at the prospect of losing his autonomy, Leo used every possible pretext to evade her web, though he finally came to live with her, intermittently and conspiratorially, in Berlin from 1901 onwards. Elżbieta Ettinger suggests that Rosa had a brief liaison with Jogiches' future biographer, Zdzisław Leder, early in 1905. Still, the union was patched up and limped on until their brief stay in Warsaw in 1906. Jogiches did not enjoy Bebel's patronage and had to rely on his own ingenuity for his escape from the Tsar's prisons. Peter Nettl suggests that Jogiches then had a liaison with a comrade who was sheltering him. Ettinger (who makes no bones of her partiality for Leo Jogiches) contests this suggestion. At all events, their intimacy ceased between 1905 and 1906. A believer in walking away with her head held high, Rosa was once bitterly critical of one of Goethe's ex-mistresses: 'God punish me, but she was a cow. In particular, when Goethe gave her the sack, she behaved like a nagging washerwoman. . . . I cleave to the idea that a woman's character doesn't show itself when love begins, but when it ends.'

Over the winter of 1906–7, Rosa Luxemburg was very close to Parvus. It is possible they were lovers. The evidence for this is as strong as the evidence for the affairs suggested by Ettinger and Nettl, and Parvus later claimed he had burned their correspondence to protect her reputation. Parvus had earned her respect as a leading member of the 1905 Petersburg Soviet (the kind of proletarian institution she saw leading a successful proletarian revolution) and as co-author with Leon Trotsky of the theory of 'permanent revolution'. On the other hand, she knew that he had already abandoned two women to indigence with children he had fathered. He had also walked out on a bankrupt publishing enterprise, leaving Marchlewski to face the creditors. Julek and Bronisława can scarcely have approved her closeness to Parvus. It illustrates how little she cared for 'petty-bourgeois' ethics.

When in the winter of 1906–7, Rosa Luxemburg suggested to Clara Zetkin that her son Konstantin might visit Berlin for a while, Rosa was certainly not thinking of another affair. But 'Kostja', as she loved to call him, was no spotty teenager but a sensitive young man, and Rosa was soon romantically involved. In January, 'Kostik, my son' received her 'greetings'. In March, 'dear Kostja' earned her 'kisses'. By May, her 'Beloved Baby' was rewarded with English love poems.

At last, Rosa felt she had a lover in whom she could confide her feelings without fear of rebuff; for a while this was so. As she served a two-month prison term for incitement in 1907, all her thoughts were on her new beloved: 'I think constantly of my little baby and press him all the time to my breast in my thoughts. What is the little one doing without me? Often it is hard for me to overcome my yearning. To see this child happy and avert his slightest pain is my dearest thought.' At other times, she tried to compensate for this rather suffocating maternal love, by setting him up as an authority over her painting: 'If only you could sit by me to criticize and judge! I only believe your judgment now, far more than Zundel's.' Rosa constantly advised Kostja on what he should read and entertained the most extravagant ambitions for his future as a writer. It was not only Leo who would have found their intimacy scandalous, and Rosa and Kostja had to resort to subterfuge to see as much of one another as possible. For a while, this put distance between Rosa and Clara Zetkin, but Clara knew better than to censure their love. Her own scandalous second union with the painter, Friedrich Zundel, eighteen years her junior, must have tempered her reaction.

When Kostja returned from his summer holidays in August 1909, he omitted to send Rosa his usual account. She knew something was wrong. When her suspicions were confirmed, she wrote a dignified, but not entirely convincing, farewell: 'A beloved friend you are and you will remain for me, as long as you want, as long as I live. Whatever concerns you is dearer to me than the rest of the world. I will say nothing more about that . . . which you wrote of to me, because every mention hurts.' In fact, she fought hard to save their intimacy, creating a vacancy at the SPD Party School in Berlin in the hope of luring him back. When this failed, she assumed the role of indulgent aunt and intellectual mentor in his life.

Rosa doted on Kostja, but he never totally absorbed her affections as Leo Jogiches had. In 1908, she took her sister Anna for a seaside holiday on the Baltic coast. For the first time, Rosa was proud of her sister: 'She knows very little about scientific socialism, but bitterly complains about my brothers, who are cowards and who have already lost all belief in the Revolution, while she holds on as fast as I do.' They picked wild flowers, spotted snails' trails, breathed the sea air and laughed together, and Rosa repented her former superior airs: 'Here I am for the first time as she deserves; for earlier I was always irritated, impatient, insufferable: this is because I am once more *I* since I am free of Leo.'

Rosa's new-found freedom was not universally welcomed by their married friends. It was in an attempt to use her friendship with Luise Kautsky as a cover for her relations with Kostja that Rosa began to arouse the *personal* hostility of Karl Kautsky. He vigorously objected to any holiday plans that might have left the two women together. 'He hates my influence over Luise', she told Kostja, 'for she has emancipated herself internally from him'. Rosa returned to the attack that autumn of 1908, boldly suggesting that Luise spend a short time in Stuttgart unchaperoned, editing *Die Gleichheit* for Clara Zetkin, who was ill.

Evidently, Rosa had overplayed her hand, for Karl forced Luise to refuse. This time, Rosa's ostensible anti-feminism sounds much more like the disappointment of a lover:

> . . . this little experiment with Luise strengthens me in my former view: Please, renounce for ever the search for a female editor, nothing will come of dealing with women, they are not free and not disciplined. You may get an unsatisfactory male editor, but you will always know with a man where you're at and there'll be no histrionics, but a sober business relationship that spares your nerves.

Rosa's most faithful companion was her cat Mimi. She made no secret of her maternal feelings for Mimi, and even lectured her friends on Mimi's pardonably neurotic nature:

> . . . Mimi is a little mimosa, a hypernervous little princess in cat's fur, . . . once, when I, her real mother, wanted to take her out of the house by force, she got cramps from the overexcitement and became quite still in my arms, and had to be carried with tearful little eyes back into the apartment and only came to hours later . . . you have no idea what my maternal heart went through.

The substitute for the child she had yearned to bear, Mimi was also a focus for the revulsion against humanity that Rosa experienced in the wake of the defeat of the Russian Revolution and the marginalization of radicalism in the SPD. As she herself recognized, 'One cleaves more to animals, when human beings are so despicable'. Page after page of her correspondence with Kostja was devoted to Mimi's adventures: the day Mimi nearly got baked in the oven, the day Rosa tried to persuade her to give up hunting birds to become a vegetarian, and the day Mimi began 'reading' the papers. Kostja played the game beautifully, sending Mimi her favourite medicinal grass from Stuttgart. Bemused by all the mail to 'Fräulein Mimi', the postman began to ask after the young lady. Even such weighty guests as Lenin had to stroke and compliment Mimi, if they were to get any response from

Rosa. Cat-lovers may still be reading Rosa's letters with pleasure when Marxists are an extinct breed.

Before the 1905 Revolution, Rosa Luxemburg had lived the life of a true revolutionary, a life without boundaries. Leo had been the kind of man who literally takes his papers to bed with him. After the defeat of the Revolution, her life became more fragmented, more 'normal', more bourgeois. One symptom of this was the energy she put into the construction of a rewarding personal life distinct from politics, with friends such as Hannes Diefenbach, who sympathized with her views, but who were personal friends rather than comrades. Another was her immersion in the fine arts, especially painting, which she practised earnestly. She also enjoyed travel, gushing over her trips to Italy with the eyes of an American sophomore. Above all, she read incessantly, especially novels. As she told Clara Zetkin, this was 'as necessary as one's daily bread to counteract the desolation of the spirit by the mundane treadmill of trade union and parliamentary struggle and the poverty of our agitation'. For the first time in her life, she also had a regular job.

The breach with Leo had finally forced her to become financially self-supporting. In view of the quarantine imposed by German bourgeois society on Social Democrats as notorious as 'Bloody Rosa', this really meant exchanging her dependence on a single Social Democrat for the more honourable, but still precarious, dependence on the editorial commissions of the SPD press. Then, out of the blue, in September 1907, she was invited to teach at the newly-founded SPD Party School in Berlin. Ironically, she was only asked to help out because the Prussian police had threatened the Dutchman, Anton Pannekoek, and the Austrian, Rudolph Hilferding, with deportation if they taught there. Rosa was at first lukewarm, suspicious of the school, mistrusting the motives of its sponsors and preferring direct agitation of the masses to the creation of a party elite.

The invitation also caught her at a moment when she had finally overcome fatigue and depression to settle down to some serious intellectual work on Marxist economics, the field in which she intended to establish her reputation as a profound Marxist

87

theoretician. After careful consideration, she realized that 3,000 Marks a year for four morning lectures a week for just six months each year would solve her financial problems and give her more time than journalism for her economic studies. She accepted. As she commented flippantly to Kostja, 'At least I am at home in the subject and at most only the first half-year will cause me work; then I shall be able to do the later courses in my sleep'. This was the first time in her adult life that she had to report for work regularly at someone else's behest, and for a short time, she keenly resented being 'chained' to an 'Egyptian slavery of forced labour'.

Rosa Luxemburg's appointment to the school convinced such SPD right-wingers as Kurt Eisner that the school was becoming a hotbed of radical pedantry, and they resolved to attack it at the 1908 Nuremburg Party Congress. Nothing was better calculated to make Rosa rise to the school's defence. She conceded that the school needed improvement; she was particularly keen on seeing the history of international socialism displace national economics as the centrepiece of the course. Yet, she continued, 'We have had the experience as teachers that the results so far are excellent, so that I couldn't wish for a better elite corps' for the party. Gradually, she began to take pleasure in the contact with a new generation of socialists and to develop her own pedagogical theory and practice.

By 1911, Rosa Luxemburg was able to boast that the history of socialism had now been introduced, and that she hoped to supplement it with a history of trade unionism. She described the liberal pedagogical methods of the Party School with pride. The courses lasted for six months, classes were small enough for discussion, and the students were allowed free time to assimilate the material. She contrasted this with the positivistic cramming which took place on the courses offered to trade union officials by the leading Revisionists. 'Aren't the "doctrinaires" and the "theoreticians" once again more practical than the alleged "practicians"?' she crowed.

During her lectures at the Party School, Rosa Luxemburg loved to return to the attack on bourgeois professors of so-called 'national economy', to refute bourgeois claims that capitalism was the normal condition of humanity, and to develop and clarify her views on the inherent limits to capitalist expansion. Her incomplete lecture notes were finally published after her death as *An Introduction to National Economy*. They are immensely readable, accessibly erudite, analytically profound and spiced with her customary humour. They begin with a devastating demonstration of the futility of bourgeois studies of supposedly isolated 'national economies'. In a brilliant piece of economic historiography, she describes how the humble inventions of the Englishmen, Arkwright and Cartwright, led inexorably to famine in Orissa, to the American Civil War, to the British occupation of Egypt, to the mushroom-like growth of the textile mills of Łódź, and so to the participation of the Polish working class in the 1905 Russian Revolution.

Rosa Luxemburg also examined the researches of such brilliant bourgeois legal, sociological and anthropological scholars as Sir Henry Maine, Lewis Morgan and Maxim Kovalevsky, for proof that capitalism was a late and aberrant fruit of human culture. Communism, she argued, albeit in its primitive agrarian forms, had been the *normal* economic system throughout human history, and while it had usually been associated with patriarchy, she also cited examples of matriarchal communism. In the final section of the lecture notes, Rosa Luxemburg provided her own demonstration of the Marxist view that capitalism was the only economic system known to human history that required a constant reserve army of labour, i.e. unemployment. She foretold its demise as a result of the exhaustion of markets, the contradictory interests of the capitalists themselves and the revolt of the exploited.

Kautsky's Nervous Breakdown

Rosa Luxemburg's reservations about the leading Marxist thinker of her day went back to the turn of the century, when Karl Kautsky had patronizingly told her that in twenty-years' time, she would think exactly as he did. 'In that case, I shall be a noddy', she replied. She frequently mocked his ignorance of people and his Panglossian optimism. By 1907, she was aware of his 'fickleness' and was finding him 'cold, pedantic and doctrinaire'. As his initial enthusiasm for the Russian Revolution was replaced by a cautious, mechanistic view of the revolutionary process, she found his writing 'a repulsive web round my brain'. They were briefly reconciled in 1909–10, when the SPD Executive tried to ban Kautsky's book, *The Way to Power*, but she found him increasingly irksome. 'He shrivels and dessicates internally more and more; nothing and no one outside his family affects him as a human being'. Rosa did all she could to support Luise Kautsky's occasional rebellions, but in the eyes of the world, Luxemburg and Kautsky were allies, until January 1910, when a storm broke out that would divide them for ever.

One of the major institutional foundations of the quasi-absolutist Hohenzollern state was the Prussian Electoral Law. No matter how many seats they might win in the Reichstag, the SPD would remain powerless so long as the parliament of Prussia, the most powerful state in Germany, was controlled by a formula that gave the richest quarter of a million electors the same representation as the poorest six million. Working-class resentment at this state of affairs was heightened by reactionary changes in the electoral law in neighbouring Hessen and by a promise of reform in Prussia by the Prussian Prime Minister and German Reich Chancellor Bethmann Hollweg. On 3 January 1910, the Prussian SPD Congress resolved to use 'all means' to achieve a democratic franchise. A month later, Bethmann Hollweg unveiled a reform bill which completely ignored the main socialist grievances. *Vorwärts* called it a 'brutal and contemptuous declaration of war'. Demonstrations followed in several Prussian cities. When even the Chancellor's modest proposals were rejected by the Prussian House of Lords, further demonstrations took place throughout Prussia. A major demonstration planned for 6 March 1910 for Treptow Park was banned; the police were shaken to find that 150,000 Social Democrats had rallied instead at the Tiergarten. Rosa Luxemburg turned up at the rally with the Kautskys and Leon Trotsky.

Rosa felt that the moment for radical demands had now arrived. Clara Zetkin opened the columns of *Die Gleichheit* to Rosa's calls for the use of the mass strike and her demand that the SPD campaign openly for a republic. When she tried to make these points in the columns of *Vorwärts* and *Die Neue Zeit* the editors rejected her articles on the grounds that the SPD Executive had forbidden any discussion of the mass strike, not to mention a republic. August Bebel justified this decision in the light of the imminence of the 1912 Reichstag elections. 'The present situation is not ripe for a mass strike; on the other hand, if we have won a glorious electoral victory next year, . . . we would have quite a different situation'.

Bebel's naïve optimism simply ignored the fact that even an overwhelming electoral victory for the SPD in the Reichstag would change nothing in Prussia. The ultimate source of the Executive's veto was the trade union leadership, which claimed that it would assume the leadership of the masses when they demonstrated sufficient militancy, while doing all they could to postpone this moment for as long as possible. Still, Rosa was confident she could force the party's hand: 'All that means nothing, since the mood in the whole country is excellent as never before, and Berlin will *have* to advance under the pressure of the provinces. *One cannot therefore operate the lever in Berlin. This 'head' will soon move if one gives it a few kicks in the rear.*' To some extent, events confirmed her optimism. The articles banned in Berlin were published by radical papers in Dortmund and Breslau and were soon circulating around the country.

Rosa Luxemburg now took leave of the Party School, and on 3 April, she began an agitational tour that took her through Breslau, Waldenburg, Kiel, Bremen, Dortmund, Bochum, Herne, Elberfeld and Barmen. While the other SPD leaders squirmed with embarrassment in Berlin, Rosa incited the German proletariat to radical action. The climax came in Frankfurt-on-Main, where she addressed an ecstatic audience of 7,000 in a circus marquee. Wherever she went, Rosa Luxemburg mocked Bethmann Hollweg's 'reforms' and condemned the 'personal regime', i.e. the Kaiser. She was unusually courteous towards the handful of sincere bourgeois democrats, but suggested that they were not 'the snowdrops of a burgeoning Spring, but rather the rare meadow-saffrons of a melancholy Indian summer'.

Listing the fearful casualties borne by the proletariat in wartime and in industrial accidents, she asked those who doubted the resolve of the masses whether they 'expect that for fear of a few fatalities we would back away from the path we have taken, from the struggle for our most elementary political rights?' A bridgehead had been won, she told her listeners, the right to demonstrate, and this must be extended along 'the whole line of struggle'. And when the Social Democrats had completed their work of enlightenment and morale building, they could leave the rest to events, 'with the certainty that history is working in our direction, and that in this struggle, as at every stage on our progress to socialism, we socialists will come out victorious – despite everything.'

While she was touring, Rosa Luxemburg received a copy of Karl Kautsky's critical article, 'What now?', in which he urged the SPD to adopt Fabian tactics of attrition. Thus, he argued, there should be demonstrations, but not at any cost, while the party line encouraging economic strikes, but forbidding political strikes, should be rigorously enforced. The party must concentrate on the Reichstag elections, aiming for an absolute majority. 'Such a victory', he claimed echoing Bebel, 'would signify nothing less than a catastrophe for the whole ruling system'. Only if force were used against the triumphant Reichstag majority, should mass action be invoked.

'I shall settle with this coward, who only finds the courage to stab others in the back', Rosa fumed to Leo Jogiches. And settle with him she did. Not all the European Left were convinced that the Prussian Goliath was ready to be felled, but no serious Marxist could read the dialectical rubbishing that Rosa Luxemburg gave Kautsky without beginning to doubt his credentials as a Marxist and a revolutionary. When she tried to cite documents proving that the Executive had smothered the mass strike discussion, he censored her articles. She retaliated by referring to his letters to her. Kautsky begged for a truce on the grounds that the Marxist Left should unite to counter the latest provocation from the Revisionists in the Baden SPD, who had approved the state budget and bent the knee to the King. But Rosa ground on remorselessly, shredding Kautsky's reputation beyond intellectual recovery.

Karl Kautsky had the misfortune to be both the leading Marxist of the Second International and a petty-bourgeois father and husband. His intellectual humiliation was compounded by the continuing cordiality of his entire family for someone who made no bones of her contempt for him. He was haunted by the fear of a verbal drubbing at the Party Congress, where Rosa's baiting would be exacerbated by the ironic support he anticipated from all those Revisionists, reformists and practicians he had lectured for so long. Rightly or wrongly, the party assumed that the nervous breakdown that kept Kautsky away from the 1910 Magdeburg Party Congress was the work of Rosa Luxemburg.

The party fathers were incensed. In Kautsky's absence, the practicians got even with Rosa, accusing her of intellectual condescension. In the words of Philipp Scheidemann, 'I am far from being as clever as Rosa Luxemburg. I cannot be so clever anyway, for you all know that I was a very ordinary worker, who had to obtain his little bit of knowledge, which Comrade Luxemburg mocks, in sleepless nights.' Reason was no match for injured *amour propre*, and Rosa wilted in the face of hostility. 'I feel *like a beaten dog*', she informed Jogiches, 'and it seems to me that I have suffered *a smashing defeat*'.

Rosa's Pyrrhic victory against Kautsky was followed by a bruising confrontation with old August Bebel himself. In the summer of 1911, an international crisis was precipitated when the German government despatched warships to Agadir in Morocco, claiming that the French were in breach of a previous agreement defining French, Spanish and German interests there. The French seemed helpless until on 21 July, David Lloyd George, the British Chancellor of the Exchequer, warned Germany that war was preferable to allowing Britain to be treated, 'where her interests were vitally affected, as if she were of no account in the Cabinet of Nations'. Pan-Germans erupted in bellicose hysteria, but Kaiser Wilhelm II and Chancellor Bethmann Hollweg knew the game was up. In November 1911, Germany withdrew her Moroccan claims in exchange for a slice of Central Africa.

The French and Spanish socialists had mobilized immediately to oppose war in massive demonstrations held on 10–12 July. Until the Lloyd George speech, the only echo in Germany came from the Stuttgart radicals, who organized a meeting addressed by Karl Liebknecht on 15 July. The SPD Executive declined to join the 12 July demonstration in Paris, while even the massive demonstration in Berlin a week *after* Lloyd George's speech was organized by the Berlin trade unions, rather than the SPD, and as a result of a visit by French socialists. In other words, the SPD leadership seems to have dragged its feet *so long as there was no danger to Germany*! It looked as though August Bebel, who saw no reason to break his summer vacation in Switzerland, saw in Bethmann Hollweg and the Kaiser stronger guarantors of peace than the Social Democratic movement. He was indeed petrified of delivering any more 'anti-national' accusations into the hands of the conservatives so close to the Reichstag elections. Rosa suspected all this, but how could she possibly *prove* it to party veterans, who venerated Bebel as their forefathers had venerated Martin Luther?

In an article published in the radical *Leipziger Volkszeitung*, Rosa shared with her readers some information she had acquired in her capacity as a Polish member of the International Socialist Bureau. She informed the German workers that within days of the arrival of the German warships in Agadir, the socialist parties of France, Spain and Britain had agreed to an international socialist conference. She continued ominously,

> Only from the German party . . . did the invitation encounter no special reciprocal cordiality. The answer was, it is true, transmitted merely by a member of the party Executive [Hermann Molkenbuhr] as his private opinion, but evidently the other members of this body associated themselves with it, for no further communication followed from this quarter; the German member of the International Bureau [August Bebel] also declared that the conference was not to be recommended for the time being [*zunächst*], and the planned meeting failed to take place for this reason.

And, in a series of biting articles, Rosa Luxemburg found the SPD seriously wanting in proletarian internationalism.

There was an explosion of self-righteous indignation that entirely evaded the charges Rosa had made. Allegedly, she had betrayed the party by releasing the text of a confidential letter, and to have falsified the intentions of both Molkenbuhr and Bebel. Most of these counter-charges were groundless or even meaningless. After all, what was a socialist party doing conducting secret diplomacy rather than arousing the masses? Yet, these red herrings were accepted by the vast majority of SPD activists at the Jena Party Congress in 1911. This time, Rosa held firm, rebutting her critics with sang-froid and good humour. Bebel betrayed his anxiety by interrupting her incessantly from the chair. But her skin had grown tougher, and she wrote reassuringly to Kostja about the good mood she shared with Clara: 'We are both very calm and good humoured, are content with the course of the Congress and care nothing for all the attacks'.

The battles of 1910–11 were a watershed in Rosa Luxemburg's relations with the SPD leadership. Thereafter, they marginalized her, purging the editorial commissions of the radical papers that had printed her articles, but that was all. They still appreciated her value as a 'token' woman and a 'token' Pole. It no more occurred to them to expel her from the SPD than it occurred to her to form a new party. It is true that she mended fences with Franz Mehring and Karl Liebknecht, held occasional meetings with other radicals and even began to publish a newsletter, but she would have nothing to do with organizing a faction and quarrelled violently with the Bremen radicals over Radek. It would take a greater cataclysm before Rosa Luxemburg would contemplate a rupture with Social Democracy. Nor were her views of the SPD leadership shared by the whole of the European Left. Lenin, in particular, failed to endorse her criticisms of Kautsky's 'centrism', and it was this that prompted the misleading suggestions in 1930 that Lenin had retreated from Bolshevism. Lenin had other, more pressing reasons for misgivings about Rosa Luxemburg in these years.

From Mendelson to Sobelsohn

Between 1907 and 1914, Leo Jogiches and Rosa Luxemburg followed a tragic course in Polish and Russian affairs that led them to a triple disaster. By 1914 their party, the SDKPiL, had shrunk to a rump, split into warring factions; Rosa Luxemburg's personal and political integrity was seriously tarnished, and the radical left within the SPD was bitterly divided. Finally, Jogiches and Luxemburg helped to rehabilitate the Mensheviks with the SPD and got embroiled in a ferocious feud with Lenin. Until recently, the piety of Rosa Luxemburg's biographers ensured that these scandals were buried. As usual, Elżbieta Ettinger exposes

Rosa's shabby conduct but puts it down to irritation caused by romantic disappointments, while swiping at those such as Bebel who dismissed Rosa as a 'quarrelsome woman'. At least as important were Rosa's rigid and doctrinaire prescriptions for the Polish proletariat, as well as her willingness to take in Jogiches' dirty linen. Both were involved in this unedifying tale.

The story begins in Poland where the working class was split five ways after 1906. The SDKPiL had, it is true, established itself as the standard-bearer of uncompromising class struggle and internationalism. Most Jewish workers continued to support the *Bund*. A new feature of Polish working-class politics was the split in the PPS, which resulted in the emergence of a class-conscious, socialist majority, the PPS-Left (*PPS-Lewica*), which demanded autonomy for Poland, and a nationalist and insurrectionary right, the PPS-Revolutionary Fraction (*PPS-Rewolucyjna Frakcja*), influenced by Piłsudski, which would settle for nothing less than total separation from Russia. All four socialist parties were completely overshadowed, however, by Roman Dmowski's bourgeois–liberal Catholic National Democratic Party, the *Endecja*. Profiting from an offer of legality for 'non-political' unions, Dmowski's protégés in the National Trade Unions succeeded in organizing a substantial section of the Polish proletariat, breaking strikes called by the socialists.

Rejecting the view of the Russian Marxists and the Socialist International that trade unions should be defensive labour organizations within which competition and collaboration might take place between socialist groups, Luxemburg and Jogiches insisted on trade unions rigidly subordinated to the SDKPiL. The determination with which they insisted on this by now fictitious 'German model' was naturally strengthened rather than weakened by the fact that, between 1905 and 1906, the German trade unions had actually succeeded in inverting this relationship and asserting a trade union veto over militant party activity. Only a few hundred Polish militants were able to defy the *Okhrana*, the Polish industrialists and the natural desire of the workers themselves for unity with other socialist trade unionists. The SDKPiL trade unions soon resembled a general staff without an army. Rosa still opposed experiments with legal trade unions, insisting that the differences of principles between Marxists, on

96

the one hand, and revisionists and nationalists, on the other, were more important than popularity: 'nothing new has happened, but on the other hand the demarcation line may be lost'.

She was equally inflexible in her dealings with the PPS-Left. When the PPS-Left admitted its past errors, she pursued them with biting scorn: 'What are the principles of a party for which the social and political development, the physiognomy of the classes, the direction of the workers' movement in Poland, in Russia and in Europe were all a book locked with seven seals?' She insisted that PPS workers should only be permitted to join the SDKPiL by recanting their errors individually and by condemning their former leaders. This was a recipe for the continued fragmentation of the Polish proletariat.

The struggle with the PPS-Left was complicated by the fact that SDKPiL had itself compromised, by mentioning 'autonomy' for Poland during the revolutionary years. Rosa decided to correct this error in a magisterial definitive statement on the 'national question', which was published in 1908. In the misleadingly entitled *The National Question and Autonomy*, Rosa Luxemburg had little to say about autonomy. The essay is perhaps the most sweeping socialist condemnation of nationalism ever made. Correctly enough, she reminded her adversaries in the RSDRP that Marx and Engels had always subordinated the freedom of the Slavonic peoples ruled by Turkey to the interests of European democracy. Unlike the founding fathers, she could detect not a single contemporary national struggle that deserved the support of Social Democrats, and precious few in history either. While she admired the personal qualities of the medieval Swiss democrats, she denounced their cause as reactionary. She even condemned the independence movements in Latin America and India as motivated by exploitative economic interests. Dogmatically, she proclaimed that, 'Social Democracy is called. . . to realize not the right of self-determination of nations, [but] solely the right to self-determination of the working class, of the exploited and down-trodden class; the proletariat.' For Rosa Luxemburg, national independence was a bourgeois fetish on a par with the 'womens' rights' she mocked with equal vehemence.

Rosa Luxemburg was also convinced that her West European comrades, as well as Marchlewski, had so far failed to define a correct Marxist approach to the peasantry. This was a problem of critical importance for democratic socialists in Poland, a country overwhelmingly populated by Catholic peasants as yet unprepared to join a Russian peasant war. Rosa hoped to address this problem, but she never found the time. Instead, she contented herself with the pious hope that the Polish proletariat 'can and must, resting on the revolutionary movement of the other popular masses, strive towards the realization of its own mission'. On this as on other Polish issues, Rosa Luxemburg was unable to create new revolutionary theory from the experience of 1905. In fairness, one must remember that Marx and Engels had also dismally failed to offer the central European peasantry any convincing reason for supporting socialism. This failure seems to be endemic in Marxism itself.

Equally serious was the *carte blanche* she gave to Jogiches in his dealings with the SDKPiL comrades, even when they began to give rise to accusations of 'dictatorship'. It was almost as though she was compensating him politically for his reduced status in her personal life. The origins of this 'dictatorship' lay in Jogiches' evident superiority over his peers, the awe he inspired in his juniors and political necessity, which obliged the underground party to delegate its powers to a small Chief Executive (*Zarząd Główny*) in Berlin. Within the Chief Executive, Jogiches was supported by Marchlewski and Warski, whose tolerance towards Leo's 'amusing idiosyncrasies' and 'rough explosions', as Warski called them, was born of two decades of shared hardship.

Younger members of the Chief Executive, such as Dzierżyński, Hanecki, Leder and Małecki, were less indulgent, but rarely united in their criticism. So long as they merely criticized his policies, Jogiches tried to co-opt them, but when they challenged his power, he set out to drive them from the party and to ruin them morally in the eyes of the Polish proletariat. Much of their opposition was created by Jogiches himself, as he demanded the impossible and then made his subordinates scapegoats for his tactical blunders. And if they fought back, he knew he could always count on Rosa's matchless prestige within the International.

The first casualty was Stanisław Trusiewicz, who had re-founded the SDKPiL at the turn of the century, but who had now become a Menshevik. It was Trusiewicz who first accused Jogiches of 'dictatorial tendencies' and 'the suppression of the independent opinion of autonomous party organizations'. Jogiches rode rough-shod over party rules to marginalize and expel him, with Rosa's entire approbation. It did not trouble them that it was inconsistent for them to expel Mensheviks from the SDKPiL while insisting that Lenin tolerate them within the All-Russian RSDRP.

At the Sixth and final Congress of the SDKPiL that met in Prague in December 1908, Jogiches was unanimously re-elected to the Chief Executive, which was armed with absolute powers. Hanecki, Małecki and Leder soon resigned to repeat Trusiewicz's charges of 'dictatorship'. Since there were no substantial *political* differences between them, Jogiches now resorted to plain defamation of character, accusing Małecki of being a pimp and Hanecki of dealings with a known police agent. Discontent within the party, especially in Warsaw, reached a peak as the Chief Executive refused to modify its tactics to take advantage of the revival of mass militancy after 1910. By the end of 1911, a new Warsaw Committee rejected the authority of the Berlin Chief Executive, unwisely embracing the label '*rozłamowcy*' (splitters), which Jogiches gave them.

Nettl blandly assures his readers that Rosa 'had nothing to do' with 'the events inside Poland itself', and that she 'disapproved of Jogiches' tactics'. It is true that she did not cause the split, but when Jogiches began his campaigns of denigration, he did so in the certainty that she was behind him. And while there were occasions when she doubted the wisdom of his attacks, on at least one occasion, she herself suggested unethical manoeuvres to him, as in April 1912, when she wrote suggesting,

> . . . a certain idea, of which I am *almost* convinced, if not quite; the Chief Executive must respond to the rebellion of the Warsaw Committee, . . . immediately now with the announcement that provocation [i.e. police infiltration] reigns in the Warsaw Committee, that no one can yet be named, but that the CE is on their track, that the CE has exhausted all party methods of struggle against this plague, however it does not want to destroy those, who have fallen into their hands solely through blindness, unwittingly, . . . I wonder whether the con-

fiscation of *Czerwony Sztandar* is not the work of a provocation, therefore of the Warsaw Committee?! This edition was highly inconvenient for them.

These tactics exactly replicated Stanisław Mendelson's tactics against Marcin Kasprzak, Rosa Luxemburg and her comrades in 1892–3.

Unfortunately for Rosa and Leo, the 'splitters' had friends in Germany, who had the temerity to draw the attention of Rosa's German admirers to the embarassing contrast between her defence of the minority in the SPD and her ruthlessness towards the opposition within the SDKPiL. The most talented, and therefore dangerous, of these was Karl Radek. Born Karl Sobelsohn in Lwów in 1885, he began his career among the Galician Social Democrats, adopting the pseudonym 'Radek' from a fictional socialist militant (who was modelled, ironically as it turned out, on the anarchist Jan Machajski). By the time Radek arrived in Berlin in 1908, he had acquired a seedy reputation and many enemies. A slovenly Bohemian, perennially unfaithful to his long-suffering German wife, Radek had once been accused of pawning a borrowed overcoat, selling a public library book and failing to account for a modest sum of money during the first Russian Revolution. Rosa had condoned much greater offences against 'bourgeois ethics' than these, notably through her intimacy with Parvus. She herself was repelled more by Radek's embarassing hero-worship of herself and by his weakness for self-dramatization. These were failing he shared with Trotsky, to whom she compared him; no compliment in her eyes.

By March 1911, Jogiches had decided to expel Radek from the SDKPiL and then get Rosa to put it to the SPD that a person expelled from one Social Democratic party had no place in another. Despite Rosa's reservations, Leo had little trouble extorting her collaboration. Jogiches revived the allegations of theft, even though Radek had already been acquitted by party courts of these charges and publicly defended by Jogiches himself. When a party tribunal made little headway with the charges, Jogiches had the Chief Executive dissolve it and expel Radek itself. When Radek continued to defend the 'splitters', Rosa called him a 'whore' who 'sticks his nose in everywhere'. Undoubtedly the strain told. In 1912, Rosa missed the SPD Party Congress; apart from depression, she was diagnosed as suffering from cystic catarrh. At the 1913 Jena Party Congress, Rosa was heard demanding Radek's expulsion from the SPD, while pleading for his right to natural justice within the party, a natural justice she and Jogiches had persistently denied him in the SDKPiL.

To chastise this standard-bearer of their errant Polish off-spring, Rosa Luxemburg and Leo Jogiches had no hesitation in placing in the hands of Friedrich Ebert, the coming bureaucratic boss of the SPD, the weapons he needed to crush their fellow radicals in German socialism. As Rosa herself admitted, 'thanks to the stupid business with Radek, the [SPD] Party Executive celebrated a cheap victory'. Even this rather obvious reflection did not deter her from dissuading German socialists from sending strike funds to Polish workers led by the 'splitters'. It is hardly surprising that Lenin was wary of supporting her against Kautsky.

The alliance between the Bolsheviks and the SDKPiL established in 1906 continued right up to 1911. In private, Rosa Luxemburg complained of Lenin's 'Tatar–Mongol nonsense', as she termed his psychological brutality towards the Bolshevik 'ultra-left' led by Bogdanov and Lunacharsky. Publicly, she endorsed Lenin's criticism of their 'revolutionism' as a symptom of 'a shameful decline in revolutionary spirit', deserving 'the most decisive rejection on the part of all revolutionary social democracy'. Yet Lenin would not indefinitely tolerate a situation which handed leadership of the RSDRP to Jogiches (whom Lenin knew as 'Tyszka'), by shackling the Bolsheviks to Mensheviks sympathetic to Bernstein's 'revisionism'. As he put it in a graphic note to Gorky, the RSDRP was like a child with boils: 'Either, if things go well, we open up the boils and let the pus out, we cure the child and bring it up. Or, if it goes badly, the child dies. Then, we'll remain childless for a while (that means we'll resuscitate the Bolshevik fraction) and afterwards bring a healthier child into the world.'

To the philosophical and tactical debates which rent Russian Marxism in the years of reaction were added disputes about money. At times, the history of the RSDRP in 1907–12 reads like the *Pardoner's Tale* in Marxist jargon. Depressed by the apparent success of Prime Minister Stolypin's reactionary policies in Russia, blaming one another bitterly for the debacle and desperately short of cash, the Russian Marxists squabbled incessantly over two large sums of money – the fruits of a bank raid and a disputed inheritance – both acquired by the Bolsheviks under questionable circumstances.

In Menshevik eyes, this money belonged to the whole RSDRP, while Lenin viewed it as the indispensable guarantee of the survival of Bolshevism. In January 1910, all elements represented on the official RSDRP Central Committee met in Paris in a final attempt to reunite the party. Finding himself outgunned, Lenin agreed to transfer the disputed sums to the trusteeship of the German socialists most respected by Russian Marxists, Karl Kautsky, Franz Mehring and Clara Zetkin, all close friends of Rosa Luxemburg at that time. Within weeks, hostilities recommenced between Martov, the leading Menshevik, and Lenin.

So long as Lenin contented himself with attempting to subordinate the Mensheviks to the revolutionary line imposed by the Poles and Bolsheviks on the All-Russian party, the Poles supported Lenin. The situation changed during 1911, as Lenin abandoned all pretence of trying to reunite the old RSDRP and began to organize a new, Bolshevik-dominated RSDRP. The Poles now tried to restrain him. At Rosa Luxemburg's behest, the trustees refused to hand back the disputed money to Lenin. This simply made him more determined to break away from Polish tutelage. Rudely ignoring financial constraints, Lenin summoned a conference of sixteen Bolsheviks and two Mensheviks to Prague in January 1912. It condemned the Poles for practising 'the worst kind of federalism', declared itself the sole representative of Russian Social Democracy and elected a Leninist Central Committee. There was to be no place for brokers, honest or not, in this purged organization. Jogiches' attempt to dominate Russian Marxism by bureaucratic means was over. In the accurate, if malicious, words of the Menshevik journalist Martynov, 'The attempt to lead the Russian fractions under a Polish umbrella past the "left" and "right ultras" to unity collapsed in the solipsism of this "little Macchiavelli".'

One of the many non-Bolsheviks heartily offended by Rosa's manipulation of Clara Zetkin was Leon Trotsky: 'Really the deepest humiliation for Russian Social Democracy has arrived,

102

when Klara, informed by Rosa, destroys Party institutions and calls new ones into life.' For their part, Jogiches and Luxemburg poured scorn on Trotsky's vain attempts to reunite the RSDRP.

After Rosa Luxemburg's heroic death, Trotsky was generous in his tributes to her, even to the point of self-reproach, admitting 'I probably did not appreciate her . . . enough at that time'. If genuine, such remorse was misplaced. If anything, it was Rosa Luxemburg who failed to appreciate Trotsky's talents. This was not just a matter of background and manners, though in this, as in other respects, it was a case of like poles repelling one another. Between the revolutions in Russia, it was Trotsky who argued against bureaucratic manipulation of the RSDRP and for a 'new type' of party led by 'conscious and independent workers' who would only act as 'professional revolutionaries' in exceptional circumstances. This echoed Rosa Luxemburg's criticisms of Lenin in 1903, criticisms she had quietly shelved once she and Jogiches became Lenin's allies.

Through Parvus, Rosa Luxemburg must have been acquainted in detail with Trotsky's leading role in the 1905 Petersburg Soviet, and she knew that the political and literary brilliance of Trotsky's account of *1905* had taken the SPD by storm when it appeared in 1909, yet she found no words of praise for him. She bitterly objected to Trotsky's airing of Russian party scandals in public, preferring such matters to be kept to the initiates. (Once again, the contrast with her own conduct within the SPD is striking.) In sum, Rosa Luxemburg saw in Trotsky a serious (and younger) rival for the intellectual leadership of the international proletariat, for the organizational leadership of the Russian party, and a critic who exposed her and Leo Jogiches to charges of hypocrisy.

At first, Rosa and Leo were muted in their hostility towards the reconstituted Bolshevik 'RSDRP'. They still needed Lenin's support for their campaign against militarism within the Socialist International, and they needed an alliance with the Bolsheviks against the Mensheviks and the PPS-Left in the 1912 elections to the Russian Duma (parliament). It was Lenin's support for the Warsaw 'splitters' that finally broke their patience. The Duma elections allowed Lenin to bite his thumb with impunity at both the Mensheviks and the SDKPiL Chief Executive. In the heartlands of the great Russian proletariat, the Bolsheviks trounced the Mensheviks, and in Warsaw, Lenin's allies, the detested 'splitters' defeated the supporters of Jogiches and Luxemburg. Lenin now intervened to support his Warsaw comrades, the men and women Jogiches and Luxemburg were denouncing as police agents, degenerates or dupes and whose only 'crime', as far as Lenin could see, was their determination to support Bolshevism. Lenin now posed as the defender of democracy within Polish Marxism at the International Socialist Bureau.

This was too much for Rosa Luxemburg, who lost control entirely, describing her Polish enemies as 'brawlers and party saboteurs'. 'The Social Democracy of Poland and Lithuania', she thundered, was 'a totally autonomous member of the All-Russian party with its own congresses, . . . into whose internal affairs a Russian member of the Bureau has as little business to interfere, as in the affairs of the Dutch or Danish party'. Perhaps this was technically correct. It was also in flagrant contradiction to her own internationalist principles. Quite apart from the role she and Jogiches had played within the RSDRP, there were few major parties of the Second International, into whose affairs Rosa Luxemburg had *not* 'interfered', and quite properly, too, in view of her conception of proletarian internationalism. Yet now she embarked on a tenacious campaign within the International to discredit Lenin and force him to reconstitute the RSDRP in alliance with the Mensheviks. It reached its climax in the summer of 1914. For the first and last time, Rosa Luxemburg found herself collaborating with Plekhanov in a campaign whose logical conclusion was the expulsion of the Bolsheviks from the Socialist International.

'Long Live Struggle!'

The SPD radicals loved to tell of the occasion when Rosa Luxemburg and Clara Zetkin were out for a ramble with the Kautskys and the Bebels. The two radical women alarmed their comrades by wandering dangerously close to an army rifle range. As they rejoined the group, Bebel speculated on the epitaph they might have earned had they been accidentally shot. He and Kautsky

104

were not amused when Rosa dryly suggested, 'Here lie the last two men of German Social Democracy'.

Until the very end, Clara Zetkin remained Rosa's comrade-in-arms and adoptive mother-figure, and Rosa joined her in Stuttgart for as many family festivals as she could. Rosa rewarded Clara's adamantine solidarity by gracing the occasional women's conference, though not without self-irony. 'Just think', she wrote to Clara in 1911, 'I've become female. The Hagen people have also given me a mandate for the women's conference, so I must go there, even if I don't know what to say'. In the event, she found words with which to record the growing involvement of working women in trade unions (150,000 by 1912) and in electoral agitation, and to attack the bourgeois feminists.

Rosa Luxemburg never 'resolved' the 'woman question' theoretically, but nor did she deny its importance, quoting with approval Fourier's words that 'in every society the degree of female emancipation is the natural measure of general emancipation'. To feminist critics of Marxist theory, she pointed out that it was not Marxism but 'the rawness and madness of the present capitalist economic order' that attached no value to women's housework. But capitalism was also to be thanked, she believed, for drawing women into production, and hence, into struggle: 'In the modern proletarian woman the wife first becomes a person, since struggle first makes people, [offering them] a share in the work of culture, in the history of humanity.'

In practice, Clara was marginalized even more effectively than Rosa. The organization of working women was gradually assumed by the reformist trade union bureaucracies, while the political women's movement, which recruited mainly from the wives and daughters of SPD members, was placed under the direction of the politically moderate Luise Zietz. After 1908, when German women acquired greater freedom of association, the political movement was amalgamated with the male-dominated local organizations of the SPD. By 1914, Clara Zetkin's sole remaining bastion was her editorship of *Die Gleichheit*.

After July 1914, Rosa Luxemburg would concede that there was indeed one more 'man' in German Social Democracy, but until the war, she remained blind to the virtues of Karl Liebknecht. A year younger than Rosa, Karl Liebknecht was only permitted to join the SPD, of which his father was co-founder, after the conclusion of his legal studies and apprenticeship. A hyperconscientious young man, Liebknecht worshipped his father, who had been one of Karl Marx's best friends. Karl Liebknecht was devastated by his father's death in 1900 and assumed his duties as head of one of the leading SPD families fully conscious of the sacrifices this might entail for himself and his family. When his first wife died young leaving him with three young children, he married a rather shy young Russian, Sonja Ryss (who was known as 'Sophie' to the Germans). From his legal training, Liebknecht derived a passion for justice, or what we would now call 'human rights'. This impelled him to defend Russian victims of Tsarist oppression and German conscripts subjected to military brutality.

In 1904, Karl Liebknecht scored a spectacular victory over both Prussian and Russian reactionaries by securing the acquittal of nine German socialists, accused of smuggling anti-Tsarist propaganda across the border into Russia. The news found Rosa Luxemburg on holiday in Switzerland. She was as delighted as anyone: 'Thunder, such a bloody verdict on Russia and Prussia is more beautiful than all the jagged mountains and smiling valleys!' Yet her respect for Liebknecht's forensic talents did not extend to his ideas, nor to his political tactics. His ideas were modest enough in all conscience: a refutation of Jaurès' claim that his late father had been a 'revisionist' and a pamphlet on militarism, of which Rosa held a poor opinion, perhaps mistakenly.

Rosa was markedly unenthusiastic towards Liebknecht's attempt to build a third force within the SPD through the antimilitarist youth organizations he tried to create, and she gave him no assistance when the party fathers suppressed them. Her reasons for distrusting Liebknecht were straightforwardly political (and verging on the sectarian). As she told Jogiches in 1910: 'Liebknecht's position is the same as ever: *one jump to the right, one to the left*. In the Prussian *provincial parliament* he proclaimed a *mass strike*, and in the *City congress* he was opposed to our resolution of *"Protest against the banning of a demonstration in Treptow"* because we had acted *"illegally"* by not obeying the ban.'

Rosa Luxemburg's ideas were more profound, and her literary talents more sophisticated than anything Liebknecht had to offer, yet his *Militarism and Anti-Militarism* (1907) contains a combination of vulgar Marxism and empirical observation that points towards the rigorous sociological examinations of militarism that have followed the Second World War. Where Rosa tended to see militarism as merely a feature of advanced capitalism, Liebknecht demonstrated its continuity throughout class societies. He saw the armed forces not simply as an instrument of national defence/aggression and class oppression, but as a vehicle for a 'military pedagogy', which continued to operate throughout the adult lives of thousands of male reservists. While he insisted that such 'pedagogy' was unsuccessful with class-conscious proletarians, who had to be coerced into submission by physical brutality, he conceded that it was much more successful with groups such as the indigent landless labourers of the Prussian estates. Transformed into spick and span bearers of proud military uniforms, 'the difference between the level of their former civilian and their military status [is] especially great and striking'.

When Liebknecht tried to propagate his anti-militarist views among working class youths, Bebel slapped him down ruthlessly. This was one of the phenomena cited by Robert Michels, the young sociologist and at that time syndicalist, in the first ever detailed empirical study of the problem of bureaucracy in a socialist party. *The Sociology of Party Life in Modern Democracy* (1911) examined the paradox that had long vexed Rosa Luxemburg. The SPD lost its will to conduct class struggle *pari passu* with its success in gathering support and particularly in building a powerful bureaucracy. Agreeing with Rosa that the SPD and trade union leaderships habitually braked the militancy of the masses, Michels found a plausible reason for this behaviour which fully anticipated (as Rosa Luxemburg did not) the debacle of August 1914. Michels detected in the socialist bureaucrats, 'The love for what has been created and the personal interest of myriads of honourable patriarchs (*Familienväter*), whose social and economic welfare is almost entirely bound up with the existence of the party and which is dominated by the fear of the dissolution of the Party by the State (always quite possible in wartime) and the consequential economic ruin, . . .' From these observations, many of them drawn directly from Rosa Luxemburg's own articles and speeches, Michels drew the conclusion from which she flinched: 'That's no longer Marxism.' Rosa Luxemburg *never* so much as mentioned Michels' study. As far as she was concerned, the man might never have existed.

Rosa Luxemburg had compelling tactical reasons for ignoring the observations of an ethical socialist whose book was dedicated to the bourgeois sociologist Max Weber, but the absence of a sociological dimension is one of the striking features of her systematic thought. (In this she was not alone among Marxist thinkers.) It was not that she disagreed with Michels' views of the party fathers and the growing bureaucratic caste. She simply believed that at critical moments, mass pressure would overthrow bureaucratic prudence. Like Trotsky, she herself despised and evaded bureaucratic work, in the mistaken belief that organizational questions were less important than strategic issues. When Fritz Ebert took over the SPD machine, following Bebel's death in 1913, she reacted with equanimity. Her underestimation of Ebert foreshadowed Trotsky's equally suicidal blindness to Stalin's gifts.

Rosa Luxemburg also felt that she was on theoretically firm ground in ignoring the conservatism of much working-class 'culture'. When she reminded the German working class that they had 'nothing to lose but their chains', she had truly been in 'bloody earnest'. An aesthetic highbrow herself, she rejected the very idea of working-class culture under capitalism. In her eyes, this was a contradiction in terms. As she observed in an article on Marxism as early as 1903, 'The working class as such stands . . . *outside* present culture, . . . it can only occupy itself in present society in this field in so far as it creates *the spiritual weapons for its liberation struggle* . . .' She knew perfectly well that many working men were national chauvinists and little Kaisers over their wives and children, often pathetically eager to wear ties and exchange visiting cards. In her eyes, these were 'chains' and not 'culture'. By definition, only their protest songs could become 'culture'. Rosa Luxemburg's acute observations on the Belgian betrayal of women's rights prove that she did not lack a sociological imagination as such. She simply had no intention of bringing aid and

108

comfort to Michels' mentor, Max Weber, who undermined socialist élan by arguing that while oligarchies might be replaced, they could never be definitively abolished.

Inspired as she was by an unrelenting sense of duty, Rosa Luxemburg considered it her task to expose the faint-hearted SPD patriarchs to those harsh capitalist realities revealed by Karl Marx, 'which through their own iron logic lead, given a certain degree of ripeness, to the collapse of the dominion of capital and the achievement of socialism . . . unless the whole of civilized society is not to evade destruction . . .' And in this tortuous caveat, she indicated that another awful possibility had begun to haunt her, the possibility of a reversion to barbarism.

By 1913, Rosa Luxemburg was a humble daughter no more. In *The Accumulation of Capital*, she dared to reassert the scientific validity of Marxism by correcting Marx himself. This allowed her to provide an ultimate sanction for both her childhood fears of Polish chauvinism and for her adult crusades against capitalist imperialism. This was the apogee of her intellectual ambition, as she dared to assume the mantle of the prophet himself. She wrote as though intoxicated, begrudging every minute lost to 'hateful' Polish business, absorbed in her work as though she were painting. Never had she worked 'so systematically and persistently'. When she had finished, she sent it to the press 'unread'. Then, it 'completely disappeared from my mind'.

The Accumulation of Capital is Rosa Luxemburg's little-read, and for most of the human race unreadable, Marxist classic. Addressed to a tiny elite versed in advanced mathematics, economics and Marxism, it continues to baffle even some of them. Such an eminent commentator as Leszek Kołakowski is forced to admit, in *Main Currents of Marxism*, his reliance on Tadeusz Kowalik's exegesis. Rosa Luxemburg's profundity amazed and delighted her friends, while it attracted predictable hostility from everyone else. Bourgeois economists were naturally unsympathetic to all attempts to validate Marxism. Most contemporary 'Marxists' were unenthusiastic about her view that the collapse of capitalism was imminent, preferring to be 'saved' but not yet. The genuinely revolutionary minority wanted the prophet's mantle for themselves.

At the risk of mocking the complexity of Rosa Luxemburg's study, one can describe *The Accumulation of Capital* as follows: the problem Rosa Luxemburg attempted to resolved was that in his descriptions of a theoretically purely capitalist economy, Marx had failed, in Rosa Luxemburg's opinion, to explain how the capitalist system as a whole can accumulate capital. In an economy totally polarized between capitalists and workers as predicted by Marx, the capitalists could not, she argued, *both* consume the entire surplus *and* accumulate capital, while the workers were, by definition, deprived of the surplus value they themselves created and were therefore incapable of offering capital in exchange for consumption. Where she had begun by arguing that Polish capitalists could not make money (more precisely 'realize surplus value') without the pre-capitalist markets of the Russian Empire, she now sought to show that capitalism as a system would collapse once pre-capitalist markets were exhausted. Capitalism had previously managed to overcome its chronic crisis by expanding into external markets, but the march of imperialism had almost exhausted those markets. Collapse was therefore imminent.

To appreciate the stature of *The Accumulation of Capital*, one must compare it with the works of her Marxist peers. Rudolph Hilferding's *Finance Capital* (1910) had already offered an encyclopaedic but strictly orthodox Marxist analysis of imperialism, which skirted the difficulties confronted by Luxemburg. Lenin's *Imperialism* (1916) is a popular pamphlet, a work of descriptive economics, which relies heavily on the radical English economist Hobson and which makes no claims to theoretical profundity. Lenin's radicalism lay rather in his political prognosis, locating the initial socialist-led revolutions of the near future on the periphery of the metropolitan capitalist countries. But then, unlike Rosa Luxemburg, he was prepared to compromise with peasant and minority national interests.

The Accumulation of Capital was a more audacious enterprise than either, offering a monumental hostage to partisan criticism. In Bukharin's view, it rested on the false assumption of constant real wages, a result of 'Rosa Luxemburg's own logical inflexibility', which condemned 'the whole theory' to collapse 'like a house of cards'. Other critics have noted her failure to allow for the possibility of borrowing and lending between manufacturers of producer goods and manufacturers of consumer goods, which permits the capitalist system to overcome cyclical crises.

The most distinguished Marxist woman economist since Rosa Luxemburg provides a more sympathetic appraisal. In her introduction to the English edition of *The Accumulation of Capital* (1951), Joan Robinson concludes:

> Rosa Luxemburg, as we have seen, neglects the rise in real wages which takes place as capitalism develops, and denies the internal inducement to invest provided by technical progress, two factors which help to rescue capitalism from the difficulties which it creates for itself. She is left with only one influence (economic imperialism) to account for continuous capital accumulation, so that her analysis is incomplete. At the same time, few would deny that the extension of capitalism into new territories was the mainspring of what an academic economist has called the 'vast secular boom' of the last two hundred years, and many academic economists account for the uneasy condition of capitalism in the twentieth century largely by the 'closing of the frontier' all over the world. But the academic economists are being wise after the event. For all its confusions and exaggerations, this book shows more prescience than any orthodox contemporary could claim.

This theoretical work was no diversion of effort, but a powerful weapon reinforcing the self-confidence of Rosa's comrades in the unremitting battles she fought against imperialism and militarism in those last pre-war years. Together with Lenin, she did all she could to commit the Socialist International to decisive action in the event of war. Relentlessly, she exposed the self-serving posturing of the SPD Reichstag fraction and the utopian inanities of the 'official' SPD theoretician, Karl Kautsky, as he sought to ward off the coming Armageddon with a benign vision of a 'United States of Europe'. Trotsky never forgot her performance at the 1913 Jena Party Congress: 'Small in height and frail in build, she dominated the congress from the rostrum, like the incarnation of proletarian revolutionary thought. By the force of her logic and the power of her sarcasm she silenced her most

111

sworn enemies.'

Rosa Luxemburg's increasingly uninhibited criticism of the German army and of Kaiser Wilhelm II now made her a heroine to the rank and file, whatever the party fathers might think. Immediately after the messy Radek business at Jena, she toured the Rhineland. Her speeches provoked a 'patriotic' journalist to denounce her to the legal authorities, who charged her with sedition. Events played into her hands when, just two months later, a foul-mouthed lieutenant caused a riot in the Alsatian town of Zabern/Saverne. The methods used by the army to suppress the 'incident' were censured by the Reichstag by 292 votes to 54. The commanding officer was then acquitted by court martial and decorated by the Kaiser. Rosa denounced the selective indignation of the parliamentarians as hypocritical, since they only objected to military abuse of Europeans: 'Where was the storm of indignation in the Reichstag, when German soldiers hunted unarmed Herero women and children [in South West Africa/Namibia] into the desert, to leave them to breath their last in madness?' She followed a republican speech by SPD deputy Ledebour with a damning indictment of 'personal government' (i.e. the Kaiser) and warned, 'The more the bourgeoisie in its political decline expires before the throne, for the sake of the flesh pots of capitalist enrichment, the more desirable a republic appears to the proletarian masses.'

At her trial in Frankfurt-on-Main on 20 February 1914, Rosa Luxemburg exploited a golden opportunity to explain Marxist ideas on war and peace (and to propagate the anti-militarist policies of the Second International) to the masses: 'When, I say, the majority of the people arrives at the conclusion that wars are a barbaric, deeply immoral, reactionary and anti-popular phenomenon, then wars have become impossible . . .' She mocked the imputation that she might evade her sentence: 'A Social Democrat does not flee. He stands by his deeds and laughs at your punishments'. She was sentenced to a year's imprisonment but left at liberty pending appeal. Her conduct in the courtroom brought her accolades from bourgeois cartoonists, and she was treated as a heroine at protest meetings in Frankfurt and Stuttgart. Her defence lawyer, Paul Levi, became one of her closest comrades and the last of her lovers.

Determined not to waste her remaining months of liberty, Rosa accepted all the speaking engagements she could get. Her continuing attacks on the army, especially her repeated allegations that officers and NCOs maltreated conscripts, earned the reward she desired. On 13 May, she informed Levi that General Falkenhayn, the Minister of War himself, had personally initiated an action against her for dishonouring the officers and NCOs. She was ecstatic: 'Just think how much material one can broadcast and validate in such proceedings, all that our donkeys in the Reichstag have failed to do'. To Falkenhayn's horror, hundreds of tortured ex-conscripts came forward to testify on Rosa's behalf: about 1,000 had appeared by 4 July, when the action was dropped.

Rosa and Paul Levi then set out to campaign on behalf of two members of the Duala people of Cameroon, who had been charged with treason for protesting against the expropriation of their ancestral lands by the German colonial authorities. On 14 June, she explicitly urged the Berlin socialists to use a mass strike against war, though this was something Bebel had always refused to allow the party to consider. This brought her yet another summons: 'Evidently, someone concerned for my worthy person wants me behind bars as quickly as possible in these unruly times.'

She now knew that she was destined to be a martyr, but the prospect did not daunt her. As she told a young comrade. 'I assure you that I would not run away even if the gallows threatened, and for the simple reason that I hold it to be entirely necessary to accustom our Party to the fact that sacrifices belong to the craft of the socialist and are to be accepted as such. You are right: "Long live Struggle!"'

5 Spartacus

Towards the Third International

Almost alone among the SPD theoreticians, Rosa Luxemburg had confidently predicted the Great War, and her initial reaction to it was correspondingly positive. She chided her current lover, Paul Levi, for his pessimism: 'One should not contemplate an historical turning point from that point of view. We are experiencing something grandiose and new, so that one must throw away all the previous mundane yard-sticks as old rubbish. . . . Despite everything one must remain fresh and cheerful; otherwise one can do nothing.' And if this now makes her appear indifferent to the carnage that was beginning, we should remember that she believed that the proletariat would soon put a stop to the war by overthrowing its authors.

Her complacency was shattered by the hysteria which followed. It brought back long-suppressed memories of 'a ritual murder atmosphere, . . . in which the policeman on the street corner was the sole representative of humanity'. In this fearful moment, the SPD Reichstag fraction decided, by 78 votes to 14, to endorse the government's appeal for war credits, though they knew that Germany had encouraged Austrian bellicosity, had declared war on Russia and invaded neutral Belgium. Eagerly adopting the pretext that this was a defensive war against Russian Tsarism, the German socialist deputies turned their backs on the example set by Bebel and Wilhelm Liebknecht in 1870. On 4 August 1914, they *unanimously* joined the bourgeois parties in the Reichstag vote. At the same time, they meekly accepted a state of siege, which was clearly directed at their own party members throughout the country.

Behind the scenes, Rosa battled ferociously, but to no avail. This trauma was like another bereavement, far worse than her trials with the PPS in 1892–3. Her adoptive home, the SPD, had betrayed her: 'The indefensibility of the whole thing impinges on

114

my consciousness every day, every hour, more painfully and sharply; this conviction just won't leave me alone, and I don't know how I can survive it. Or more correctly, how the party will survive it.' And as anti-Russian and then anti-English xenophobia seeped onto the pages of the SPD press, she lamented, 'This party prostitutes itself in such a matter-of-course way and with such good conscience as to deprive one of all illusions.'

Like other women, Rosa was also tormented by more personal fears for the safety of such beloved younger comrades as Kostja and Maxim Zetkin, Hannes Diefenbach, Brandel Geck and Kurt Rosenfeld. She tried to comfort them with letters that were bright and gay, while she sought solace in the arts. But not even in music could she escape the trauma. She loathed Brahms' *German Requiem* ('born cannon fodder', she snorted), and she found Richard Strauss' *Ein Heldenleben* 'indescribable rubbish'. Even as she listened to her adored Beethoven, a 'cold hatred of the human gang amongst whom I am forced to live ripened in me'. She dreamt of escape, of being 'alone with Mimi and walking and reading . . . whenever I like, and working scientifically for myself quietly. . . .' Such moods made little difference, for 'quite mechanically I jump back into struggle and prepare endless upsets for myself'. At least she had finally acquired a worthy ally in Karl Liebknecht.

The outbreak of war had caught Liebknecht on holiday in Switzerland. He arrived back in Berlin just in time for the meeting of the SPD Reichstag fraction. He spoke with the minority opposed to voting for war credits, but he accepted party discipline with the rest. The minority were not just intimidated by patriotic hysteria. They were emotionally unprepared to break the party discipline of which they themselves had always been the most vociferous champions. They hoped to win over a majority of their comrades in subsequent meetings. They knew that the German working class was not yet ready to support 'splitters'. For the time being, Liebknecht declined to join Rosa in a joint statement explaining their position.

Early in September 1914, Liebknecht spent eight days in Belgium, ostensibly on a humanitarian mission tracking down his wife's relations. He took the opportunity to assess at first hand Belgian allegations of brutality against the German army and to

115

discuss the antecedents of the war with Belgian and Dutch socialists. His empirical assessment of the outbreak of war now coincided with Rosa Luxemburg's theoretically derived analysis. 'Until then I had unfortunately not yet taken up close relations' with her, he remembered. Reprimanded in his absence for his mission by the SPD fraction (which failed even to take note of a 'patriotic' mission to neutral countries by a right-wing socialist), he joined Rosa, Franz Mehring and Clara Zetkin in a declaration to the neutral socialist press dissociating them from the policy of the SPD majority.

From then on, Karl and Rosa were politically inseparable, to such an extent that Rosa began to complain that Liebknecht, 'an excellent chap', was wasting her valuable time endlessly dragging her off to meetings. The first fruit of their association was Liebknecht's *November Theses*. The *Theses* presented an analysis of the outbreak of war expressed in Liebknecht's customary blend of popular Marxism and keen empiricism. The demand for immediate peace and the re-assertion of the right to 'the self-determination of nations' were pure Liebknecht, but Rosa's influence was perceptible in his assertion that 'in the era of imperialist world politics . . . there can be no more real national wars'.

The *November Theses* were written to convince the minority of the SPD Reichstag fraction to join Liebknecht in voting against war credits when they were reconsidered in December 1914. In this purpose they failed. At the fraction meeting, the vote was 82 to 17, but only Liebknecht defied the SPD whip to cast a lonely vote against the entire Reichstag on 2 December 1914. He and Rosa were now committed to striking out on their own, though they had, as yet, no intention of leaving the party. Calling themselves the 'International Group' – though they soon became known as the Spartacists – they resolved to publish their own paper and prepared a series of Guiding Principles or *Leitsätze* for their movement.

It was agreed that Rosa Luxemburg would write a pamphlet to explain and justify the *Leitsätze*. To avert the draconian penalties provided for by the state of siege, Rosa adopted the pseudonym 'Junius', the name of the Roman republican who had overthrown the Tarquins, a name already adopted by the famous eighteenth-century critic of George III. The pamphlet became famous throughout the socialist world as the 'Junius Brochure', though its true title was *The Crisis of Social Democracy*.

The Crisis of Social Democracy owed much to Rosa's discussions with Karl Liebknecht, just as his *Theses* had to her ideas. The profundity and style were inimitably hers. Her evocation of the hysteria of August 1914 and the contrast with the drab depression of early 1915 is brilliant journalism, yet much of the pamphlet is devoted to a serious historical analysis of imperialism and of its inevitable dénouement in world war. She explained how the Franco-Prussian War of 1870 had left the European powers polarized into rival armed camps, whose antagonisms became ever more intense as their opportunities for extra-European compensation declined. Thus, Japan had thwarted Russia's Far Eastern ambitions, forcing her to reassert her Balkan interests, while Germany's attempts to frustrate the French annexation of Morocco had re-ignited Franco-German enmity in Europe.

'Junius' unflinchingly described the German contribution to the catastrophe. Hohenzollern Prussia had provoked the wars of 1866 with Austria and of 1870 with France, she argued. Hohenzollern Germany had precipitated the final division of Africa and Asia. Imperial Germany was the paradigm ('*Reinkultur*') of imperialism, with its cartels and banking trusts, its posturing, quasi-absolutist monarchy, weak parliamentary opposition and bourgeois solidarity against socialism. By building a battle fleet, Germany had pointlessly thrown down the gauntlet to the British Empire, even though the latter was still a willing market for German goods. Finally, Germany had insisted on Austria's provocative ultimatum to Serbia, in order to launch a preventive war to forestall French and Russian military reforms. She even included a brilliant prediction of the Second World War. There was nothing exclusively Marxist in this analysis. British and French liberal historians accepted large parts of it even then. To state it so uncompromisingly in Germany in 1915–16 required the special moral courage that stemmed from a lifetime's dedication to internationalism and an unshakable faith in the scientific validity of the prophecies of Karl Marx.

The remarkable insight into the dynamics of imperialism demonstrated in the 'Junius Brochure' was not matched by any corresponding percipience about the debacle of German socialism. Why had the German socialists capitulated to Hohenzollern imperialism? Early on in the pamphlet, Rosa Luxemburg seemed to admit that 'what is now in question is the whole of the last forty-five-year instalment in the development of the modern workers' movement' and to demand 'self-criticism, ruthless, cruel, fundamental self-criticism'. There were limits, of course. She had already insisted that 'If, however, it had to happen like that then Marxism is completely innocent of it'. The argument in the pamphlet is confused. At one point, 'Junius' suggests that the proletariat can only learn by its own mistakes. 'No predetermined, once-and-for-all valid scheme, no infallible guide shows it the path to follow'. Yet, only a few lines later, she describes Marxism as 'a compass', enabling the working class 'to find its way in the confusion of daily events, so as to adjust its tactics of struggle at each moment in the light of the unshakable final goal'.

Since Marxism could not be faulted, and since she continued to take at face value the pre-war SPD's commitment to it, there was nothing to be gained from a reconsideration of Michels' critique of the SPD bureaucracy. (Michels' own bizarre political evolution towards Italian social patriotism, and ultimately to fascism, was an added disincentive.) Nor would Rosa Luxemburg yet entertain in public the possibility that Bebel himself had contributed to the catastrophe. She needed to use his matchless prestige to argue that the German leaders should have behaved in 1914 as Bebel had in 1866 and 1870. She therefore misrepresented the extent of Bebel's anti-imperialist militancy at the time of the 1911 Morocco Crisis. She even quoted with approval the pre-war pacifism of the right-wing social-patriot Eduard David. True, she found some muted words of criticism for Karl Kautsky, but far from looking the bitter truth in the face, Rosa Luxemburg completely ignored all *her own* pre-war criticisms of the SPD.

Rosa Luxemburg's 'ruthless self-criticism' of the SPD concludes unconvincingly that 'An event of this consequence is certainly no matter of chance. Deep and far-reaching objective causes must lie behind it. But these causes can also lie in mistakes of the leader of the proletariat, Social Democracy, in the abdication of our will to struggle, of our courage, our fidelity to our convictions.' So the crisis of social democracy finally came down to the personal cowardice of 78 Reichstag deputies on 3–4 August 1914!

In order to exaggerate the extent of the 'betrayal', Rosa Luxemburg resorted to her customary insistence that her own idiosyncratic interpretations of the resolutions of the Second International were the only possible yardsticks by which to judge the SPD deputies. Yet, as she knew very well, it was precisely Bebel himself, who had rephrased the anti-war resolution at the Stuttgart International Socialist Congress in 1907 to exclude any precise description of what the parties should do in the event of war. She also knew that virtually no one shared her views on the 'self-determination of nations' under capitalism or denied the consequential right to national self-defence, which the SPD majority invoked in support of their actions. Despite Rosa Luxemburg's immense civic courage, her 'Junius Brochure' set a precedent for subsequent official 'Marxist' explanations which exonerate Marxism and Marxist regimes, blaming all their demonstrable failings on the *personal* limitations of small leadership groups.

In a private letter written between the writing and the publication of the 'Junius Brochure', Rosa was more frank:

At the first moment, then on 4 August [1914], I was disgusted, almost broken; since then I have become quite calm. The catastrophe has assumed such dimensions, that the normal scales of human guilt and human pain are inadequate; elemental disasters have something calming precisely in their grandeur and blindness. And finally, if things [in the SPD] were really like that and the whole peacetime glory was simply a will-o'-the-wisp on the swamp, then it is better that things come into the open . . . The pathetic quality of our vacillating friends, about which you groan, is nothing more than the fruit of the whole corruption, over which the edifice which gleamed so proudly in peacetime collapsed . . .

Of course it is wrong to judge the 'Junius Brochure' as an academic debate with Max Weber. It was a political act, a desperate attempt to remind the German workers of their duty. It was not because *she* was an outsider, a lame Polish–Jewish woman and intellectual, that she failed to confront the SPD's legacy of patriarchal bureaucracy or that love of 'discipline'

119

which the party shared with the Prussian army. She had never been inhibited by considerations such as these. Now something of a mother-figure to many in the German left, she was addressing herself with maternal solicitude to 'the flower of manhood and youthful strength, hundreds of thousands, whose socialist schooling in England and France, in Belgium, Germany and Russia was the product of the decades-long work of enlightenment and agitation'. These were her sons and her last hope if civilization had any future at all. She implored them finally, 'to wake up from the intoxication, reach out fraternally to one another and drown out the bestial chorus of the imperialist warmongers . . . with the old powerful battle cry of the workers: "Proletarians of the world, unite!"'

The twelve *Leitsätze* adopted by the 'International Group' in January 1916 were not recommendations for action but merely principles on which the socialist movement might eventually be recreated. They described the events of 4 August 1914 as a 'betrayal', while Liebknecht now accepted that the root of all evil was the endorsement by the Second International of the 'right of self-determination of nations', so that 'in the era of this uninhibited imperialism there can be no more national wars'. Henceforth, Rosa Luxemburg would make this proposition a minimum condition for collaboration, both in Germany and internationally. Lenin made short work of a position which was arguably false, and which cut Rosa Luxemburg off not only from the growing minority of pacifists in the SPD, but also from the European radical Left, which included Lenin, Radek's old friends in the SPD radical strongholds of Bremen and Hamburg and the SDKPiL 'splitters' and PPS Marxists in Poland.

The *Leitsätze* insisted that there was no going back to distinct national parties with their own policies. 'The only guarantee and the only support of world peace is the revolutionary will and the capacity for political action of the international proletariat'. The 'International Group' therefore proposed a Third International, firmly committed to socialist internationalism and rigidly centralized. *It*, and not the national parties, would decide policy on militarism, colonial and trading questions, the May Day festival and the conduct of its national sections in wartime. 'The duty of discipline towards the decisions of the International precedes all other organizational obligations'.

There were many on the left who found this prescription puzzling. Faced with the abdication of the centralized, bureaucratic and highly disciplined SPD, Rosa Luxemburg and Karl Liebknecht seemed to be proposing an even more centralized (and inevitably more bureaucratic?) international party. They did not begin to explain how it could be made invulnerable to 'capture' by the government controlling its headquarters or its largest party or section. In private, Rosa was more realistic. What really mattered to her was not the *immediate* recreation of an International – she did her best to postpone the attempts of the European Left to do so, at least until they accepted the *Leitsätze* – so much as the '*inner* clarification in each national party'.

Rosa's 'Contemporary'

On 18 February 1915, Rosa Luxemburg was taken to the women's prison on Barnimstrasse. Unlike the Russian gendarmes, who showed a certain respect for 'politicals', the Berlin policemen hustled her into the green van like a common criminal. She was surprised by her arrest and abashed that 'I had to camp without my nightie and without having combed my hair'. She felt a pang of sympathy for Schiller's Mary, Queen of Scots, but thanks to the 'angelic goodness and patience' of Karl Liebknecht, she soon acquired her nightclothes and toiletries and established 'a regular life'. She remained in the Barnimstrasse women's prison for precisely a year, the term to which the Frankfurt court had sentenced her in 1914. Released in February 1916, she was taken into 'protective custody' in July 1916 and sent to fortress prisons in Poznania and Silesia, to be released only after the November 1918 German Revolution.

For Rosa Luxemburg, a 'regular life' meant more than regular hours and well-brushed hair. Above all, it meant work. To begin with, there was the 'Junius Brochure', which she finished in April 1915. Then, she worked on her *Anti-Criticism*, a sequel to *The Accumulation of Capital*, which answered Marxist critics of her major theoretical work, earning her another comparison with Marx from Franz Mehring. She was pleased with the *Anti-Criticism*:

121

That is an achievement about which I am to some extent proud and which will certainly outlive me. It is much more mature than the *Accumulation* itself; the form reduced to the utmost simplicity, without any irrelevancies, without any flirting and juggling, unpretentious, reduced to the merest outlines, I might say 'naked' like a block of marble. This is now my aesthetic direction in general, in scientific work as in art, which is only to treasure the simple, calm and magnanimous, for which reasons, for example, the famed first volume of Marx's *Capital*, with its rococo ornamentation in Hegel's style is now an abomination (for which from the party point of view I've earned five-years' imprisonment and ten-years' loss of reputation . . .).

She also returned to the preparation of her lecture notes for publication under the title *An Introduction to National Economy*. Both works were ready for the press by July 1916, when she returned to jail. Getting them published was quite another matter. During her second imprisonment, she spent more time reading for pleasure. She devoured Gerhart Hauptmann and Thomas Mann, Shaw, Shakespeare, Anatole France, Tolstoy, Gonfalonieri, Ségur's *Julie de l'Espinasse*, Voltaire and Gorky. The prominence of authors from 'enemy' countries was no accident. She also read the verses of Ricarda Huch, her fellow alumna of Zurich University. Huch's female eroticism rather shocked her, putting her in mind of Ignatz Auer's words, 'One does not talk about something like that, one does it'.

In April 1915, Rosa Luxemburg resumed the botanical studies she had first begun in 1913. She described them as 'my passion and best recuperation after work'. She even took pleasure in the miserable weeds in the exercise yard. She envied her friends at liberty their freedom to visit botanical gardens and begged them to do so on her behalf. Her friends caught on and sent her flowers and plants, 'so I've got a whole winter garden in the cell and must spend not a little time watering and spraying all my population every morning'. Sonja Liebknecht's visit to the Berlin Botanical Garden in May 1918 provoked Rosa to an outburst of enthusiasm about her beloved plants. 'Most city folk are basically crude barbarians. With me, on the contrary, the inner growing together with organic nature – *en dépit de l'humanité* – takes on almost pathological forms, which is connected with the state of my nerves'.

Apart from the plants, there were birds and insects to divert her. It was a major event when she found a peacock butterfly lifeless on the bathroom window. She warmed it with her hands, and pushed flowers gently towards its antennae until it revived. She collected stray birds' feathers and became expert at recognizing their songs and guessing their moods, or so she persuaded herself. She remembered her mother's faith in King Solomon's talents with renewed sympathy and developed her own anthropomorphic preferences: 'The resounding lecture of the nightingale is too much like a prima donna for me, it admonished the audience too much, intoxicating triumphs, captivating hymns of praise.'

Her favourite was the robin with its 'small, tender little voice', which 'performs an individual, intimate melody, which rings like a prelude, a little bit of reveille'. It recalled for her 'the distant trumpet call of deliverance in the prison scene in *Fidelio*, which also splits the night'. Towards the end of her imprisonment, she was able to charm the pigeons in the Breslau prison to such an extent that they comforted her by perching beside her as she lay in bed. And there was always the sky, 'above all the clouds! What an inexhaustible basis for captivating a pair of human eyes!' It was on these riches that Rosa drew in the letters of comfort she wrote to Hannes Diefenbach, Kostja Zetkin, Luise Kautsky and Sonja (Sophie) Liebknecht.

When Rosa first got to know Diefenbach in 1908, his apparent superficiality irritated her. In a characteristically premature judgment, she informed Kostja that her picture of Hannes was 'already complete'. In time, she was conquered by his impeccable manners, exquisite taste and readiness to act as her foil. With Hannes, she finally learnt to relax. 'Hänschen', she wrote in January 1917, 'when will we experience again our beautiful evenings in Südende, when you read me Goethe between countless cups of tea, and I gave myself happily over to laziness with Mimi on the sofa . . .?'

In Rosa's heart, Luise Kautsky retained not just a small corner, as Lulu modestly supposed, but 'the fine little room with Mimi'. Rosa protested when doctors proposed removing Luise's gall bladder, '*This time* I am for a "strategy of attrition",' she joked, 'And then, you're right, what is a person without a gall bladder? And especially now, to do without a gall bladder *now*!! No, that would finish even an angel, and we never wanted to be angels.' And she advised Luise not to upset herself thinking about politics:

I find nothing more comical than that. Don't you understand that the whole miserable business is much *too big* to groan over? I can be afflicted when Mimi is sick on me, or when there's something wrong with you. But when the whole world goes off the rails, then I just try to *understand* what and why it's happened, and if I've done my duty, then I'm calm and fine.

Sonja Liebknecht was not made of martyr material, but Rosa did her best to maintain her morale. 'You are mistaken', she wrote, 'if you think that I could not understand or [would] undervalue any traits in your character. You don't yet know me: nothing human, and also nothing feminine, is foreign and indifferent to me'. Sometimes Rosa lectured Sonja on her duty to her imprisoned husband. 'In these four years, you must gain an inner control so that Karl Liebknecht can find you as a little queen, before whom he can bend his head. For that, only inner discipline and self-respect are necessary, and you must master them. You owe it to yourself, and to *me*, who loves and respects you'.

In prison, Rosa's detachment about her own achievements grew. She insisted to Luise, 'I must have *someone*, who believes me when I say that I thresh about in the whirlpool of world history out of duty, but I was really born to herd geese'. Once more, she mocked her own frivolity:

Tomorrow you see *Figaro*! You see I am incorrigible. I've "relearnt" nothing. "North and West and South divide, thrones explode, empires shake" – and I think of *Figaro*. Yes and feed industrious mice and magpies. To the latter – my sole audience here – I present the most earth-shattering ideas and solutions and then let them fly off again! . . . But devil take it, even they will veer round to Scheidemann, I detect it already: natural drives are stronger than all learnt wisdom.

Her disappointment in the German proletariat, clearly visible in this reference, led her to a more elitist view of the relations between the masses and leaders:

There is nothing more inconstant than human psychology. At any one moment the psyche of the masses conceals, like Thalatta, the eternal sea, all latent possibilities; deathly calm and blustery storms, the basest cowardice and the wildest heroism. The mass is always what it *must* be according to the circumstances of the time, and it is always on the point of becoming something quite different to that which it appears. [It would be] a fine captain, who steered only according to the momentary appearance of the water's surface and failed to grasp from signs in the sky and in the depths, that he should look out for storms to come!

Despite her indifference to religion, Hauptmann's portrayal of Christ in *Emmanuel Quint* struck a chord as

the tragedy of the man who preaches to the crowd and feels how each word, the moment it leaves his mouth, is vulgarized and ossified and becomes a caricature in the brains of his listeners; and then the preacher himself is nailed fast to this caricature and is finally encircled and deafened with rude noise: 'Show us the miracle! You taught us. Where is your miracle?'

But for her own epitaph, she still chose the final lines of Conrad Meyer's poem, 'Hutten's Confession':

I regret accepting my duty too late.
I regret my heart was too feebly enflamed.
I regret I didn't enter my feuds
With sharper blows and bolder deeds.
I regret I've only once been exiled,
I regret I've often known human fear.
I regret the day I didn't inflict a wound.
I regret the hour I was out of harness,
I regret, I confess it with a sense of contrition,
That I was not three times more brave.

All this forced detachment and courage did not save her from moments of acute misery. The cry of a goose reminded her of her unfreedom: 'Then everything in me quivers with nostalgia, I don't know what for, simply for distance, for the world!' She mourned dead friends, including Hugo Faisst the painter, Jean

125

Jaurès and Marie-Edouard Vaillant. The February Revolution in Russia cheered her briefly, but when the German proletariat failed to respond, she was plunged into depression and, at times, nervous collapse. She felt all too like the pathetic, abused Romanian buffaloes she saw in the prison yard, dragged from their age-old freedom on the Romanian plains and yoked to German army carts.

Then she suffered the hardest blows of all. Her beloved Mimi died in Spring 1917, but her friends simply could not bring themselves to tell her, until, frantic with anxiety at their silence, she finally 'nailed' them with her questions. Worse followed when the impractical and undemanding Hannes Diefenbach fell in France on the very eve of the Bolshevik Revolution. (She must have felt that the German proletariat might have saved him and themselves.) She shared her loss with Diefenbach's sister:

> I have also lost the dearest friend, who understood and sympathized with every one of my moods and experiences like no one else. In music, painting and literature, which were as vital to both of us as air, we had the same gods and made joint discoveries. I've just read from the wonderful correspondence of Mörike and his wife for recuperation, and at every point of beauty, I thought to myself out of habit, 'I must draw Hannes' attention to that!' I can't get used to the idea that he has vanished without trace . . .

During all these trials, Rosa's living link with the outside world was the unassuming Mathilde Jacob, an impoverished and initially non-political typist, whose life was illuminated and then embittered by Rosa, who was unable fully to reciprocate her devotion. Rosa treated Mathilde as a subordinate, though her letters suggest a steady increase in esteem and affection. Leo Jogiches now assumed the responsibility for distributing the appeals of the 'International Group', or 'Spartacists', as they began to call themselves, throughout Germany, a fitting role for his talents. Mathilde Jacob came to spend long hours in his company. Like Sonja Liebknecht, Mathilde found Jogiches a mellower man, and she was able to bring Leo and Rosa together as friends once more. Gradually, Rosa Luxemburg was coming to value aspects of her past she had once despised.

126

Nowhere was this more apparent than in her work on Vladimir Korolenko's *History of My Contemporary*. The most comprehensive of all personal histories of the nineteenth-century Russian intelligentsia, Korolenko's *History* appeared in 1906–10. Rosa loved it at once and translated an episode for Clara Zetkin's *Die Gleichheit*. Her long final imprisonment allowed her to translate the entire mammoth work into German and to furnish it with an introduction that belongs to the most sensitive and magnanimous Marxist criticism of Russian literature.

Like most Russian intellectuals, Rosa had little to say about the founder of the intelligentsia, Catherine the Great, the woman whose extraordinary career so remarkably counterpoints her own. (It has taken Isobel de Madariaga a lifetime to rescue Catherine, humiliated at her death by her own son, from the mixture of male resentment and radical sectarianism which buried her achievements for so long). For Rosa Luxemburg, it was precisely the *oppositional* character of the Russian intelligentsia and its literary tradition that demanded admiration. In other respects, the essay is full of revaluations, including a generous tribute to Jean Jaurès' 'unerring instinct for the truth'. This is a work totally unlike the coldly partisan contributions of many Russian Marxists. In a brilliant analysis of Russian literature from Pushkin to her own time, she finds words of praise for the Populist Mikhailovsky, words of extenuation for the 'decadent' Leonid Andreyev, and she pays fulsome tribute to Chekhov and Gorky, whose worth she has finally recognized.

The introduction to Korolenko's *Contemporary* was also an indirect form of autobiography. In this work of great economy, Rosa Luxemburg significantly returns to two themes with unmistakable biographical relevance for her. One is the theme of physical handicap, not considered a suitable subject for sympathetic artistic treatment by many artists at that time. Korolenko's cripple paradoxically proclaims that 'men are *obliged* to be happy', while his blind musician, 'becomes spiritually "sighted", in so far as he steps out of the egoism of his own inescapable misery, to make himself a loudspeaker for the physical and spiritual misery of all the blind'.

The other theme that is repeated concerns the reaction of the young Korolenko himself to the competing claims of Polish,

Ukrainian and Russian nationalism. In Rosa Luxemburg's words, 'From the conflict of the three nationalities, whose field was his Volhynian homeland, he saved himself in humanity' – just as she had. Once, Rosa had vied with Lenin in her biting comments on the All-Russian intelligentsia. The wartime conduct of the Germans, intellectuals and proletarians alike, had made her once more proud of that Russian tradition which had asserted universal human values, despite everything.

The Russian Revolution

Paul Levi made sure that every politically educated citizen of the mid-twentieth century would remember Rosa Luxemburg as the most eloquent socialist critic of Leninism. In *Organizational Questions of Russian Social Democracy* (1903), she had mocked Lenin's model Bolshevik party as the 'ego' of the Russian revolutionary. In *The Russian Revolution*, which she wrote in prison in 1918, she attacked the abrogation of political freedoms in Bolshevik Russia, answering Bolshevik self-justification with a proposition that echoed J. S. Mill at least as much as Karl Marx:

> Liberty only for supporters of the government, only for members of one party, however numerous they may be, is no liberty. Liberty is always liberty for those who think differently. Not for the sake of a fetish for 'justice', but because everything enlivening, healing and cleansing in political liberty depends on this quality, and its effectiveness fails when 'liberty' becomes a privilege.

It is obviously quite legitimate to apply this yardstick to Soviet practice (then and later), especially if one applies the same yardstick to other regimes, as, for example, Amnesty International does. Students of Rosa Luxemburg will also need to ask whether her celebrated attacks on Leninism, seen in the context of her own political practice, justify the suggestion that she successfully indicated a method for achieving radical social change without Bolshevik authoritarianism. It is difficult to avoid the suspicion that she found it no easier to stick to her high principles than the rest of humanity.

128

In 1903, Rosa Luxemburg, had disingenuously raked up organizational grounds for opposing Lenin's 'Jacobin' concept of the party, because she could not stomach the RSDRP's views on the 'self-determination of nations'. Following the 1905 Revolution, she and Leo Jogiches had behaved as dictatorially towards dissent in the SDKPiL as Lenin had ever done in the RSDRP. In other words, her arguments had been partly meretricious, and she had failed to practice what she preached. There was no equivalent covert sectarian motive for *The Russian Revolution*, but the German Revolution would soon submit Rosa's principles to a rigorous test and find them wanting.

The first half of *The Russian Revolution* is almost entirely laudatory about her former Bolshevik rivals (and her private correspondence confirms that there was nothing tactical or contrived about this). She praised the Bolsheviks for achieving 'the immortal historical accomplishment of proclaiming for the first time the final goals of socialism as an immediate programme'. With equal magnanimity, she acknowledged that,

> Whatever a party may demonstrate in an historical moment in courage, vigour, revolutionary farsightedness and consequentiality, Lenin, Trotsky and comrades have totally achieved. The entire revolutionary honour and capacity for action which failed the Social Democracy in the West was incorporated in the Bolsheviks. Their October Revolt was not only an actual salvation for the Russian Revolution, but also a salvation for the honour of international socialism.

The third section of the pamphlet rehearses her long-held differences with Lenin over the peasantry and the self-determination of nations. She understood that Lenin's encouragement to the Russian peasantry to seize the great estates had been little more than a bribe to gain peasant support for his revolution. This did not in her eyes justify a step with serious long-term implications for socialist economics: 'A socialist government which has come to power must, however, do one thing at least: take measures which point, in their fundamental premises, in the direction of a later socialist reform of agrarian relations; it must at least prevent anything which blocks the path to those measures.' In practice, she asserted (foreseeing Stalin's difficulties), 'The Leninist agrarian reform has created a new powerful popular stratum of enemies on the land, whose resistance will be far more dangerous and tenacious than that of the noble estate owner was.' The trouble with this purely negative criticism was that Rosa Luxemburg, following faithfully in the footsteps of Engels and other distinguished Marxists, had completely failed to explain how socialist revolutions could succeed at all in the overwhelmingly peasant societies of Eastern Europe if revolutionaries did not embrace this risk.

Rosa Luxemburg's summary of the disastrous effects on the Russian Revolution of the adoption by the Bolsheviks of the 'self-determination of nations' was still just about plausible in 1918. She pointed out correctly that the doctrine she abhorred had encouraged the Finns, Ukrainians and Baltic peoples to secede not just from Russia, but from the Revolution. As she herself conceded, however, the presence of the German Army in those territories was the decisive factor. Reluctant to admit Engels' argument that modern military technology might change the terms on which a 'people' can challenge a foreign army, Rosa Luxemburg was one of those socialists who erroneously believed a citizen militia capable of beating a modern army.

As the Russian Civil War ground on, Bolshevik acceptance of the 'self-determination of nations' undermined the Russian Whites in the borderlands of the former Empire, secured the benevolent neutrality of Finland, the Baltic states and eventually even Piłsudski's Poland, while still permitting the Bolsheviks to reincorporate the Ukraine, the Caucasus, Central Asia and Siberia. Even more important, it committed the socialist revolution internationally to alliance with national liberation struggles by the non-European peoples against European imperialism, while remaining free to rally national resistance to fascism during the Second World War. Pressed to a conclusion that she was anxious to avoid, Rosa Luxemburg's views, if adopted by socialists everywhere, would have given international socialism the choice between a *de facto* alliance with imperialism or neutrality in many of the crucial struggles of the twentieth century.

It is evident that this is no exaggeration if one considers her conduct at the 1907 Stuttgart Congress of the Socialist International. Rosa Luxemburg refused to support Marchlewski's demand that the International back colonial struggles for freedom. Of course, she was not entirely wrong. Socialism has indeed paid a high price for the adoption of the 'self-determination of nations'. It is no longer possible to envisage the socialist revolution as a continuous worldwide event or chain of events. Socialism's compromise with nationalism also created the possibility of eventual conflicts between 'socialist' states of the kind that erupted between the USSR and Yugoslavia in 1948 and between the USSR and China in the 1960s.

A number of factual errors in the contentious fourth section of *The Russian Revolution* confirm the allegations by Clara Zetkin and Lenin that Rosa Luxemburg had lacked accurate information from Russia when she wrote it. She misdates the election and dissolution of the All-Russian Constituent Assembly, Russia's only democratically elected parliament. While accepting some of Lenin's and Trotsky's criticisms of this body, she countered by arguing that, 'the medicine that Trotsky and Lenin have discovered, the abolition of democracy altogether, is even worse than the disease it is supposed to cure'. This is because it hampered the real corrective, 'that active, untrammelled, energetic, political life of the broadest masses of the people'.

Worse still, the Bolsheviks had abolished the freedom of association and the freedom of the press. 'It is a manifest, incontrovertible fact', she insisted, 'that without a free, uninhibited press, without an unrestricted life of association and assembly, it is precisely the sovereignty of the broad masses that is completely unthinkable'. And without it there can be no socialism! Only if socialism were a recipe revealed to an elite could it emerge under such conditions. On the contrary, she insisted, socialism could only emerge through a process of free experimentation. The alternative (as Communist reformers since Khrushchev have repeatedly confirmed), was grim:

Public life slowly goes to sleep, a dozen party leaders of inexhaustible energy and boundless idealism direct and govern, underneath them in reality a dozen leading heads direct, and an elite of the workers is summoned from time to time to assemblies, to applaud the speeches of the leaders, to approve resolutions laid before them unanimously, basically therefore, a clique economy; a dictatorship if you will, but not the

131

dictatorship of the proletariat, but the dictatorship of a handful of politicians, i.e. dictatorship in the purely bourgeois sense, in the sense of Jacobin rule. . . .

The correct path, Rosa Luxemburg argued, was not to abolish bourgeois democracy, but to infuse it with a revolutionary socialist content:

> We always distinguished the social kernel from the political form of bourgeois democracy, we always exposed the harsh kernel of social inequality and unfreedom under the sweet smell of formal equality and freedom, not to overthrow the latter, but to provoke the working class not to content itself with the shell; rather to conquer political power, to fill it with a new social content.

She closed by exonerating the Bolsheviks from all blame provided they desisted from making a virtue of necessity. The Bolshevik dilemma 'could not be resolved in Russia, it could only be resolved internationally. And in this *sense* the future everywhere belongs to "Bolshevism".'

'I dared to do it'

Until 1917, Rosa Luxemburg's conditions of detention were fairly mild. She borrowed books from the Royal Prussian Library in Berlin; she entertained a lively correspondence on non-political topics with her friends and received regular visitors, who smuggled her articles out of prison. These articles then appeared under pseudonyms in the *Spartakusbriefe* (Spartacus Letters) and as equally illegal leaflets. Since her pre-war political activities had been largely literary, imprisonment was not a total barrier to her participation in German political life.

As Rosa had anticipated, the patriotic fervour of 1914 gradually evaporated, and this allowed a pacifist tendency to manifest itself in the SPD. In the third Reichstag vote on war credits in March 1915, Otto Rühle joined Liebknecht in voting against, while thirty others abstained. Kautsky and Bernstein now joined forces to argue for a reunification of the pre-war Socialist International and met French socialists in Bern, while the Left Wing radicals Georg Ledebour and Johann Hoffman joined the European Left at the Zimmerwald Conference in September 1915. In November, the first anti-war demonstration was held in Berlin; the following month, eighteen SPD members of the Reichstag, including SPD Co-Chairman Hugo Haase, joined Liebknecht and Rühle in the vote on war credits, while a further twenty-two socialist deputies left the chamber to avoid voting.

The apparent dogmatism of the *Leitsätze* of 1916 had been deliberate. It had established a demarcation line between the 'International Group' and the SPD pacifists, whom Rosa Luxemburg derisively called the 'Marsh', after the pathetic moderates of the French Revolution. She pointed out that the eighteen had only voted against war credits on the grounds that 'The frontiers of our country have been secured'. Not only did this suggest that they might vote *for* war credits once more if, for example, the Russians reinvaded East Prussia. It also provided French and Belgian socialists with a perfect argument for supporting war credits in their countries, whose frontiers had been overrun by the German Army. Even in opposing their government, the German 'Marsh' had sinned against that fatherland Rosa Luxemburg had inherited from Ludwik Waryński: she promised never to betray it: 'The world fraternity of the workers is for me the most sacred and paramount on earth, it is my guiding star, my ideal, my fatherland; I would rather lose my life than be untrue to this ideal!' She was confident that 'whoever seriously and sincerely desires the resurrection of socialism will come to us, if not today, then tomorrow'.

In March 1916, the SPD Reichstag fraction expelled the eighteen who had opposed war credits. Haase, Ledebour and Wilhelm Dittmann then organized a 'Socialist Labour Association' (*Sozialistische Arbeitsgemeinschaft*: SAG) as a separate Reichstag fraction. As Liebknecht ironically noted: its first action 'as a foetus' was to excommunicate him. In April, Liebknecht was assaulted in the Reichstag. He and Rosa (then enjoying her last six months of wartime liberty) decided that the time had come to provoke mass action. On 1 May 1916, an anti-war demonstration on Berlin's Potsdamer-Platz attracted several thousand participants. Liebknecht's shouts of 'Down with the War! Workers of the World, Unite!' were followed by his arrest and sentence to two-years' imprisonment, *increased* on appeal to four-years' imprisonment and six-years' subsequent loss of civil rights. Marchlewski, Rosa Luxemburg, Ernst Meyer and Franz Mehring were all arrested shortly afterwards, leaving Leo Jogiches to maintain a vestigial existence for the 'Spartacus Group', as they called themselves after January 1916. His conspiratorial talents were now put to good use.

Liebknecht's persecution elicited a slight response from the German working class. On the day he first went to court, an emerging group of revolutionary shop stewards (*Obleute*) led a strike of 55,000 metal workers in Berlin; there was also a major strike in Brunswick. Rosa's feverish demands for more action during the appeal hearing received no response. She now expressed herself bitterly, not just about the SPD leaders, but about the German proletariat itself:

> If the workers remain silent and calm, if they do not raise their voice loudly against the scandalous sentence, then the Reich military court will utter a verdict not just against Liebknecht, but against the immediate future of the working class in Germany . . . And if they should play the role of cannon fodder bravely to the end, then they may bear the entire costs and burdens of the war as pack-donkeys, and put up with the kicks of the reaction[aries] in addition.

At least, she consoled herself, it must now be clear to them that there was nothing more to be had from the Reichstag. They must look to themselves.

More disappointments followed. In the Spring of 1917, peace moves were in the air, only to be followed by a savage intensification of the fighting. 'The socialist proletariat has once more failed', she fumed, ' . . such an abdication by a social class of its historical tasks is quite unprecedented'. She now saw the German masses as 'degraded' by 'centuries of bourgeois class rule'. Then came the spectacle of German proletarians in uniform (who had fraternized with the rebellious Russian soldiers at the behest of their bourgeois officers) crushing the Finnish revolution and suppressing the soviets in the vast expanse of Eastern Europe ceded to Germany by Soviet Russia in the treaty of Brest-Litovsk. By June 1918, Rosa Luxemburg had begun to hate the

German working class: 'Over the bones of Russian, Ukrainian, Baltic and Finnish revolutionary proletarians, over the national existence of the Belgians, Poles, Lithuanians and Romanians, over the economic ruin of France, the German worker stamps forward, wading in blood over his knees, to plant the victory standards of German imperialism everywhere.' And she warned these 'executioners of foreign liberty' that they would soon *have* to rebel against their own handiwork, 'because iron historical laws do not let themselves be mocked'.

Rosa had nothing but contempt for the 'Marsh', as she called the SAG, but she had a kind of respect for the SPD leaders, Fritz Ebert and Philipp Scheidemann, 'who have the desperate courage of renegades who have burnt all the bridges between themselves and an honourable past'. Despite this, she steadfastly refused to contemplate the formation of a new party. 'You might as well resign from the human race', she reproved Kostja. As late as March 1916, Karl Liebknecht expressed their position just as uncompromisingly: 'Not splitting or unity, not new or old party is the slogan, but the reconquest of the party from below upwards by the rebellion of the masses, which must take the organization and its resources into their own hands.'

Yet Ebert and Scheidemann countered by suspending and reorganizing party branches wherever the SAG won a majority. Luxemburg remained adamant. In January 1917, she wrote an 'Open Letter to the Like-Minded', attacking the Bremen and Hamburg radicals, who were setting up independent groups of 'International Socialists'. However worthy their motives, she argued,

> Flight remains flight, to us it is a betrayal of the masses, who are floundering and choking in the strangling noose of the Scheidemanns and Legiens, handed over to the bourgeoisie for better or for worse. One can 'resign' from small sects and conventicles. It is nothing but immature fantasy to hope to free the whole mass of the proletarians from this heaviest and most dangerous yoke of the bourgeoisie by a simple 'resignation', and to go ahead of them with a brave example in this way.

She pledged herself to await the 'general showdown' that would occur at the end of the war, and with an oddly fatalistic meta-

135

phor, she echoed Martin Luther: 'The decisive throw of the dice in the class struggle in Germany will be cast for decades in this general showdown with the authorities [*Instanzen*] of Social Democracy and the trade unions, and then for all of us to the last man, it will be a matter of: "Here I stand, I can do no other!"'

The trouble was that Ebert and Scheidemann were never going to let this happen at an open congress of all German socialists. In the Spring of 1917, they expelled the SAG, whose members then convened in Gotha to constitute a distinct Independent Social Democratic Party of Germany (*Unabhängige Sozialdemokratische Partei Deutschlands*: USPD). The 'Spartacists' could hardly remain in a party totally controlled by Ebert and Scheidemann, but it pained them having to join the USPD, a party they thoroughly despised. Despite the mockery of the 'left radicals', they gritted their teeth and placed themselves under USPD colours, an involuntary testimony to the fact that until such time as the masses followed them, they would have to stay with the masses. They consoled themselves with the role of 'warning conscience' of the USPD, merely awaiting the sharpening of social tensions to bid for its 'real leadership'.

Rosa Luxemburg's critique of the USPD leaders, Haase, Ledebour and Dittmann, centred on their failure to criticize their own past. In an echo of the 'Junius Brochure', she insisted that 'Only from the source of self-criticism, of a cruel, fundamental examination of one's own mistakes in programme, tactics and organization can the clear guidelines for the future be won'. This time, she followed her own advice, in an implicit self-criticism of her own: 'It must be clear for every child, that under the flag of the party programme and the Congress decisions, the whole workers' movement had taken a false direction which led to the abyss . . .' She demanded illumination of the *praxis* (the implicitly rationalized practice) of the pre-war SPD, of its obsession with purely parliamentary action and bureaucracy – 'nothing but parliamentarism' and 'bureaucratism'. For the *only* time in her career, Rosa Luxemburg associated herself with specific *organizational* remedies, including the demands for referenda and political autonomy for local groups made by the 'International Group'. This contrasted sharply with her earlier demands for a rigidly centralized International and illustrates the subordinate import-

136

ance she continued to attach to organizational questions.

By October 1918, the German High Command had come to recognize that it would lose the war. Ludendorff hoped that the Allies would offer better terms to a 'democratic' government, so the liberal Prince Max von Baden was appointed Reichschancellor, while the SPD supplied two Secretaries of State (Bauer and Scheidemann). In return, the SPD sanctioned a diplomatic breach with Soviet Russia and undertook to discourage talk of revolution. They promised a democratic monarchy and, in a gesture to the Left, demanded the liberation of Karl Liebknecht. Liebknecht's return to Berlin was greeted by 20,000 cheering workers, but the signal for revolution was given neither by Liebknecht nor by the revolutionary shop stewards, who felt that the industrial workers were still unready for decisive action.

At the beginning of November 1918, the German Naval High Command decided on a last desperate assault on the British Royal Navy. The men got to hear of it, and sick of heroics, they mutinied at Kiel and elected a *Rat* (council) after the model of the Russian soviets. Between 6 and 8 November, revolution broke out in many of the major proletarian centres in Germany; everywhere, soldiers and workers elected soviets. Berlin was the last to fall, but on 9 November, strikes broke out 'spontaneously', i.e. without a formal instruction from any recognized political group. The SPD leader, Fritz Ebert, was appointed first socialist Reichschancellor; the Kaiser then abdicated and left for Holland. In a portent of things to come, Philipp Scheidemann proclaimed a Republic from the Reichstag building, while Karl Liebknecht proclaimed a 'free, socialist Republic' from the Charlottenburg Palace.

Meanwhile, Ebert had already concluded a secret agreement with General Groener, guaranteeing the continuation of hierarchical authority in the army and civil service, the defence of Germany's pre-war frontiers, particularly against the Poles, hostility to Bolshevism and the postponement of all social reforms until the convocation of a democratically elected National Assembly. Liebknecht took part in the negotiations between the SPD and USPD over the formation of an interim cabinet, withdrawing only when it became clear that neither party would countenance a government responsible to the soviets. The misleadingly named 'Council of People's Commissars' (*Rat der Volks-beauftragten*) that emerged comprised three representatives from each socialist party: Ebert (Reichschancellor), Landsberg and Scheidemann (SPD), and Barth, Dittmann and Haase (USPD).

No one doubted that the proletariat had made the revolution, but it was equally apparent that a substantial section of the German working class still trusted SPD leaders who were determined to thwart what Liebknecht called 'the real political domination of the proletariat'. There were also substantial monarchist units that retained their arms and bided their time. The situation bore some resemblance to that in Russia in February 1917, with the crucial difference that while Leibknecht and Luxemburg were not convinced that they had much to learn from Lenin, Ebert and Scheidemann were determined to avoid repeating Kerensky's mistakes.

While at least some of her hopes were finally being consummated, Rosa Luxemburg was forced to remain frustratingly on the periphery in prison in Breslau. She was only released on 8 November 1918, arriving in Berlin two days later. Her spirits were depressed by the continuing strength of the SPD and by the tragic news that her young comrade, Brandel Geck, had fallen in the final days of the war. She was reminded of her own vulnerability: 'We all stand under blind fate, only the grim thought comforts me that I shall also perhaps be promoted to the other side – perhaps by a bullet of the counter-revolution, which lowers from all sides.'

Such gloomy reflections were swiftly banished by the atmosphere she discovered in Berlin. From the moment of her arrival, she was surrounded by her closest comrades, Karl Liebknecht, Leo Jogiches, Paul Levi, now forgiven for his recent marriage, and by scores of younger comrades. She instantly assumed the editorship of *Die Rote Fahne*, the paper hurriedly produced by the Spartacus League in the commandeered offices of the former gutter press *Lokal-Anzeiger*. On one occasion, she even had to jump on a table to harangue their military guards, who had been suborned with alcohol supplied by the *Lokal-Anzeiger*'s former staff and had turned their guns on the revolutionaries they were supposed to be guarding.

Gradually, Rosa's feverish efforts produced a paper, which

even the radical wing of the USPD came to prefer to their own party's *Freiheit*. Rosa was also keen for Clara Zetkin to supply a women's section, but Clara was frail and transport uncertain, and the two great friends never met again. There were repeated anonymous threats to Rosa's life, and to Liebknecht's (which had to be taken seriously, in view of the mood of some monarchist units), and on top of the endless conferences, mass-meetings and journalism came incessant changes of residence that exhausted her already mentally and physically debilitated frame. The Revolution was now her only home.

Just over a week after her release, Rosa Luxemburg effectively cancelled her unpublished criticism of the dissolution of Russia's democratically-elected Constituent Assembly by the Bolsheviks. Like Lenin, she had come to see the issue as a straightforward choice between socialism or barbarism, and she echoed the arguments Lenin had advanced in 1917–18: 'Today, it is not a matter of democracy or dictatorship. The question placed on the agenda by history is: *bourgeois* democracy or *socialist* democracy. For the dictatorship of the proletariat is democracy in a socialist sense.' In an article explaining the programme of her comrades, 'What does the Spartacus League want?', she argued for the 'Abolition of all parliaments and local councils and the takeover of their functions by workers' and soldiers' soviets . . .' Yet, she disclaimed any desire to erect a one-party minority dictatorship: 'The Spartacus League will never take over the power of government, except through the clear, unambiguous will of the great majority of the proletarian mass.' She did not succeed in explaining how in practice her continuing hostility to the use of 'terror' could be reconciled with her demand that the proletarian masses 'smash the ruling class on the head like Thor [with] his hammer'.

Painstakingly, Ebert and Scheidemann cut the ground from under the feet of their USPD coalition partners. The army took a new oath of loyalty to the cabinet, disregarding the soviets. When the General Congress of Worker and Soldier Soviets met on 16–21 December, the USPD could muster only a quarter of the votes, and the Spartacists and 'left radicals' no more than 20 between them. The Congress meekly voted power back to the

139

cabinet pending the election of a National Assembly, on the basis of a democratic franchise for all men and women over twenty.

Learning from the complacency of the Russian Provisional Government of 1917, the SPD leaders were determined to convoke the Assembly quickly. They were equally determined to destroy, or at least intimidate, Germany's equivalent of the Russian Kronstadt: this was the People's Naval Division, the men who had first mutinied at Kiel, the shock troops of the German proletarian revolution, and who were now installed in the Palace and Royal Stables in Berlin. On Christmas Eve 1918, monarchist troops attacked the People's Naval Division without warning on the instructions of SPD cabinet members. The furious USPD ministers now abandoned the cabinet in protest. As the red sailors defended themselves from further attacks, the Spartacus League demanded that the USPD convene a party congress by the end of the month. When this was refused, as they knew it would be, a conference of Spartacists already scheduled for the New Year became the founding Congress of the Communist Party of Germany (the KPD(S) or Spartacists).

In Warsaw, Rosa's old comrade, Adolf Warski, had just presided over the unification of the SDKPiL and PPS-Left in a new Communist Workers' Party of Poland (KPRP), and Karl Radek now arrived in Berlin with Lenin's demand that the Spartacists, the Bremen 'International Communists' and, if possible, the revolutionary shop stewards unite in a German Communist Party. The syndicalist mood of many delegates wrecked these hopes. Rosa was not too downhearted. She disagreed with her young comrades, but she understood them. As she informed Clara, 'Don't forget that the "Spartacists" are, to a large extent, a fresh generation, free from the befuddling traditions of the "old, time-honoured party", and that must be accepted with its bright and dark sides'. By a margin of 62 to 23, the 'Spartacists' rejected the appeals of Luxemburg, Liebknecht and Jogiches in favour of the party's participation in the elections to the National Assembly. A substantial minority also wanted to make membership in the Communist Party incompatible with membership in the existing trade unions. The revolutionary shop stewards were appalled by the tone of both these discussions and refused to join the Communist Party, which therefore remained a revolutionary sect with a minimal following among the employed industrial workers.

One of the remarkable features of Rosa Luxemburg's speeches at the Congress was a posthumous debate with Friedrich Engels, the man whose patronage of Polish patriotism had blighted her entry into international socialist politics twenty-six years earlier. Now she took Engels to task for having endorsed the SPD's decision in the 1890s to rely exclusively on parliamentary methods of struggle: 'Now Party comrades, today we experience the moment, when we can say: we are with Marx again, under his banner . . . once again where Marx and Engels stood in 1848, when they first unfurled the banner of international socialism.'

On 4 January 1919, the SPD government sacked Emil Eichhorn, the radical USPD Police Chief of Berlin, who had refused to follow his party comrades into opposition. Radical militants resolved to back him up, and on the following day Karl Liebknecht joined Eichhorn and Däumig, a leading shop steward, in a protest demonstration. Where Lenin and Trotsky had organized the capture of the real centres of power, the Spartacist crowd 'spontaneously' occupied the offices of the SPD organ, *Vorwärts*, which had traduced them for so long. Perhaps Rosa thought ruefully of Hauptmann's Christ, but misled by the apparent militancy of the demonstrators and by reports of military support, Liebknecht's intense sense of honour obliged him to join Paul Scholze and Ledebour in a Revolutionary Commission, which declared the Ebert government deposed, but did little to disarm it or control its activities. In the event, the Commission failed to gain even the active support of the People's Naval Division, and they failed to carry the revolutionary shop stewards.

Several witnesses suggest that Rosa Luxemburg was horrified at Liebknecht's impetuosity, and Levi reports her as chastising him with the words, 'Karl, is that our programme?' Yet Rosa had argued for decades that the proletariat need not lose in such situations. They might take power, or they could learn a painful lesson, which would point them in the direction of future victory. At first, she did all she could to sharpen the conflict, denouncing 'plum-soft elements', who favoured conciliation, and urging the Commission to,

141

Act! Act! Courageously, determinedly, consequentially: that is the damned duty and obligation of the revolutionary shop stewards and of the honest socialist party leaders. To disarm the counter-revolution, to arm the masses, to occupy all positions of power. Act *fast*! The revolution obliges. Her hours count for months in world history and her days for years. May the organs of the revolution be conscious of their high responsibilities!

The Commission appeared at first to follow her advice, but when their isolation became too obvious to ignore, they allowed Haase, Kautsky and others to try mediation. By 8 January 1919, aware at last of the grave dangers facing the German Revolution, Rosa Luxemburg began to counsel the withdrawal of the Communists from the Revolutionary Commission, though in public she still demanded an end to negotiations, the maximum revolutionary use of the few institutions controlled by the 'Spartacists' and mass action on the streets. Discounting all evidence of proletarian division and uncertainty, she declared:

> The masses are ready to support every revolutionary action, to go through fire and water for the cause of socialism. One must give them clear slogans, [and] demonstrate a consequential, determined attitude. The idealism of the workers, the devotion of the soldiers to the revolution can only be strengthened by the determination and clarity of the leading organs. And today that is a policy which knows no hesitations, no half-measures, but only the principle [*Leitmotiv*]: Down with Ebert–Scheidemann!

Then she turned her old criticism of the SPD bureaucracy on its head:

> Germany was the classic country of organization and yet more organizational fanaticism, yes of organizational obscurantism. For the sake of 'organization', they gave up the spirit, the goals and the capacity for action of the movement. And what do we experience today? In the most important moments of the revolution, it is the famed 'organizational talent' that abdicates first in the most deplorable manner . . . The organization of revolutionary actions must and can only be learnt in the revolution itself . . . That is why historical experience exists! But one must at least *learn* from experience.

As the rising collapsed, Jogiches and Luxemburg forced Liebknecht to resign from the Revolutionary Commission, leaving the USPD Left wing to secure an orderly withdrawal, and washing the hands of the Communists in the entire affair. In Rosa's view, 'learning' now meant learning to mistrust 'this rotting corpse' – the USPD – and the revolutionary shop stewards and to trust only the Communists, whose every martyr recruited a hundred new members for the KPD, and she proclaimed that she hoped to see

> the masses of the proletariat assemble ever more densely around the flag of ruthless revolutionary struggle. Even though isolated layers may be intoxicated and captured by demagogy and phrases of 'unity', so tomorrow they will stand more firmly and faithfully, after a new disappointment and sobering-up, once more beside the sole Party, which knows no compromises and no vacillations, which goes its own historically preordained way, without looking to right or left, without counting enemies or fellow-travellers – to victory.

Rosa and Karl Liebknecht were now exposed to the vengeance of the victorious monarchist troops. As they took refuge in the house of their comrades, the Marcussons, Rosa Luxemburg concluded her extraordinary career with a last defiant article entitled 'Order Reigns in Berlin!' She closed with a warning to the bourgeoisie: 'Tomorrow the Revolution will arise to its full rattling height and will announce, to your terror, like the call of a trumpet: I was, I am, I shall be!'

The European bourgeoisie never forgave Alexander Kerensky for 'failing' to assassinate or execute Lenin and Trotsky after the first Bolshevik rising, the 'July Days' of 1917. It was, in fact, unthinkable for that typical Tolstoyan intellectual, who had personally signed the law abolishing the death penalty, even to consider such an act seriously. Rosa Luxemburg had herself contrasted the relative indifference of the German revolutionaries towards the death penalty, whose abolition was put off until the National Assembly: 'Oh, how German is this revolution: German! How prudent, pedantic it is, without élan, without glamour, without grandeur. The forgotten death penalty is only a small individual characteristic. But how the inner spirit of the whole

143

takes care to betray itself precisely in such small characteristics.'

Ebert, Scheidemann and the new SPD Defence Commissar, Gustav Noske, did not repeat any of Kerensky's 'mistakes'. On 13 January, the SPD organ, *Vorwärts*, carried the following verse:

> Many hundreds of dead in a row,
> > proletarians . . .
> Karl, Rosa, Radek & Company,
> None of them are there, none of them are there,
> > proletarians!

Two days later, Karl and Rosa were dead.

The murderers probably saved Karl and Rosa from an agonizing and acrimonious appraisal of the disaster, turning them instead into martyrs and eventually even icons, whose actions few socialists had the stomach to criticize. Only in the 1970s and 80s, finally, did such Western socialists as Pierre Broué and Manfred Schorrer begin to examine the 'Spartacist Rising' in a critical spirit. Broué concluded that, 'The leadership of the Communist Party had not been capable of preventing the destruction of a movement, which it had helped to unleash, and which it had done nothing to prevent or halt.'

The suggestion of sectarianism, of dogmatism, even of irresponsibility is not entirely unjust, and Rosa Luxemburg certainly shared these failings from time to time with the movement she tried to lead. Like Joan of Arc, she also demonstrated an unshakable commitment to her beliefs and boundless civic and physical courage. Our current world may have less confidence in Marxism and less sympathy for socialism, but if humanity is to survive, the need for internationalism is as great as ever it was. Rosa Luxemburg earned the everlasting gratitude and admiration of internationalists everywhere, including many non-socialists, for her stand during the First World War. And as she waited for Otto Runge's rifle butt, she knew that she had earned the right to recite the inspiring lines of the poem she loved so well, Meyer's 'Confession' of the Swiss Democrat, Ulrich von Hutten, and to say with him,

> Ich hab's gewagt

> I dared to do it.

Guide to Political Parties and Factions

Bund (Algemener Yiddischer Arbeter-Bund): General Jewish Workers' League
(1897–1920). Marxist organization of the Jewish proletariat,
particularly active in the western provinces of the Russian
Empire. Hosted the first Congress of the RSDRP in Minsk
(1898), but barred from second Congress in 1903 because of its
insistence on a federal party and on 'national cultural autonomy' for the Jews of Russia. Rejoining the RSDRP at the
Stockholm (Unification) Congress of the party in 1906, the
Bund was closely allied to the Russian Mensheviks, many of
whose leaders (e.g. Julius Martov) had emerged from the *Bund*.
Its best-known leader was Mark Lieber, a prominent member
of the 1917 Petrograd Soviet. It was proscribed by the Bolsheviks during the Civil War.

Endecja (Polska Partia Nacjonal-Demokratyczna): Polish National Democratic Party. Main party of the Polish bourgeoisie and peasantry in Russian Poland. Founded by the Russophile Roman
Dmowski in 1905, it remained significant in independent Poland after 1918 as the Polish People's Party.

KPD(S) (Kommunistische Partei Deutschlands (Spartakisten)): Communist
Party of Germany (Spartacists). Name adopted by the German
Communist Party at its foundation by Rosa Luxemburg and
Karl Liebknecht in January 1919. Banned by Hitler, the KPD
was merged on Stalin's orders with the East German SPD in
1946 to create the Socialist Unity Party (SED), the ruling party
of the German Democratic Republic.

KPRP (Komunistyczna Partia Robotnicza Polski): Communist Workers'
Party of Poland. Original name of Polish Communist Party
formed on Lenin's advice by Adolf Warski (SDKPiL) and
Maksymilian Horwitz-Walecki (*PPS-Lewica*) in December
1918. Banned by Piłsudski, suppressed and purged by Stalin
and persecuted by the Nazis, in 1948 it was merged on Stalin's
orders with the PPS to create the Polish United Workers' Party
(PZRP), the ruling party of the Polish People's Republic.

PPSD (*Polska Partia Socjal-Demokratyczna Galicji i Śląska Górniego)*): Polish Social Democratic Party of Galicia and Upper Silesia. Founded in 1892 by Ignacy Daszyński for the socialists of Austrian Poland, it enjoyed a federal relationship with the Austrian Socialist Party until 1919, when it amalgamated with the PPS and the PPS of Prussia.

PPS (*Polska Partia Socjalistyczna*): Polish Socialist Party. Formed on initiative of Stanisław Mendelson following November 1892 Paris Conference, its leaders included the conspirator and founder of its military wing, Józef Piłsudski, later dictator of Poland, and the Marxist theoretician, Kazimierz Kelles-Krauz. In 1905–6, the PPS split into a nationalist 'Revolutionary Fraction' (*Rewolucyjna Frakcja*) and a Marxist 'Left' (*Lewica*). In 1919, the PPS absorbed the PPSD and the PPS of Prussia. The major socialist party of inter-war Poland, it was merged in 1948 with the Polish Communist Party to form the ruling Polish United Workers' Party. An attempt to re-establish an independent PPS in Poland was made in 1988.

PPS-Lewica (PPS-Left): Between 1906 and 1919 it pursued a path between the SDKPiL and the PPS-*Rewolucyjna Frakcja*. In 1918, some of its leaders joined the KPRP, while others rejoined the PPS, where they constituted a left-wing in inter-war Poland. Leaders included Maksymilian Horwitz-Walecki, Maria Kostrzewa, etc.

PPS-Rewolucyjna Frakcja (PPS-Revolutionary Fraction): The PPS nationalists who, after 1906, supported Piłsudski's nationalistic brand of socialism. They included such enemies of Rosa Luxemburg as Witold Jodko-Narkiewicz.

PPS Zaborzu Pruskiego (PPS of the Prussian Partition): Founded in 1892 by Stanisław Mendelson as an affiliate of the SPD for Polish-speaking subjects of Prussia, Rosa Luxemburg joined it in a vain attempt to stem its nationalist tendencies in 1898. In 1919, it amalgamated with the PPS and PPSD.

Proletariat I (*Międzynarodowa Socjal-Rewolucyjna Partia 'Proletariat'*): International Social Revolutionary Party *Proletariat* (1882–6). The first quasi-Marxist party of the Russian Empire, founded by Ludwik Waryński.

Proletariat II (As above, 1888–92): The shadowy successor to *Proletariat I*, whose members included the sociologist Ludwik Krzywicki,

Marcin Kasprzak and the young Rosa Luxemburg.

RSDRP (*Rossiiskaia Sotsial-Demokraticheskaia Rabochaia Partiia*): Russian Social Democratic Workers' Party. Never much more than an aspiration, the 'RSDRP' was the umbrella name accepted by all Marxists of the Russian Empire between 1898 and 1918. In practice, it amounted to a loose association of Russian factions and of national groupings of Jews, Poles, Latvians and Georgians. Its first congress (1898) left little but a name and a manifesto. Its second congress (1903) gave rise to the celebrated split between Bolsheviks (Lenin, etc.) and Mensheviks (Martov, etc.), expelled the *Bund* and provoked Rosa Luxemburg to her famous critique of Leninism entitled *Organizational Questions of Russian Social Democracy*. Between 1906 and 1910, Leo Jogiches acted as arbiter of the uneasily reunited RSDRP, but he lost this role when Lenin began to campaign against all the other groups within the RSDRP in 1910. In 1912, the Bolsheviks declared themselves the RSDRP, capturing a considerable following among the proletariat of the major centres of Great Russia, Kharkov, Baku, etc. Menshevik and national groupings of the RSDRP retained a strong following in the borderlands of the Empire. From 1912–14, Rosa Luxemburg tried to force Lenin to reunite with the Mensheviks by invoking the authority of the Socialist International.

SAG (*Sozialistische Arbeitsgemeinschaft*): Socialist Labour Association. Name taken by the pacifist wing of the SPD, led by Hugo Haase, Karl Kautsky and Eduard Bernstein between 1916 and 1917. Later became the USPD.

SDKP (*Socjal-Demokracja Królestwa Polskiego*): Social Democracy of the Kingdom of Poland. Formed by Rosa Luxemburg, Leo Jogiches, Adolf Warski and Julian Marchlewski in 1892–3 to combat the nationalist PPS. It was destroyed by the Russian *Okhrana* (political police) in 1896.

SDKPiL (*Socjal-Demokracja Królestwa Polskiego i Litwy*): Social Democracy of the Kingdom of Poland and Lithuania. When Stanisław Trusiewicz and Feliks Dzierżyński founded the SDKPiL in 1900, they considered they were merely continuing the work of Rosa Luxemburg and the SDKP. She herself and Leo Jogiches rejected this view until 1901 when they captured the new (or re-formed) party, which they ruled dictatorially until 1914. In December 1918, it amalgamated with the *PPS-Lewica* to form the Polish Communist Party (KPRP).

147

SFIO (Section Française de l'Internationale Ouvrière): French Section of the Workers' International. Party uniting revolutionary Marxist and reformist wings of French socialism and led by Jean Jaurès, formed at the behest of the 1904 Amsterdam Congress of the Socialist International (at which Rosa Luxemburg played an influential part). Discredited by the support of its parliamentarians for the Vichy regime in 1940 and the Algerian War in the 1950s, it merged with other groups to form the present French Socialist Party in 1969.

'Spartacists' *(Spartakisten)*: Name adopted by Rosa Luxemburg, Karl Liebknecht and Clara Zetkin for their supporters in the International Group (1915), which became the Spartacist Group (1916). Until 1917, it was a faction within the SPD, but it remained within the USPD following the party split, becoming the Spartacist League in 1918. One of the founding groups of the German Communist Party (KPD(S)).

SPD (Sozialdemokratische Partei Deutschlands): Social Democratic Party of Germany. Founded by August Bebel and Wilhelm Liebknecht as the Socialist Workers' Party of Germany in 1868, the SPD became the model party of the Second International and the sole party of German socialism until 1917. During the First World War, the nationalist majority, led by Fritz Ebert and Philipp Scheidemann, future President and Chancellor of Weimar Germany, expelled the pacifists, led by Hugo Haase and Georg Ledebour, who established their own USPD (Independent SPD). The 'Spartacists' remained within the USPD until December 1918, while the 'International Socialists' formed their own group. The major party of the Weimar Republic, the SPD was banned by Hitler. It re-emerged in 1945 to become one of the two major parties of the German Federal Republic. In East Germany it was merged with the Communists in 1946 to form the Socialist Unity Party *(SED)*, the governing party of the German Democratic Republic.

USPD (Unabhängige Sozialdemokratische Partei Deutschlands): Independent Social Democratic Party of Germany. Name adopted by pacifist wing of SPD upon their expulsion from the party in 1917. Led by Hugo Haase, Emil Barth, etc., it rejoined the SPD in 1922, though many of its supporters joined the German Communist Party.

Note: Throughout the text, I have used the word 'faction' to refer to an informal tendency within a political party, while the word 'fraction' is reserved for the parliamentary delegation of a party, or a distinct party.

Chronology

1870	5 March, Rozalia (Róża) Luksenburg born in Zamość; fifth child of Eljasz (Edward) Luksenburg and Lina née Loewenstein.
1873	Luksenburg family move to Warsaw. Róża's hip dislocation misdiagnosed leading to permanent disability.
1884	Róża Luksenburg enters Second Women's Gymnasium, Warsaw.
1887	Róża Luksenburg joins socialist group under the influence of Marcin Kasprzak. She leaves school but is refused a gold medal.
1889	Róża Luksenburg leaves for Switzerland.
1890	On registration at Zurich University, she alters her name to Rosa Luxemburg. Leo Jogiches arrives in Switzerland; they become intimate.
1892	May, general strike and revolt in Łódż (subject of Rosa's first articles).
1893	Julian Marchlewski arrives in Zurich and joins Rosa at International Socialist Congress. Daszyński gets Rosa's mandate rejected, but delegates read her *Report*. Rosa Luxemburg, Leo Jogiches, the Warskis and Marchlewski resolve to form their own party, the SDKP.
1894	Rosa arrives in Paris to study economics; is befriended by Cezaryjna Wojnarowska; assumes editorship of *Sprawa Robotnicza* (The Workers' Cause). First Congress of SDKP in Warsaw adopts theses drafted by Rosa.
1896	Warsaw SDKP smashed by police; sympathizers advised to join PPS. Rosa attacks PPS in *Die Neue Zeit*, but fails to persuade International Socialist Congress in London to oppose the 'self-determination of nations'.
1897	Rosa obtains doctorate with thesis, *The Development of Industry in Poland*. Rosa's mother, Lina Luksenburg, dies.

1898	19 April, Rosa enters marriage of convenience with Gustav Lübeck. 16 May, Rosa arrives in Berlin. She joins PPS affiliate of SPD for electoral agitation in Silesia. She writes article series *Social Reform or Revolution*. At SPD Party Congress in Stuttgart, she attacks 'Revisionism' of absent Bernstein. Rosa briefly edits *Sächsische Arbeiterzeitung*, Dresden.
1899	August, Rosa moves to Berlin-Friedenau; she is befriended by Bebel, Karl and Luise Kautsky, Clara Zetkin, etc. Rosa takes father on holiday in Silesia. At Hannover SPD Congress, she again attacks Bernstein.
1900	S. Trusiewicz and F. Dzierżyński refound SDKPiL, which falls under influence of Wojnarowska, who favours Polish autonomy. Rosa begins attacks on Jean Jaurès, 'the Great Corrupter'. She attends International Socialist Congress in Paris. Her father, Edward Luksenburg, dies in Warsaw.
1901	Jogiches joins Rosa in Berlin, then departs for Algeria with dying brother. September, Rosa fined 100 Marks for attacking 'Prussification' of Polish schoolchildren. November, Tsarist police arrest Trusiewicz and Dzierżyński, allowing Jogiches and Rosa to recapture control of SDKPiL.
1902	March, Belgian socialists form alliance with liberals at expense of demand for women's franchise; Rosa denounces them.
1903	Rosa obtains divorce from G. Lübeck. She edits SDKPiL publications *Przegląd Socjaldemokratyczny* (Social Democratic Review) and *Czerwony Sztandar* (Red Flag); publishes 'In Memory of Proletariat'. July, Fourth Congress of SDKPiL lays down conditions for merger with RSDRP. Rosa orders SDKPiL delegation at Second Congress of RSDRP in Brussels to break off negotiations. She defends herself from Wojnarowska's criticism by writing *Organizational Questions of Russian Social Democracy*. At Dresden SPD Party Congress, Rosa secures virtual expulsion of Prussian PPS from SPD and supports motion designed to enforce unification of French Socialists and avert further 'Millerand cases'.
1904	February, Rosa attends Amsterdam Congress of Socialist International, which instructs French socialists to unite, leading to formation of SFIO under Jaurès (1905). Rosa drafts SDKPiL programme *Czego Chcemy?* (What do we want?). Rosa serves two-months' imprisonment for *lèse majesté* in Zwickau,

where she studies Marxist economics and writes first prison letters to Kautskys.

1905   January, Miners strike in Ruhr; 'Bloody Sunday' in St Petersburg; Polish workers join protest strikes. March, German Trade Union leaders ban discussion of mass strikes. Jogiches moves to Kraków. Rosa suffers pleurisy, but writes for Polish and German press, collects funds, etc. September, at Jena Party Congress of SPD, Rosa secures acceptance of mass strikes as defensive weapon. Bebel appoints Rosa associate editor of *Vorwärts*. October, mass strikes in St Petersburg, Moscow, Warsaw secure October Manifesto guaranteeing freedom of association and press and representative Duma. December, uprisings in Moscow and Baltic provinces suppressed. 29 December, Rosa returns to Warsaw.

1906   Rosa publishes *Z doby rewolucyjnej: Co dalej?* (In the revolutionary hour: what next?). 4 March, Rosa and Leo Jogiches arrested in Warsaw. Rosa held in Warsaw Citadel. April, Fourth 'Unification' Congress of RSDRP, Stockholm; SDKPiL joins RSDRP. August, Rosa bailed; visits St Petersburg, Finland, and then returns to Germany. September, her speech at Mannheim SPD Congress earns sentence of two-months imprisonment for incitement; she writes *Mass Strike, Party and Trade Unions*. Rosa close to Parvus; visits Italy with Kautskys.

1907   January, in chauvinistic 'Hottentot' elections to Reichstag, SPD suffers first reverse. Rosa's affair with Kostja Zetkin begins. May, Rosa and Jogiches attend Fifth Congress of RSDRP in London; Rosa attacks Plekhanov and Mensheviks with authority of SDKPiL and SDP. 12 June, begins two-month prison sentence in Barnimstrasse Prison, Berlin. At Stuttgart Congress of Socialist International, Bebel refuses to commit SPD to specific action in event of war; Rosa helps to agenda demand for women's franchise, but opposes unconditional support for colonial independence. October, she begins work at SPD Party School, Berlin, and works on economic studies.

1908   Rosa takes sister, Anna, on holiday and befriends Hannes Diefenbach. Rosa takes up oil-painting. She publishes *The National Question and Autonomy* (Polish) and helps consolidate Jogiches' 'dictatorship' at Sixth SDKPiL Congress in Prague.

151

1909   Rosa visits Italy and Switzerland; she misses SPD Congress.

1910   6 March, 150,000 Berlin workers attend banned demonstration at Tiergarten. April, Rosa departs on agitational tour throughout Germany. Bitter polemic between Rosa and Karl Kautsky, increasing tension in Kautsky marriage and causing Kautsky's nervous breakdown. At Magdeburg SPD Congress, Rosa is bitterly attacked by majority. She begins to treat cat Mimi as child substitute.

1911   Rosa criticizes inactivity of SPD leadership and is denounced by Bebel at Jena Party Congress. August, Rosa moves to Berlin-Südende (away from Kautskys). Warsaw Committee of SDKPiL rejects authority of Chief Executive in Berlin; party split into Warsaw 'splitters' (*rosłamowcy*) and 'executivites' (*zarządowcy*).

1912   January, Lenin holds all-Bolshevik Sixth RSDRP Conference in Prague; breaks with Mensheviks, *Bund*, SDKPiL Chief Executive. Rosa supports Jogiches' intrigues against *rosłamowcy;* campaigns against Radek in SPD, against Lenin in International Socialist Bureau. Rosa too ill to attend SPD Congress. In Russian elections, *rosłamowcy* successful. Victories for SPD in Reichstag elections reinforce influence of parliamentarians. Rosa attends Emergency Congress of Socialist International in Basel, which reissues anti-war declaration.

1913   Rosa takes up botany. August, death of Bebel; Rosa pays tribute. Fritz Ebert takes over SPD party machine. At Jena Party Congress, Rosa secures expulsion of Radek from SPD. Rosa tours Rhineland denouncing militarism. Rosa, F. Mehring, Marchlewski publish first number of *Sozialdemokratische Korrispondenz*. Rosa publishes major theoretical work *The Accumulation of Capital*.

1914   February, Rosa tried for sedition at Frankfurt-on-Main; sentenced to one-year's imprisonment; begins love affair with her defence counsel, Paul Levi. Rosa continues to attack militarism. Summoned by Defence Minister General v. Falkenhayn. Rosa secures proof of torture of recruits forcing Falkenhayn to drop the case. Receives additional summons for incitement. Rosa continues to campaign for expulsion of Bolsheviks from International, unless they reunite with Mensheviks. As war begins, Rosa returns from Brussels to Berlin. 4 August, SPD Reichstag fraction votes for war credits. Russians advance into

East Prussia saving Paris; Germans defeat Russians at Tannenberg and begin occupation of Poland. 10 September, Rosa, Karl Liebknecht, Mehring, Zetkin dissociate themselves from SPD majority.

1915   18 February, Rosa imprisoned in Barnimstrasse Women's Prison, Berlin, for one year. She resumes botanical studies and works on her *Anti-Criticism* (a reply to the critics of her *Accumulation of Capital*) and *Introduction to National Economy*. She also writes *The Crisis of Social Democracy* under pseudonym 'Junius' (not published until 1916). She contributes to first number of *Die Internationale*, which is immediately suppressed.

1916   January, First Reich Conference of 'International Group' ('Spartacists') adopts Rosa's *Leitsätze* (Guiding Principles) foreshadowing Third International. 18 February, Rosa released from prison. March, formation of SAG. 1 May, Liebknecht arrested after anti-war demonstration. July, Rosa, Marchlewski, Mehring taken into 'protective custody'; Rosa will not be released until 8 November 1918. Jogiches runs underground Spartacist group. October, Rosa, transferred to Wronke fortress, Poznania. She continues to publish in *Spartakusbriefe* illegally. She begins translation and introduction of V. G. Korolenko's *History of My Contemporary*. Rosa attacks Bremen radicals for 'deserting' SPD.

1917   February/March, 'bourgeois' revolution in Russia. May, founding Congress of USPD in Gotha. Rosa, Spartacists reluctantly join USPD. May, death of Rosa's beloved cat Mimi. July, Rosa transferred to Breslau Prison. Bolshevik revolution in Petrograd.

1918   Mass strikes begin in Germany. 3 March, Treaty of Brest-Litovsk. Rosa bitterly attacks German proletariat for inaction. Autumn, Rosa writes *The Russian Revolution*. October, German High Command prepares for defeat. Prince Max v. Baden becomes Reichschancellor; SPD deputies Bauer and Scheidemann join government. 3–4 November, Naval mutiny at Kiel. 6–8 November, Revolution and election of soviets all over Germany. 8 November, Rosa released from Breslau prison. 9 November, revolution in Berlin. Kaiser Wilhelm II abdicates. Fritz Ebert becomes Reichschancellor and chair of 'Council of People's Commissars', a coalition of SPD and USPD. Scheidemann proclaims 'republic'; Liebknecht proclaims 'free, socialist republic'. 10 November, Rosa reaches Berlin and assumes

153

editorship of *Die Rote Fahne* (The Red Flag). Rosa now denounces democratically elected National Assembly in favour of soviet system. She writes *What does the Spartacus League Want?* 29–31 December, First Congress of KPD(S) in Berlin. Rosa fails to persuade party to take part in National Assembly elections; Rosa explains KPD programme and criticizes Engels.

1919 10–12 January, 'Spartacist' rising suppressed. 14 January, Rosa's last article 'Order reigns in Berlin' published in *Die Rote Fahne*. 15 January, Murder of Karl Liebknecht and Rosa Luxemburg. 8 May, court-martial of Vogel and Runge. 17 May, Leo Jogiches murdered. 31 May, Rosa's body discovered. 13 June, Rosa's funeral attended by tens of thousands of Berlin workers.

1921 Paul Levi expelled from KPD; he publishes Rosa's *Russian Revolution*.

1924 Lenin dies. Fifth Comintern Congress discusses Rosa's ideas.

1929 Rosa not mentioned at Sixth Comintern Congress.

1931 First part of Gerchikov's biography of Rosa published. Stalin stops further discussion.

1939 P. Frölich publishes biography of Rosa.

1951 DDR President Wilhelm Pieck pays tribute to Rosa.

1956 At Soviet Twentieth Party Congress, Khrushchev denounces Stalin. W. Gomuľka takes over in Poland. Warski et al. rehabilitated. Barriers to study of Rosa's career removed.

1959 Rosa's martyrdom officially commemorated in DDR.

1966 Peter Nettl publishes first (and until now only) full biography of Rosa.

1968 Students in Western Europe invoke memory of Rosa in demonstrations against Viet Nam War.

1986 Margarethe von Trotta's film, *Rosa Luxemburg*, starring Barbara Sukowa.

1988 Mikhail Shatrov's play, *On and On*, reacquaints Soviet public opinion with Rosa's criticisms of Bolshevism.

Bibliography

Guide to Further Reading

The major obstacle confronting serious students of Rosa Luxemburg's career is the continuing absence of a complete edition of her works and letters. For readers of English, there are handy anthologies of a limited number of her political writings by Robert Looker (See Section I below) and Dick Howard (I), while Elżbieta Ettinger has recently provided key extracts from her correspondence with Leo Jogiches (I). Earlier editions of her letters from prison to Luise Kautsky and other friends and of her principal writings on economics are also available in academic libraries.

A major step forward in the study of Rosa Luxemburg's life and thought was taken in the 1970s, when Dietz Verlag, the publishing house of East Germany's ruling Socialist Unity Party, began to publish an academic edition of her works painstakingly prepared by Annelies Laschitza and Günter Radczun (I). They followed this up with an equally distinguished and beautifully indexed edition of her *Collected Letters* (I). It is from these two multi-volume editions that I have made my own translations for the purposes of quotation (in some cases after checking with Polish originals, which merely increased my respect for the work of Laschitza and Radczun).

Unfortunately, if understandably, Laschitza and Radczun were obliged to limit their editions to those of Rosa Luxemburg's writings that are of significance for the history of the *German* labour movement. I was therefore obliged to consult the Polish editions of her *Selected Works* (*Wybór Pism*, Section I) and of documents on the history of the SDKPiL (eds Buzek and Tych, Section II) for her early journalism and for such important theoretical works as her final essay on 'Autonomy and the National Question'. Even these useful collections omit many interesting shorter works, while Rosa Luxemburg's letters to those outside the German labour movement have been published in dribs and drabs, if at all. Fortunately, Laschitza and Radczun were able to include all Rosa Luxemburg's letters to Leo Jogiches, in view of his role in the creation of the Spartacist Group and the German Communist Party.

The extent of the difficulties that still confront the conscientious reader is illustrated by the fact that the only version of Rosa Luxemburg's pamphlet on 'The Church and Socialism' I could locate was a slightly abridged German translation of an edition published in English by the Communist Party of Ceylon (undated), which appeared in an enterprising anthology entitled *Rosa Luxemburg, Ein Leben für die Freiheit*, edited by Frederik Hetmann (Frankfurt: Fischer, 1980). Italian readers are slightly better served by Lelio Basso's edition of the *Scritti Politici* (Rome: Riuniti, 1967). To savour all the nuances of Rosa Luxemburg's letters to Jogiches, one should ideally read the Polish originals published by Feliks Tych (Section I), who is not to be blamed for the poor quality of the paper and other materials employed.

The bibliography is divided into eleven sections as follows: (I) Rosa Luxemburg's works and letters; (II) published collections of documents in which Rosa Luxemburg figures; (III) the Marxist classics, the works of her Marxist peers, together with George Lichtheim's illuminating history of Marxism and Leszek Kołakowski's indispensable three-volume work; (IV) the section on biographical materials which have not yet been fully assimilated into the secondary literature, including the tantalising and tragically premature attempt at a 'scientific biography' by the Soviet historian, Gerchikov, Feliks Tych's essay on Rosa Luxemburg's final visit to Warsaw and Verena Stadler-Labhart's sketch of her student days in Zurich. Section V includes the more politically significant appraisals of Rosa Luxemburg. The best recent appraisal in English is by Norman Geras, but Italian (and Spanish) readers have the advantage of access to Lelio Basso's appreciations, one of which is mentioned here.

Amongst the biographies (Section VI), Peter Nettl's two-volume work remains without rival after twenty years, though Elżbieta Ettinger has recently added to our knowledge of Rosa Luxemburg's personal life. Ettinger was able to draw on unpublished correspondence in Amsterdam and Stanford. She also benefited, as I have tried to do, from the publication of Zdzisław

Leder's short biography of Jogiches published in *Archiwum Ruchu Robotniczego* in 1976 (VI) and from the release by the West German Archiv der Sozialen Demokratie of Rosa Luxemburg's letters to Paul Levi, which, coming just as Laschitza and Radczun were going to press with the final volume of Rosa Luxemburg's letters, had to be accommodated uncomfortably as an appendix to volume 5 of the *Collected Letters* (Section I). On the other hand, Ettinger evidently decided to ignore Scharlau and Zeman's work on Parvus (Section IX).

The remainder of the bibliography is organized thematically into sections on 'Women and Socialism' (VII), 'Nationalism and Socialism in Eastern Europe' (VIII), 'German Socialism, 1870–1925' (IX), 'The Second International' (X) and 'Economics and Imperialism' (XI). I found the works by E. Lima and G. Fiume and by Richard J. Evans (both section VII) particularly helpful on the history of the German proletarian women's movement; Dale Spender's passage on Emma Goldman (much of which applies also to Rosa Luxemburg) explains why many East European revolutionary women are still regarded with ambivalence by Anglo-Saxon radical feminists (VII).

Robert Wistrich (VIII) provides a revealing, if slightly harsh, account of Rosa Luxemburg's attitude towards the Jewish people, while G. W. Strobel's monumental account of the SDKP/SDKPiL clarifies the unhappy birth and painful evolution of the internationalist current in Polish socialism (VIII), subsequent tragic chapters of which have recently been opened up to Western readers by Teresa Toranska's interviews with those she terms 'Stalin's Polish Puppets' (VIII). Marian Żychowski's study of Polish socialist thought (VIII) and the still incomplete *Polski Słownik Biograficzny* (VI) are indispensable aids for those seeking to unravel the complex threads of Polish socialism. An unexpected, indirect shaft of light on Rosa Luxemburg's traumatic debut in Polish socialism has recently been thrown by John Slatter's article in *Irish Slavonic Studies* (VIII), which describes Michael Davitt's participation in a court of honour considering the accusations against Rosa Luxemburg's mentor, Marcin Kasprzak.

The received interpretation of the history of the SPD was, until recently, the critical view expressed by Carl Schorske's *German Social Democracy 1905–1917. The Development of the Great Schism*

(Cambridge: Harvard, 1955) and which found more elaborate expression still in Dieter Groh's thesis of 'negative integration' (IX). Both followed a tradition going back to Robert Michels (IX) and to Rosa Luxemburg herself. My own studies and experiences render me receptive to Richard Evans' argument that the German proletariat (or perhaps merely German proletarians) was able to achieve significant and worthwhile objectives through the pre-1914 SPD (VII). Pierre Broué (IX) and Manfred Schorrer (IX) have subjected the SPD radicals to criticism as remorseless as Schorske's criticism of the SPD leadership, occasionally and hyperbolically appearing to allocate all the blame for the failures of the German left to the radicals. If one wishes to escape the retrospective wisdom of post-1914 (and post-1933) commentators, it is worth consulting such contemporary accounts of the SPD as those of Bertrand and Alys Russell (VII) and Robert Michels (IX). Helmut Trotnow and Heinz Wohlgemuth (both IX) provide sharply contrasting interpretations of the career of Karl Liebknecht, each author seeing in Liebknecht the precursor of his own humanist-socialist or Marxist-Leninist views.

The Second International has earned authoritative and comprehensive studies in Russian and German from Communist and post-1918 Social Democratic interpretations (X). English readers are well served, as always, by the engaging study by James Joll (X). Of the technical literature on Rosa Luxemburg's economic writings, I found Hermann Lehman's introduction to the fifth volume of Rosa Luxemburg's *Collected Works* (XI) and Jan Dziewulski's study (which deserves a good English translation) (XI) the most helpful. English readers can, however, rely on Kołakowski's abstract of Tadeusz Kowalik's monograph (III).

I. *Rosa Luxemburg's Works and Letters*:

(As yet no complete edition exists)
Luksemburg, Róża, *Wybór Pism*, 2 vols, Warsaw: Książka i Wiedza, 1959
——, *Listy do Leona Jogichesa-Tyszki*, ed. Feliks Tych, Warsaw: Książka i Wiedza, 1968–71
——, 'Listy Róży Luksemburg do Cezaryjny Wojnarowskiej

(1896–1906)', Z *Pola Walki,* No. 1 (53), 1971

Luxemburg, Rosa, *Gesammelte Werke,* ed. Annelies Laschitza and Günter Radczun, 6 vols, Berlin: Dietz, 1970–5

——, *Selected Political Writings of Rosa Luxemburg,* ed. Dick Howard, New York–London: Monthly Review Press, 1971

——, *Selected Political Writings,* ed. Robert Looker, London: Jonathan Cape, 1972

——, *Comrade and Lover. Rosa Luxemburg's Letters to Leo Jogiches,* ed. Elżbieta Ettinger, London: Pluto, 1979

——, *Gesammelte Briefe,* ed. A. Laschitza and G. Radczun, 5 vols, Berlin: Dietz, 1982–4

II. *Documents:*

Carat i Klasy Posiadające w Walce z Rowolucją 1905–1907 w Królestwe Polskim, Warsaw: Państwowe Wydawnictwo Naukowe, 1956

Congrès International Ouvrier Socialiste, Zurich 6–12 Août 1893 . . ., Geneva: Minkoff Reprint, 1976ff.

Dokumente und Materialien zur Geschichte der Deutschen Arbeiterbewegung, Berlin: IML of SED, 1958–67

Der Gründungsparteitag der KPD, Protokoll und Materialien, ed. Hermann Weber, Frankfurt/M–Vienna: Europa Verlag, 1969

Piatyi (Londonskii) s'ezd RSDRP, aprel'–mai 1907 goda. Protokoly, Moscow: IML of the KPSS, 1963

Protokoll(e) des Ersten (usw) Kongresses der Kommunistischen Internationale, Berlin–Hamburg: Carol Hoym/KPD, 1919–24

Protokoll(e) über die Verhandlungen des Parteitages der Sozialdemokratischen Partei Deutschlands, Berlin: SPD, 1889–1913

Socjaldemokracja Królestwa Polskiego i Litwy: Materiały i Dokumenty, ed. H. Buzek and F. Tych, 2 vols, Warsaw: Książka i Wiedza, 1957–

III. *Marxist Theory and Praxis:*

Kołakowski, Leszek, *Main Currents of Marxism,* 3 vols, London: Oxford University Press, 1978

Lenin, V. I., *Collected Works,* 45 vols and 2 index vols, Moscow–

159

London: Progress–Lawrence and Wishart, 1960–80

Lichtheim, George, *Marxism. An Historical and Critical Study*, London: Routledge & Kegan Paul, 1961

Liebknecht, Karl, *Gesammelte Reden und Schriften*, 10 vols, Berlin: Dietz, 1958–68

Marchlewski, Julian, *Ludzie, Czasy, Idze*, ed. N. Michta, Warsaw: Książka i Wiedza, 1973

——, *Pisma Wybrane*, ed. T. Daniszewski et al., Warsaw: Książka i Wiedza, 1952

Marx, Karl, and Frederick Engels, *Collected Works*, Moscow–London: Progress–Lawrence and Wishart, 1975–

Plekhanov, G. V., *Sochineniia*, ed. D. Riazanov, 24 vols, Moscow–Petrograd: Inst. K. Marksa i F. Engelsa, 1923–7

Warski, Adolf, *Wybór pism i przemówień*, 2 vols, ed. T. Daniszewski, Warsaw: Książka i Wiedza, 1958

IV. Biographical Materials:

Badia, Gilbert, *Rosa Luxemburg, Journaliste, Polémiste, Révolutionnaire*, Paris: Éditions Sociales, 1975

Gerchikov, I. V., *Roza Liuksemburg*, Part I: *Genezis i oformlenie sotsial'no-politicheskikh vozzrenii, 1870–1898* (only part ever published), in *Uchënye Zapiski Saratovskogo Gosudarstvennogo universiteta imeni N.G. Chernyshevskogo*, vol. IX: *Pedagogicheskii fakul'tet*, Saratov: 1931

Hannover-Druck, Elisabeth, and Heinrich Hannover (eds), *Der Mord an Rosa Luxemburg und Karl Liebknecht: Dokumentation eines politischen Verbrechens*, Frankfurt/M: Suhrkamp, 1967

Laschitza, Annelies, and Günter Radczun, *Rosa Luxemburg. Ihr Wirken in der deutschen Arbeiterbewegung*, Berlin: Dietz,ʼ 1971

Schiel, Ilse, and Erna Milz (eds), *Karl und Rosa: Erinnerungen zum 100. Geburtstag von Karl Liebknecht und Rosa Luxemburg*, Berlin: Dietz, 1971

Semkovskaia, N. (*alias* Irena Izvol'skaia), *Roza Liuksemburg*, Kharkov: Proletar', 1925

Stadler-Labhart, Verena, *Rosa Luxemburg an der Universität Zürich, 1889–1897*, Zurich: Verlag Hans Rohr, 1978

Tych, Feliks, 'Ostatni pobyt Róży Luksemburg w Warszawie', in

Warszawa Popowstaniowa 1864–1918, part 1 (Studia Warszaw-skie, vol. II), Warsaw: Inst. Historii Polskiej Akademii Nauk, 1968

V. Appraisals of Rosa Luxemburg's Significance:

Basso, Lelio (ed. and intro.), *Rosa Luxemburg e lo sviluppo del pensiero marxista*, vol. II of *Annali* of the Fondazione Lelio e Lisli Basso–Issoco, Rome, 1976

Ciołkosz, Adam, *Róża Luksemburg a Rewolucja Rosyjska*, Paris: Instytut Literacki, 1961

Geras, Norman, *The Legacy of Rosa Luxemburg*, London: New Left Books, 1976

Gradowski, Ryszard, 'Róża Luksemburg – Teoretyk i Działacz Międzynarodowego ruchu robotniczego', *Z Pola Walki*, No. 3 (55), 1971

Guérin, Daniel, *Rosa Luxemburg et la spontanéité révolutionnaire*, Paris: Spartacus, 1982

Kautsky, Karl, *Rosa Luxemburg, Karl Liebknecht, Leo Jogiches: Ihre Bedeutung für die deutsche Sozialdemokratie*, Berlin: 'Freiheit', 1971

Lenin, V. I., 'Notes of a Publicist', *Collected Works*, vol. 33, Moscow–London: Progress–Lawrence and Wishart, 1966, pp. 204–11

Levi, Paul, 'Introduction' to *Rosa Luxemburg, Eine kritische Würdigung*, Berlin: Verlag Gesellschaft und Erziehung, 1922

Lukács, Georg, 'The Marxism of Rosa Luxemburg', in his *History and Class Consciousness*, London: Merlin, 1968

Pieck, Wilhelm, 'Introduction', in Rosa Luxemburg, *Ausgewählte Reden und Schriften*, 2 vols, Berlin: Dietz, 1951

Slutskii, A. G., 'Bol'sheviki o germanskoi sotsial-demokratii v period eë predvoennogo krizisa', *Proletarskaia Revoliutsiia*, No. 6, 1930

Stalin, J. V., 'Some Questions regarding the History of Bolshevism' (Letter to the Editors of *Proletarskaia Revoliutsiia*), in Stalin, Joseph, *Leninism*, vol. 2, London: Modern Books, 1933

Trotsky, Leon, 'Hands off Rosa Luxemburg' and 'Rosa Luxemburg and the Fourth International', in *Rosa Luxemburg Speaks*, ed. Mary A. Waters, New York: Pathfinder, 1970

——, *Martyrs of the Third International: Karl Liebknecht, Rosa Luxemburg*, London: Prinkipo, 1971

——, *Political Profiles*, London: New Park, 1972

Zetkin, Clara, *Um Rosa Luxemburgs Stellung zur russischen Revolution*, Hamburg: Verlag der Kommunistischen Internationale, 1922

VI.   *Biographies of Rosa Luxemburg and Leo Jogiches*:

Ettinger, Elżbieta, *Rosa Luxemburg. A Life*, London: Harrap, 1987

Evzerov, R. Ia., and Inessa S. Iazhborovskaia, *Roza Liuksemburg: Biograficheskii ocherk*, Moscow: Mysl', 1974

Frölich, Paul, *Rosa Luxemburg, ideas in action*, London: Left Book Club, 1940; reprinted and annotated, London: Pluto Press, 1972

Leder, Z. (*alias* W. Feinstein), 'Nieznana praca biograficzna członka kierownika SDKPiL Zdzisława Ledera o Leonie Jogichesie-Tyszce', *Archiwum Ruchu Robotniczego*, vol. 3, 1976

Nettl, John Peter, *Rosa Luxemburg*, 2 vols, London: Oxford University Press, 1966

Pilch, Andrzej, 'Jogiches, Leon', in *Polski Słownik Biograficzny*, vol. 11, Wrocław, etc: Polska Akademia Nauk, 1973

Roland–Holst van der Schalk, Henriette, *Rosa Luxemburg. Ihr Leben und Wirken*, Zurich: Jean–Christophe Verlag, 1937

VII.   *Women and Socialism*:

Bebel, August, *Die Frau in der Vergangenheit, Gegenwart und Zukunft*, Zurich: Verlags–Magazin, 1897, etc.

Braun, Lily, *Die Frauenfrage; ihr geschichtliche Entwicklung und wirtschaftliche Seite*, Leipzig: Hirzel, 1901

Dunayevskaya, Raya, *Rosa Luxemburg, Women's Liberation and Marx's Philosophy of Revolution*, Atlantic Highlands, NJ–Brighton: Humanities Press–Harvester, 1981

Engels, Friedrich, *The Origin of the Family, Private Property and the State*, London: Lawrence and Wishart, 1940

Evans, Richard J., *Sozialdemokratie und Frauenemanzipation im deutschen Kaiserreich*, Berlin–Bonn: J. H. W. Dietz, 1979

Lima, E., and G. Fiume, '*Gleichheit* e la contradizione femminile nella Socialdemocrazia tedesca (1891–1896)', Università di Palermo, *Facoltà di Lettere. Istituto di Lingue e letterature straniere*, vol. 14, 1980

Moszczeńska, J., 'Die Geschichte der Frauenbewegung in Polen', in *Handbuch der Frauenbewegung*, vol. I, eds. Helene Lange and Gertrud Bäumer, 5 vols, Berlin: W. Moeser, 1901

Niggemann, Heinz, *Emanzipation zwischen Sozialismus und Feminismus: Die sozialdemokratische Frauenbewegung im Kaiserreich*, Wuppertal: Peter Hammer, 1981

Russell, Alys, 'Social Democracy and the Woman Question in Germany', in Bertrand Russell, *German Social Democracy, Six Lectures*, London: Longman, 1896

Spender, Dale, *Women of Ideas (and what men have done to them)*, London: Ark, 1982 (see section on Emma Goldman, pp. 497–507)

Stites, Richard, *The Women's Liberation Movement in Russia; Feminism, Nihilism and Bolshevism, 1860–1930*, Princeton: Princeton University Press, 1978

Vogel, Lise, *Marxism and the Oppression of Women: Towards a Unitary Theory*, London: Pluto, 1983

Zetkin, Clara, *Zur Geschichte der proletarischen Frauenbewegung Deutschlands*, Berlin: Dietz, 1958

VIII. *Nationalism and Socialism in Eastern Europe*:

Blejwas, Stanislas A., *Realism in Polish Politics: Warsaw Positivism and National Survival in Nineteenth Century Poland*, New Haven: Yale Consortium, 1984

Blobaum, Robert, *Feliks Dzierżyński and the SDKPiL: A Study of the Origins of Polish Communism*, Boulder, Colo.–New York: Columbia University Press, 1984

Daszyński, Ignacy, *Pamiętniki*, 2 vols, Krakow: Nakład Z.R.S.S. 'Proletariat', 1925–6

Deutscher, Isaac, *The Non-Jewish Jew and other Essays*, London: Oxford University Press, 1968

Frankel, Jonathan, *Prophecy and Politics: socialism, nationalism and the Russian Jews, 1862–1927*, Cambridge: Cambridge University

Press, 1981

Getzler, Israel, *Martov, A Political Biography of a Russian Social Democrat*, Melbourne–Cambridge: Melbourne and Cambridge University Presses, 1967

Geyer, Dietrich, *Kautskys Russisches Dossier. Deutsche Sozialdemokraten als Treuhänder des russischen Parteivermögens 1910–1915*, Frankfurt–New York: Campus Verlag, 1981

Historia polskiego ruchu robotniczego 1864–1964, vol. 1, ed. F. Tych et al., Warsaw: Książka i Wiedza, 1967

Kalabiński, Stanisław, and Feliks Tych, *Czwarte Powstanie czy Pierwsza Rewolucja: Lata 1905–1907 na ziemiach polskich*, Warsaw: Wiedza Powszechna, 1969

Lerner, Waren, *Karl Radek: The Last Internationalist*, Stanford: Stanford University Press, 1970

Marx, Karl, 'On the Jewish Question', Karl Marx and Friedrich Engels, *Collected Works*, vol. 3, Moscow–London–New York: Progress–Lawrence and Wishart, 1975

Mendelsohn, E., *Class Struggles in the Pale: The Formative Years of the Jewish Workers' Movement in Tsarist Russia*, Cambridge University Press, 1970

Mill, John, *Pionern un Boier*, New York, 1946–49 (in Yiddish)

Naimark, Norman, *The History of the 'Proletariat': The Emergence of Marxism in the Kingdom of Poland, 1870–1887*, Boulder–New York: Columbia University Press, 1979

Najdus, Walentyna, *SDKPiL a SDPRR 1893–1907*, and *SDKPiL a SDPRR 1908–1918*, Wrocław, etc: Ossolineum, 1973–80

Pilsudski, Joseph, *The Memories of a Polish Revolutionary and Soldier*, London: Faber, 1931

Rosdolsky, Roman, 'Engels and the "Nonhistoric" Peoples: The National Question in the Revolution of 1848', *Critique*, No. 18–19, 1986

Schumacher, Horst, and Feliks Tych, *Julian Marchlewski–Karski*, Berlin: Dietz, 1966

Slatter, John, 'An Irishman at a revolutionary court of honour: from the Michael Davitt papers', *Irish Slavonic Studies*, No. 5, 1984

Strobel, G. W., *Die Partei Rosa Luxemburgs, Lenin und die SPD*, Wiesbaden: Franz Steiner Verlag, 1974

Tims, Richard W., *Germanizing Prussian Poland: The H–K–T Society* and the Struggle for the Eastern Marches in the German Empire, 1894–1919, New York: Columbia University Press, 1941

Tomicki, Jan, Polska Partia Socjalistyczna 1892–1948, Warsaw: Książka i Wiedza, 1983

Toranska, Teresa, Oni: Stalin's Polish Puppets, London: Collins–Harvill, 1987

Trotsky, Leon, My Life: An Attempt at an Autobiography, London: Penguin, 1975

Wistrich, Robert, Revolutionary Jews from Marx to Trotsky, London: Harrap, 1976

Żychowski, Marian, Polska myśl socjalistyczna ix i xx wieku (do 1918 r.) Warsaw: Państwowe Wydawnictwo Naukowe, 1976

IX. German Socialism, 1870–1925:

Broué, Pierre, Révolution en Allemagne, 1917–1923, Paris: Minuit, 1971

Drakhovitch, Milorad M., and Branko Lazitch, The Comintern: Historical Highlights: Essays, Recollections, Documents, Stanford–New York: Praeger, 1966

Groh, Dieter, Negative Integration und revolutionärer Attentismus: Die deutsche Sozialdemokratie am Vorabend des Ersten Weltkrieges, Frankfurt/M–Berlin: Ullstein, 1973

Kautsky, Karl, Erinnerungen und Erörterungen von Karl Kautsky, ed. Benedikt Kautsky, The Hague: Mouton, 1980

Levi, Paul, Zwischen Spartakus und Sozialdemokratie. Schriften, Aufsätze, Reden und Briefe, Frankfurt/M–Vienna: Europa, 1969

Maehl, William Harvey, August Bebel, Shadow Emperor of the German Workers, Philadelphia: American Philosophical Society, 1980

Mayer, Thomas, Bernsteins Konstruktiver Sozialismus: Eduard Bernsteins Beitrag zur Theorie des Sozialismus, Berlin–Bonn: J. H. W. Dietz, 1977

Michels, Robert, Zur Soziologie des Parteiwesens in der Modernen Demokratie: Untersuchungen über die Oligarchischen Tendenzen des Gruppenlebens, Leipzig: Klinkhardt, 1911

Müller, Richard, Vom Kaiserreich zur Republik. Ein Beitrag zur Geschichte der revolutionären Arbeiterbewegung während des Welt-

krieges, 3 vols, Vienna: Malik–Verlag, 1924–5

Noske, Gustav, *Aufstieg und Niedergang der deutschen Sozialdemokratie*, Zurich: Aeroverlag, 1947

Salvadori, Massimo, *Karl Kautsky and the Socialist Revolution, 1880–1938*, London: New Left Books, 1979

Scharlau, W., and Z. A. B. Zeman, *Freibeuter der Revolution: Parvus–Helphand: Eine politische Biographie*, Cologne: Verlag Wissenschaft und Politik, 1964

Scheidemann, Philipp, *Memoiren eines Sozialdemokraten*, 2 vols, Dresden: Carl Reissner Verlag, 1928

Schleifstein, Josef, *Franz Mehring. Sein marxistisches Schaffen, 1891–1919*, Berlin: Rütten und Loening, 1959

Schorrer, Manfred, *Die Spaltung der deutschen Arbeiterbewegung*, Stuttgart: Cordeliers, 1985

Trotnow, Helmut, *Karl Liebknecht. Eine politische Biographie*, Cologne: Kiepenhauer und Witsch, 1980

Ulbricht, Walter et al., *Zur Geschichte der Deutschen Arbeiterbewegung*, 8 vols, Berlin: Dietz, 1966

Wheeler, Robert F., *USPD und Internationale: Sozialistischer Internationalismus in der Zeit der Revolution*, Frankfurt/M: Ullstein, 1975

Wohlgemuth, Heinz, *Die Entstehung der Kommunistischen Partei Deutschlands, 1914 bis 1918. Überblick*, Berlin: Dietz, 1968

——, *Karl Liebknecht. Eine Biographie*, Berlin: Dietz, 1973

X. *The Second International*:

Adler, Victor, *Briefwechsel mit August Bebel und Karl Kautsky*, ed. Friedrich Adler, Vienna: SPÖ, 1954

Baron, Samuel, *Plekhanov, the Father of Russian Marxism*, London: Routledge & Kegan Paul, 1963

Braunthal, Julius, *Victor und Friedrich Adler. Zwei Generationen Arbeiterbewegung*, Vienna: Verlag der Wiener Volksbuchhandlung, 1965

——, *Geschichte der Internationale*, 3 vols, Hannover: J. H. W. Dietz, 1961–71

Correspondence entre Lénine et Camille Huyssmans 1905–1914, ed. G. Haupt, Paris–The Hague: Mouton, 1963

Istoriia vtorogo Internatsionala, 2 vols, eds L. I. Zubov et al., Mos-

cow: Institut Istorii AN SSSR, 1965–6.
Joll, James, *The Second International*, London: Routledge & Kegan Paul, 1955
Liebman, Marcel, *Les Socialistes belges 1885–1914. La Révolte et l'organisation*, Brussels: Vie Ouvrière, 1979
O'Hare, Kate Richards, *Selected Writings and Speeches*, ed. Philip S. Foner and Sally M. Miller, Baton Rouge–London: Louisiana State University Press, 1982
Voigt, Christian, *Robert Grimm. Kämpfer, Arbeiterführer, Parlamentarier*, Bern: Zytglogge, 1980
Willard, Claude, *Le Mouvement Socialiste en France (1893–1905) Les Guesdistes*, Paris: Éditions Sociales, 1965

XI. *Economics and Imperialism*:

Daszyńska–Golińska, Zofia, *Rozwój i Samodzielność Gospodarcza ziem polskich*, Warsaw–Kraków: J. Mortkowicz, 1914
Dziewulski, Jan, *Wokół Poglądów Ekonomicznych Róży Luksemburg*, Warsaw: Książka i Wiedza, 1972
Hilferding, Rudolf, *Das Finanzkapital: Eine Studie über die jüngste Entwicklung des Kapitalismus*, Frankfurt/M–Vienna: Europäische Verlagsanstalt, 1968
Hobson, John A., *Imperialism: a study*, London: James Nisbet and Co., 1902
Kowalik, Tadeusz, *Róża Luksemburg. Teoria Akumulacji i Imperializm*, in *Monografie z dziejów nauki i techniki*, vol. 74, Wrocław, etc: Wydawnictwo Polskiej Akademii Nauk, 1971
Lehmann, Hermann, 'Vorwort', in Rosa Luxemburg, *Gesammelte Werke*, vol. 5: 'Ökonomische Schriften', Berlin: Dietz, 1975
Lenin, V. I., *On the Development of Capitalism in Russia*, in *Collected Works*, vol. 3, Moscow–London: Progress–Lawrence and Wishart, 1960–80
——, *Imperialism, The Highest Stage of Capitalism*, in *Collected Works*, vol. 22
Marx, Karl, *Capital*, 3 vols, Moscow–London: Foreign Languages PH–Lawrence and Wishart, 1961–2
——, *Theories of Surplus Value*, London: Lawrence and Wishart, 1951

Robinson, Joan, 'Introduction' to Rosa Luxemburg, *The Accumulation of Capital*, London: Routledge & Kegan Paul, 1951; reprinted in her *Collected Economic Papers*, vol. 2, Oxford: Blackwell, 1960

Sweezy, Paul, *The Theory of Capitalist Development: Principles of Marxian Political Economy*, New York–London: Modern Reader Paperbacks, 1942

Zawadzki, Józef, *Poglądy ekonomiczne Róży Luksemburg*, Warsaw: Książka i Wiedza, 1982

Index

Accumulation of Capital, The, 3, 109–11, 121–2
Adler, Victor, 37, 42, 48, 58, 66, 68
Afghanistan, 52
Africa, 19, 93, 112–13, 117
Agadir, Morocco, 93–4
Alexander II, Tsar of Russia, 2, 16, 18, 24
Alexander III, Tsar of Russia, 29, 32
Algeria, 57
Allemane, J., 42
Allies, 137 f
Alps, 25
Alsace–Lorraine, 42, 112
America, Latin, 97
America, North, 19
American Civil War, 27, 89
Amnesty International, 128
Amsterdam, 64–5
Anarchists, 36, 66
Andreyev, Leonid, 127
Anna Karenina, 20
Anti-Criticism, 121–2
'Anti-Socialist Laws', 25, 45, 68, 70
Arkwright, R., 89
arts, fine, 4, 87, 115
Asia, 117, 130
Association of Polish Social Democrats Abroad, 42
Auer, Ignatz, 48, 51, 54, 122
Austria, 22, 33, 36, 37, 87, 114, 117
  socialists of, 37, 43, 48
Autocracy, Russian, 31
Avksentiev, N.D., 77
Axelrod, P.B., 31

Baden, 92
Baden, Prince Max von, 137
Bakunin, M.I., 2
Balakhovskaya, Sofia, 51
Balkans, 117
Baltic peoples, 130, 135
  provinces, 79
barbarism, 109
Barent brothers, 26
Barmen, 91
Barnimstrasse Women's Prison, 121
Barth, E., 138
Basso, Lelio, 15
Bauer, G.A., 137
Bavaria, 48, 60, 70

Bavarian Soviet Republic, 11
Bebel, August, 4, 25, 36–7, 45, 48, 53, 55, 58, 60, 64ff, 68–9, 74, 76, 80, 93ff, 104, 107f, 113f, 118f
Becker, K., 7
Beethoven, Ludwig van, 115
Beijing, 62
Belgium, 4, 62, 66, 114–15, 120, 135
  socialists, 66–8, 116, 133
Beria, L.P., 14
Berlin, 6–10, 45–7, 53, 57, 68f, 72, 78, 83f, 85, 87, 91, 93, 98, 100, 113, 115, 122, 132ff, 137–45
Bern, 132
Bernstein, Eduard, 25 ,42, 57–61, 63, 75f, 101, 132
Bethmann Hollweg, T. von, 90–1, 93–4
Bettelheim, Bruno, 1, 57
Bierut, B., 14
Bismarck, Otto von, 25, 45, 49, 65
Blackwell, Emily, 51
Bochum, 91
Bogdanov, (Malinovsky) A.A., 101
Bohemia, 42
Bolshevism, 13, 73–4, 79–82, 101f, 103f, 128–32, 137
Bömelburg, Th., 75
bourgeoisie/bourgeois, 18, 39–40, 58, 62ff, 67f, 73, 79–80, 87, 88–9, 91, 97, 109, 114, 117, 132, 135, 139, 143
Brahms, J., 115
Braun, (née von Gisicki), Lily, 55, 66–7
Bremen, 49, 91, 95, 120, 135, 140
Breshkovskaya, E.K., 24
Breslau (Wrocław), 52, 56, 91, 123, 138
Brest-Litovsk, Treaty of (1918), 10, 134
Britain, 36, 43, 45, 49, 57–8, 60–1, 70, 81, 89, 93–4, 117, 120, 137
Brogan, Sir Denis, 63
Brosse, Minister, 52
Broué, P., 144
Brunswick (Braunschweig), 134
Brussels, 68, 72–3
Bukharin, N.I., 110
Bülow, Prince B. von, 81
Bund, 42, 70, 80, 82, 96

169

bureaucracy, 76, 102, 107–8, 119, 136, 142

Cameroon, 113
Canaque, Louise la, 17
Canaris, Admiral W.W., 9
Capital, 21, 122
Cartwright, E., 89
Catherine II, Tsarina of Russia, 127
Catholics, 49–50, 62, 66, 96, 98
Catholic Clerical Party, 66
Caucasus, 130
Central Asia, 130
Central Committee of RSDRP, 80, 102
Central Union of Women and Girls of Germany, 52
Chassidism, 2, 17–18
Chekhov, A.P., 127
Chernyi Peredel, 31
China, 131
Christ, 30, 141
Chrzanowska, Jadwiga, *see* Warszawska, J.
Cologne, 75
Combes, E., 63
Comintern *see* International, Third
Commune, Paris (1871), 17, 40 73, 68
Communism, 89
Communist Manifesto, The, 34, 75
Communist Party of Germany, *see* KPD
Communist Party of Poland, *see* KPRP
Conservatives, Belgian, 17; German, 81, 94
Constituent Assembly, the All-Russian, 10, 131–2, 139
Council of People's Commissars (German), 138
Crisis of Social Democracy, The, *see* 'Junius Brochure'
culture, proletarian, 108
Czech lands, 66
Czerwony Sztandar (Red Flag), 69, 79, 99

Dąbrowa, 18
Dąbrowski, Gen. Jarosław, 17, 21
Danes, 104
Darwinism, 3
Daszyńska, Zofia, 24, 37, 40
Daszyński, Ignacy, 36–8, 42, 48, 74
Däumig, Ernst, 141
David, Dr. Eduard, 118
Davitt, Michael, 34

death penalty, 143–4
'Decembrists', 24
Deutsch, Lev G., 31, 33
Deutscher, Isaac, 20
Development of Industry in Poland, The, 40
Diefenbach, Johannes ('Hannes'), 87, 115, 123, 126
Dittman, W., 133, 136, 138
Dmowski, Roman, 96
Dortmund, 91
Draft Programme of the Polish Socialist Party, 35
Dreger, Rifleman, 7–8
Dresden, 64–5
Dreyfus, Capt. Alfred, 62–3
Duala people, 113
Duma, 80, 103
Dunayevskaya, Raya, 16, 55, 76–7
Dutch, 65, 87, 104, 116
Dzierżyński, Feliks, 50, 69, 72, 80, 98

Ebert, Friedrich (Fritz), 8, 101, 108, 135–6, 137, 138–40, 142, 144
Economic theory, Marxist, education in, 21, 26
Bernstein's views on, 58
Lenin's views on, 10, 12, 110
Luxemburg, R., views on, 3–4, 39–40, 58–60, 87–9, 109–11, 121–2
Eden Hotel, Berlin, 6–10, 14
Egypt, 89
Eichhorn, Emil, 141
Eintracht Club, Zurich, 25
Eisner, Kurt, 88
Eissner, Clara, *see* Zetkin, Clara
Elberfeld, 91
Electoral Law, Prussian, 90
Elizavetgrad, 18
Emancipation of Labour Group, 31–2
Emmanuel Quint, 125
Endecja, 96
Engels, Friedrich, 3, 11, 19, 32, 34–5, 37, 46, 57, 66, 98, 130, 141
Enlightenment, 2
Ethiopia, 52
Ettinger, Elżbieta, 16, 19, 83–4, 95

Faisst, Hugo, 125
Falkenhayn, Gen. E. von, 113
famine, 33
Federation of German Women's Unions, 52
Fidelio, 123
Figaro, 124

Finance Capital, 110
Finland, 130, 134
Fischer, Ruth, 11
Fourier, C., 105
France, 4, 17, 32, 36, 40, 62–5, 70, 74, 76, 93–4, 117, 120, 133, 135
France, Anatole, 122
Franco-Prussian War, 16–17, 76, 114, 117
Frankfurt/Main, 91, 112, 121
freedom of the press, 131
Freud, Sigmund, 20
Frölich, Paul, 14

Galicia, 22, 48, 100
Gallifet, Gen. the Marquis of, 63
Geck, Brandel, 115, 138
General Commission of German Free Trade Unions, 75, 81
General Cóngress of Worker and Soldier Soviets of Germany, 139
General Jewish Workers' League, *see* Bund
General Strike, *see* Mass political strike
Geneva, 21, 29, 31–3
Geneva, Lake, 39
George III, King of England, 117
Gerchikov, I.V., 13–16
Gerisch, A., 48
German Requiem, A, 115
Germany, 27, 46, 49, 67, 70, 73ff, 77, 81, 93–4, 96, 136f
   army, 111–13, 115, 120, 130, 133, 139
   Communism, 3–4
   Great War and, 114–18, 120, 126
   intelligentsia, 73–4, 128
   National Assembly, 137, 139–40, 143
   Revolution, 129, 137–42
   socialism, 3, 25, 45–6, 64–5, 80–1, 93–4, 114–19
   trade unions, 60–1, 74–6
   women's movement, 52–4, 105
   workers, (proletariat), 18, 58, 74, 108, 120, 124, 126, 134–5
Geyer & Co., 41
GKSD (*Garde-Kavallerie-Schützen-Division*), 6–9
Gleichheit, Die, (Equality), 46, 54, 86, 90, 105, 127
Głos (Voice), 28
Goethe, 83–4, 123
Golde-Strożecka, Estera, 24
Gonfalonieri, 122
Gorky, Maxim, 101, 122, 127
Gotha, 136

Graudenz (Grudziądz), 27
Guards Cavalry Rifle Division, *see* GKSD
Guesde, Jules, 62, 65
Guiding Principles, *see* Leitsätze
Guillaume-Schack, Countess Gertrud, 53
Guttman, Bronisława, *see* Marchlewska, B.

Haase, Hugo, 133, 136, 138, 142
Hagen, 105
'Hakatists', 49
Hamburg, 41, 49, 81, 120, 135
Hands off Rosa Luxemburg, 13
Hanecki, Jakub, 72, 77, 98–9
Hannover, 61
Haskalah (Enlightenment), 2
Hauptmann, Gerhard, 122, 125, 141
Hegel, G.W.F., 122
Heine, Konrad, 60
Heinrich, W., 26
Heldenleben, Ein, 115
Helfman, Hessia, 18, 24
Heligoland, 28
Helphand, Alexander, *see* 'Parvus'
Herero people, 112
Herne, 91
Hessen, 90
Hilferding, Rudolph, 87, 110
History of My Contemporary, The, 4, 127–8
Hitler, A., 9
Hobson, J.A., 36, 110
Hoffmann, J., 133
Hohenzollern, House of, 30, 64, 90, 117–18
Holland, 137
Huch, Ricarda, 122
Hué, Otto, 77
Hutten, Ulrich von, 25, 144
'Hutten's Confession', 125, 144
Huyssmans, Camille, 68
Hyndman, H.M., 34–5

Ihrer, Emma, 51, 53
Imperialism, 110
Independent Socialist Party of Germany, *see* USPD
India, 97
intelligentsia, 25, 29, 36, 42, 73–4, 127–8
International, First Socialist (International Workingmen's Association), 2
International, Second (Socialist and Workers'), 3, 22, 32, 35–7, 42–3, 46, 51, 54, 64–5, 66, 92, 96, 103,

171

111–12, 119f
Congresses of,
  Paris (1889), 22, 33, 54
  Zurich (1893), 35–8
  London (1896), 42–3
  Paris (1900), 51, 54
  Amsterdam (1904), 64–5
  Stuttgart (1907), 119, 130–1
Luxemburg, R. in, 69, 104
International, Third (Communist),
  11–13, 114, 120–1, 136
'International Communists', 135
'International Group', 116, 120, 126,
  133, 136
International Social Revolutionary
  Party *Proletariat, see Proletariat*
International Socialist Bureau, *see*
  ISB
'International Socialists', 135
Introduction to National Economy, An, 4,
  122
Ireland, 42, 49
ISB (International Socialist Bureau),
  51, 65, 68, 94, 104
Iskra (The Spark), 71–2
Italian Socialist Party, 11
Italy, 36, 57, 87
Izvolskaya, Irena, 23

Jacob, Mathilde, 126
Jacobins, 73, 132
Jankowska, Maria, 24, 33
Japan, 117
Jaurès, Jean, 4, 33, 63–5, 67, 106,
  125ff
Jena, 75–6, 94, 101, 111
Jeszcze Polska, 68–9
Jewish people, 2, 17–20, 22, 28–30,
  42, 57, 62, 96, 114, 119
Joan of Arc, 144
Jodko-Narkiewicz, Witold, 42
Jogiches, Leo (alias Grosovsky, Jan
  Tyszka, etc.), 3–4, 8–9, 28–35,
  40–5, 47, 50–1, 55–7, 61, 65,
  69–72, 77, 79–80, 82, 83–5, 87,
  92–3, 95–6, 98–104, 106, 126,
  129, 134, 138, 143
Jorns, Investigator, 8–10
Julie de l'Espinasse, 122
'July Days', 143
'Junius Brochure' (*The Crisis of Social
  Democracy*), 117–19, 121, 136
Junkers (Prussian landowners), 31, 49

Karski, *see* Marchlewski, Julian
Kasprzak, Marcin, 21–2, 27, 34, 37,
  41, 77, 100
Kautsky, Karl, 3, 22, 42, 46, 55, 58,

61, 64, 65, 68, 73, 76, 79, 85–6,
  89–90, 92–3, 95, 101–2, 104, 111,
  118, 132, 142
Kautsky, Luise (née Ronsperger), 1,
  4, 11, 22, 54, 79, 85–6, 90, 123–4
Kazan Cathedral demonstration, 31
Kerensky, A.F., 138, 143–4
Khrushchev, N.S., 15, 131
Kiel, 91, 137
Kiev, 18
Kołakowski, L., 109
Kollontai, Alexandra M. (née
  Domontovich), 16
Kopelzon, Lev, 29
Korolenko, V.G., 1, 4, 127–8
Koszutska, M. (alias Kostrzewa),
  12, 24
Kovalevsky, M.M., 89
Kowalik, T., 109
KPD (*Kommunistische Partei
  Deutschlands*), 3–4, 6, 11–12,
  140–4
KPRP (*Komunistyczna Partia Robotnicza
  Polski*), 13–14, 140
Kraków, 27
Kronstadt, 140
Kruszyńska, *see* R. Luxemburg
Kulturkampf, 49

Łada, Olympia, *see* Lübeck, O.
Landsberg, O., 138
Latin America, 97
Latvian Social Democrats, 80, 82
Ledebour, Georg, 112, 133, 136, 141
Leder, Zdzisław (alias, Feinstein,
  Władysław), 83, 98–9
Legien, Carl, 135
Leipziger Volkszeitung, 55, 58, 76, 94
Leitsätze (Guiding Principles), 116,
  120, 133
Lenin, V.I. (alias Ulyanov), 1, 4, 10,
  12, 13, 15, 19, 28–9, 39, 55, 69,
  71–2, 73–4, 79, 82–3, 86, 95,
  101–4, 110, 111, 120, 128–32,
  138, 140, 141, 143
Lessons of October, The, 13
Levi, Paul, 9, 10–12, 73, 112–14,
  128, 138, 141
liberals, Belgian, 66–8; British and
  French, 117; German, 81; Swiss, 26
Lichtheim, George, 61
Liebknecht, Karl, 3–4, 6–8, 11, 45,
  93, 95, 105–7, 115–17, 120, 121,
  124, 132–5, 137–44
Liebknecht, Sonja (née Ryss), 1, 106,
  122–4, 126
Liebknecht, Wilhelm, 25, 33, 48, 106,
  114

172

Limanowski, Bolesław, 4, 35
Lithuania, 28–30, 135
Lloyd George, David, 93
Łódż, 18, 27–8, 41, 89
Loewenstein, Lina see Luxenburg,
  Lina
Lokal-Anzeiger, 138
London, 33–5, 41, 42, 58, 73, 80, 82
Lübeck, Carl, 25
Lübeck, Gustav, 46, 83
Lübeck, Olympia (née Łada), 25, 46
Lud Polski (People of Poland), 21
Ludendorff, Gen. Erich, 137
Lunacharsky, A.V., 101
Luther, Martin, 94, 136
Luxemburg, Rosa (née Luxenburg,
  Rozalia; alias, Kruszyńska, Junius,
  etc.)
  Bebel, A. and, 55, 64–5, 69, 93–6,
    104, 118
  Bolshevism, views of, 72–3, 82–3,
    101–4, 128–32
  Diefenbach, H. and, 87, 123, 126
  Ebert, F. and, 101, 139–44
  economic theories of, 3–4, 35–6,
    38–40, 88–9, 109–11
  Engels, F. and, 3, 21, 24, 141
  'International Group' and, 116,
    120–1, 126, 136
  internationalism of, 3–4, 133, 144
  International Socialist Congresses
    and, 35–8, 42–3, 51, 64–6, 119,
    130–1
  ISB (International Socialist
    Bureau) and, 68, 104
  Jaurès, J. and, 63–5, 127
  Jogiches, L. and, 3–4, 26, 28–30,
    41–5, 56–7, 69–70, 83–4, 87,
    126, 138
  journalism of, 4, 41, 117, 132,
    138–9
  Kasprzak, M. and, 21–2, 27, 41,
    77
  Kautsky, K. and, 3, 55, 65, 76,
    85–6, 89–90, 92–3, 104, 118
  Kautsky, L. and, 1, 4, 85–6,
    123–4
  KPD (Communist Party of
    Germany) and, 3–4, 140–1
  Lenin, V.I. and, 4, 10, 12, 69,
    71–4, 82–3, 95, 102–4, 120,
    128–32, 139
  Levi, P. and, 11–12, 73, 112–14,
    128, 138, 141
  Liebknecht, K. and, 3, 95, 105–7,
    115–17, 121, 124, 133–5, 140–4
  Liebknecht, S. and, 1, 122–4, 126
  Marchlewskis, J. and B. and, 26–8

  Marx, K., view of, 3, 21, 24, 38,
    141
  Mehring, F., and, 3, 55, 64, 95,
    102, 116, 121
  Menshevism and, 12, 79–80, 95,
    98–9, 102–4
  Parvus (A. Helphand) and, 27, 84,
    103
  Plekhanov, G.V. and, 31, 79–82,
    104
  Polish patriotism and, 3, 20, 35–6,
    39–40, 42–3, 48, 50 ,57
  PPS (Polish Socialist Party) and,
    35–8, 42–3, 48, 51, 72, 82–3,
    97, 103, 114
  PPS ZP(PPS of Prussia) and,
    48–50
  Proletariat I and, 2, 20–1, 71
  Proletariat II and, 21–2
  Radek, K. and, 31, 95, 100–1
  RSDRP and, 71–2, 79–82, 102–3
  Russian Revolution (1905) and,
    77–9
  Russian Revolution (1917) and,
    126, 128–32
  SDKP and, 3, 35–6, 40
  SDKPiL and, 50–1, 69, 71–2, 77,
    79–80, 95–104
  'Spartacists' and, 26, 134, 139–44
  SPD and, 3, 48–62, 69, 75–7, 80,
    89–95, 101, 104–9, 111–13
  SPD Party School and, 87–8
  Sprawa Robotnicza and, 41
  Trotsky, L.D. and, 102–3
  USPD and, 136, 140 ,143
  Warskis (Warszawskis), A. and J.
    and, 26–8, 40–1
  Wojnarowska, C. and, 40, 50, 72
  women, views on, 4, 23–4, 51–2,
    54–5, 57, 66–7, 71, 86, 105
  writings of:
    Accumulation of Capital, The, 3,
      109–11, 121–2
    Anti-Criticism, 121–2
    'Celebration of May Day 1892 in
      Łódż,' 28, 41
    Crisis of Social Democracy, The,
      (alias 'Junius Brochure'),
      117–19, 121, 136
    Development of Industry in Poland,
      The, 40 ,43
    Introduction to National Economy,
      An, 4, 122
    Introduction to V.G. Korolenko,
      The History of My Contemporary,
      4, 127–8
    'Junius Brochure,' see The Crisis
      of Social Democracy

Leitsätze (Guiding Principles), 116–17, 120, 133
Letters, 38
Mass Strike, Party and Trade Unions, 81
National Question and Autonomy, The, 97
'Order Reigns in Berlin,' 143
Organisational Questions of Russian Social Democracy, 73, 128–9
Report (to the Third International Socialist Workers Congress in Zurich, 1893, on the Condition and Progress of the Social Democratic movement in Russian Poland 1889–1893), 35–7, 39–40
Russian Revolution, The, 73, 128–32
Social Reform or Revolution, 58–60
'Two Methods of Trade Union Policy,' 81
'What does the Spartacus League want?' 139
Works, 38
Zetkin, Clara and, 54–5, 76, 81, 84–5, 87, 90, 95, 102, 104–5, 139–40
Zetkin, Konstantin and, 83–6, 115
Luxenburg, Anna, 23, 85
Luxenburg, Edward, (Eljasz), 16–18, 23, 55–6
Luxenburg, Lina (née Loewenstein), 16–18, 23, 45, 56
Lwów, (L'vov, L'viv), 100

Machajski, Jan W., 100
Madariaga, Isabel de, 127
Magdeburg, 93
Main Currents of Marxism, 109
Maine, Sir Henry, 89
Małecki, A. (Rubinstein), 98–9
Mann, Thomas, 122
Manuilsky, D.Z., 12
'March Action' (1921), 11
Marchlewska, Bronisława (née Guttman), 26–8, 84
Marchlewska, Marta, 28
Marchlewski, Julian, (alias 'Karski'), 26–8, 35–7, 41, 46, 69, 72, 77, 84, 97–8, 130–1, 134
Maroggia, 45
'Marsh', 133, 135
Martov, Julius (Tsederbaum), 18, 71, 102
Martynov, A., 102
Marx, Karl, 1ff, 11, 19–20, 21, 24,

36–8, 58–9, 64f, 95, 98, 106, 109–10, 117, 122, 128, 141
Mary, Queen of Scots, 121
Maskalim, 17
mass (political) strikes
Belgian, 66–8; German, 75–6, 81; Prussian, 90–2; Russian, 73–4, 77, 79, 81
Matschke, Anna, *see* Luxemburg, R.
May Day, 35, 41, 81, 120
Mehring, Franz, 3, 55, 64, 95, 102, 116, 121, 134
Mendelson, Stanisław, 33–5, 37, 49, 71, 95, 100
Menshevism, 12, 18, 73, 79–81, 95, 98–9, 101–4
Meyer, Conrad F., 25, 125, 144
Meyer, E., 134
Michels, Robert, 107–8, 118
Mickiewicz, Adam, 2, 18
Mikhailovsky, N.K., 127
militarism, 103, 106–7, 111–13, 120
Mill, J.S., 128
Millerand, Alexandre, 63–5, 76
Mimi (Rosa Luxemburg's cat), 4, 86, 115, 123–4, 126
Minsk, 72
Molkenbuhr, Hermann, 94
Morgen, Lewis, 89
Morgenstern, Lina, 52
Mörike, E., 126
Morocco, 76, 93–4, 117–18
Moscow, 11, 18, 62, 79
Mozart, W.A., 20
Munich, 46, 69

Namibia, (formerly German South West Africa), 112
Narodnaia Volia, 71
National Democratic Party (of Poland: *Endecja*), 96
national question, the , *see* self-determination of nations
National Question and Autonomy, The, 97
National Trade Unions (of Poland), 96
Nazis, 10 ,25
Nechaev, S.G., 32
Negroes, 19
Nettl, John Peter, 15, 17, 21–2, 83–4, 99
Neue Zeit, Die (New Era), 3, 42, 46, 58, 63, 90
New Economic Policy (NEP), 13
Newton, Isaac, 64
New York, 51
Nicholas II, Tsar of Russia, 77
1905, 103

Noske, Gustav, 8, 60, 144
November Theses, 116–17
Nuremburg, 88

Obleute, see shop stewards
Odessa, 18
Okhrana (Russian political police), 29, 34, 96
'Opportunism,' 58, 66, 70, 74, 82
'Order Reigns in Berlin,' 143
organic incorporation, theory of, 36
Organisational Questions of Russian Social Democracy, 73–4, 128–9
Origins of the Family, Private Property and the State, 53
Orissa, 89
Ott, Herr, 8
Otto-Peters, Luise, 52
Our Differences, 31
Oxford University Press, 15

Pabst, Capt. W., 6–8, 30
pacifism in SPD, 120 ,132
Pannekoek, Anton, 87
Pardoner's Tale, 101
Paris, 17, 28, 34–5, 40–1, 43–4, 51, 56, 93, 102
Parti Socialiste de France, 64
Parti Socialiste Francqis, 64
Parvus (alias Helphand, Alexander), 27, 46, 58, 77, 84, 100, 103
patriarchy, 89, 107–8, 119
peasantry, 4, 31, 70–1, 80, 97–8, 129–30
pedagogy, 88
People's Naval Division, 140–1
Peretz, Isaac L., 18
'permanent revolution', 84
Perovskaya, Sofia, 24
Petit Sou, Le, 64
Petry, Captain, 6
Pfannkuch, Wilhelm, 48
Pflugk-Harttung, Captain H. von, 6–7, 9
Pieck, Wilhelm, 14–15
Pilate, Pontius, 30
Piłsudski, Bronisław, 28, 35
Piłsudski, Jósef, 14, 27, 28–9, 35, 37, 41, 42, 96, 130
Plekhanov, G.V., 2, 4, 29–33, 36–7, 42, 43, 55, 58, 64, 71, 77, 79–82, 104
Poland, 17, 29, 30, 39–40, 49–51, 68–71, 74, 95–104, 120, 137
Communism in, 13–15, 141
independence of, 12, 34, 36, 40, 42–3, 96, 135
Luxemburg, R. and, 16–22, 25–8,

39–41, 77–80, 119
nationalism of, 16–17, 20–1, 34–8, 42, 48–51, 68–9, 96, 109, 127–8
oppression of, 20, 25–6, 49–50, 57
revolts in, 16–17, 20–1
socialism in, 4, 20–2, 24, 33–8, 41–2
SPD and, 46, 49 ,60
Polish People's Party (of Germany), 49
Polish Socialist Party, *see* PPS
pogroms, 2, 18–19, 114
Poppe, Rifleman, 7
Populists, Russian, 28–9, 31, 43, 71
Positivism, 2, 18, 45
Potsdamer-Platz demonstration, 133–4
Poznań (Posen), 41, 49, 121
PPS (Polish Socialist Party), 33–7, 42–3, 48, 51, 70, 72, 76, 77, 80, 82–3, 97, 114
PPS-Left, 80, 96–7, 103, 120, 140
PPS-Revolutionary Fraction, 96
PPSD, 36, 48, 100
PPS ZP (PPS of Prussia), 49–50, 64
Prague, 99, 102
Prawda (Truth), 28
Preconditions for Socialism and the Task of Social Democracy, The, 58
proletariat (the industrial working class), 27, 32–3, 54, 64f, 68, 75, 79, 103, 105, 107, 108, 141–3
French, 64
German, 54, 74, 124–6, 128, 133–5, 138–9, 141–3
Polish, 27–8, 42, 48–9, 68–9, 74, 79, 98
Russian, 32, 74, 79
Proletariat I, 2, 20, 29, 71
Proletariat II, 21, 28, 33
Prussia, 16–17, 25, 27, 29, 30, 45, 46, 48, 49, 52, 78, 90–2, 106, 107, 117, 120, 133
Przedświt (Dawn), 33
Przegląd Socjaldemokratyczny (SD Review), 69
Pushkin, Alexander I., 127
Putamayo River (S. America), 19

Radek, Karl (Sobelsohn), 31, 95, 100–1, 112, 120, 140
radicalism (in SPD), 75–6, 86, 93, 95, 101, 104, 105, 135–6, 139–40
Rappoport, Charles, 64
Rat, Räte, see soviets
Ratyński, Kazimierz, 27, 40
Reichstag (German parliament), 45,

48–50, 53, 54, 64, 76, 80–1, 90–2, 94, 111–14, 118–19, 133–4, 137
Report (to the Third ISC Zurich 1893), 35, 37–8
Revisionism, 57–8, 60–1, 63–5, 76, 88, 92–3, 96, 101, 106
Revolutionary Commission, 141–3
Rhineland, 112
Riga, 35
Right, 30
Robinson, Joan, 111
Robotnik (The Worker), 37, 41
Roland-Holst van der Schalk, Henriette, 65–6
Romans, 116
Romanian, 126, 135
Rosa Luxemburg (film), 16
Rosenfeld, K., 115
Rostamowcy, see splitters
Rote Fahne, Die, (The Red Flag), 8, 138–9
Rousseau, J. J., 39
Równość (Equality), 33
Royal Prussian Library, 132
RSDRP, 71–3, 79–83, 99, 101–4, 129
Rückersfeldt, Augusta von (Marchlewska), 27
Rühle, Otto, 132–3
Ruhr, 49, 74
Runge, Otto, 6–10, 14, 144
Russell, Alys, 53
Russia, 2, 4, 16–25, 28–33, 43, 52, 54, 60, 67, 71–4, 96–7, 101–3, 106, 110, 120, 128, 137, 140
    Revolution of 1905, 10, 74–81, 86, 89, 100
    Revolution of 1917, 126, 128–32, 134
    War, Great, and, 114, 117, 133–5
Russian Revolution, The, 10, 12, 73, 128–32
Russification, 20, 27
Ryazanov, D. (Goldenblatt), 12, 29
Ryss, Sonja, *see* Liebknecht, Sonja
Rzewuski, E. von, 6–7

Sächsische Arbeiterzeitung, 76
SAG (Socialist Labour Association), 133, 135–6
Saint Mandé Programme, 63
St Petersburg (Petrograd/Leningrad), 17–18, 20, 31, 35, 74, 77, 80, 84, 103
San Salvatore, 45'
Saratov, 31
Saverne (Zabern), 112
Saxony (Sachsen), 46

Scheibler & Co, 41
Scheidemann, Philipp, 8, 93, 124, 135–9, 142, 144
Schiller, F. von, 2, 18, 121
Schlüsselburg Fortress, 20
Schoenlank, Bruno, 55, 58, 60
Scholze, P., 141
Schorrer, M., 144
sciences, natural,, 2, 4, 23, 26, 87, 122–3
SDKP (Social Democracy of the Kingdom of Poland), 3, 35–8, 40, 42–3, 50, 69
SDKPiL, (Social Democracy of the Kingdom of Poland and Lithuania), 50–1, 65, 69–74, 77, 80–3, 95–104, 120, 129, 140
Second Women's Gymnasium, Warsaw, 20
Ségur, P., Marquis de, 122
self-determination of nations, right of, 42–3, 71–2, 80, 97, 116, 119, 120, 129–31
Serbia, 117
SFIO (French Section of the Workers' International), 65
Shakespeare, W., 122
Shatrov, M., 15
Shaw, G.B., 122
shop stewards (*Obleute*), 134, 137, 140–1, 143
Siberia, 24, 45, 69, 130
Sielicki, W., 29
Silesia (Schlesien/Śląsk), 49–50, 56, 121
Singer, Paul, 48, 55
Skłodowska, Maria (Marie Curie), 51
Slavonic peoples, 97
Slutsky, A.G., 13
Sobelsohn, K., *see* Radek, K.
Social Democratic Party of Germany, *see* SPD
Social Democracy in Poland, *see* SDKP and SDKPiL
Social Democracy, Russian, *see* RSDRP
Social Democrats, Latvian, 80
Social Reform or Revolution, 58
Socialism and the Political Struggle, 31
Socialist Labour Association, *see* SAG
Socialist Party of Belgium, 66–8
sociology, 108
Sociology of Party Life in Modern Democracy, The, 107–8
South West Africa (Namibia), 112
Soviets, German, 137–9; Russian, 84, 103, 134
Spain, 93–4

Spartacist Group/League, 6, 11, 116,
126, 134, 136, 138–44
Spartakusbriefe, 132
SPD (Social Democratic Party of
Germany), 11, 28, 36, 43, 45–50,
57–61, 64–5, 77, 81–2, 86, 95,
100–1, 103, 106–7, 114–16,
118–21, 132–6, 137–44
'Anti-Socialist Laws' and, 25, 45,
70
Executive (*Vorstand*) of, 45, 48,
50–1, 64, 90–3, 101
government of, 8–9, 137–44
Luxemburg, R. in, 3, 48–62, 69,
75–7, 80, 89–95, 104–9,
111–13
Party School, Berlin, 85, 87–8, 91
Reichstag fraction of, 91–4, 111,
114–16, 119, 132–3
women and, 51–55, 66, 105
Spinoza, B., 20
'splitters' (*rostamowcy*), 99–101,
103–4, 120
spontaneity, revolutionary, 68, 73
Sprawa Robotnicza (The Workers'
Cause), 35–8, 41
Stalin, J.V. (Dzhugashvili), 13–15,
108, 129
Stock, Emmy, 54
Stockholm, 80
Stolypin, P.A., 101
Strauss, Richard, 115
Strożecki, Jan, 37
Stuttgart, 46, 54, 58, 60, 85, 93, 105,
112, 119, 130
Sukowa, Barbara, 16
Switzerland, 25–6, 36, 57, 76, 94, 97,
106, 115
Luxemburg, R., resides in, 22, 25,
43, 46
szlachta (Polish gentry), 2, 18, 21

Tagebuch, Das, (The Diary), 10
Tarquins, 116
Tashkent, 18
Tell, William, 25
Teutonic Knights, 49
Thalheimer, August, 12
Thiers, A.-L., 17
Tolstoy, L.N., 2, 20, 33, 122
trade unions, 76, 87, 88, 91, 93, 107,
134, 136, 140–1
British, 36, 61
German, 60–1, 74–5, 77, 81, 88,
91
Polish, 27–8, 96–7
Russian, 81
women and, 53–4, 105

Trotsky, L.D., 1, 13, 15, 20, 77, 84,
90, 100, 102–3, 108, 111, 129, 131,
141, 143
Trotta, Margarethe von, 16
Truck Acts, 53
Trusiewicz, Stanisław, 50, 69, 98–9
Tsederbaum, Alexander, 18
Tsederbaum, Julius, *see* Martov, J.
Turati, F., 36
Turin, 12, 16
Turkey, 97
Turner, J., 23
'Two Methods of Trade Union
Policy, The,' 81
Tych, Professor Feliks, 15
Tygodnik Powszechny (Universal Daily),
28
Tyszka, Jan, *see* Jogiches, L.

Ukraine, 128, 130, 135
Ulyanov, A.I., 28–9, 35
Ulyanov, V.I., *see* Lenin, V.I.
Union of Polish Socialists Abroad,
34–5, 37
Union of Polish Workers (ZRP),
27–8
Union for the Representation of the
Interests of Working Women, 53
United States of America, 52
'United States of Europe', 111
USPD (Independent Social
Democratic Party of Germany), 8,
136–9, 140–1, 143
USSR, 131

Vaillant, M.-E., 42, 64–5, 126
Vandervelde, Emile, 36, 66, 68
Vandervelde, Lalie, 67
Vertrauensmänner/personen, 70
Victoria, Queen of England, 28
Vienna, 48, 66
Vladivostok, 18
Vogel, Lt. K., 7–9
Volhynia, 128
Vollmar, Georg von, 60, 63, 70
Voltaire, F.-M.A. de, 122
Voronezh, Congress of, 31
Vorwärts (Forwards), 45–6, 74, 76–7,
90, 141, 144

Waldeck-Rousseau, R., 63–4
Walki Klas (Class Struggles), 33
War, Great, (1914–18), 3, 105, 107,
114, 117–120, 126, 134, 137, 144
War, Second World (1939–45), 107,
117, 130
War and Peace, 20
Warsaw, 2, 17–19, 20–1, 28, 34–5,

40–1, 51, 79–80, 83, 99, 103–4
Warski, A., *see* Warszwaski, Adolf
Warszawjanka, 68
Warszawska, Jadwiga (née
  Chrzanowska), 26–8, 40–1
Warszawski, Adolf, 14–15, 26–8, 35,
  40–1, 69, 72, 80, 98, 140
Waryński, Ludwik, 3, 20–2, 33–4,
  40, 71, 133
'Watergate', 62
Way to Power, The, 90
Weber, Max, 108, 119
Weber, Rifleman, 7
Wesełowski, Bronisław, 27, 40
Westminster Palace Hotel, 34
What does the Spartacus League want?,
  139
What is to be Done?, 73
What now?, 92
Whites, Russian, 130
Wilhelm II, German Emperor, 28,
  30–1, 91, 93–4, 111–12, 137
Wilna (Vil'no, Vilnius), 28–9, 35
Winter, August, 49
Wiślicki, Feliks, 26
Włocławek, 27
Wojnarowska, Cezaryna, 24, 40, 42,
  50–1, 66, 69, 72
Wolf, Prof. Julius, 26
Wolfstein, Rosi, 14
Woman, in the Past, Present and Future,
  53–4
Women, 2, 53, 57, 71, 77, 84
  Belgian, 66–8, 108

franchise for, 4, 25, 66–7
German, 46, 52–4, 76, 105
Luxemburg, R., on, 54–5, 86, 95,
  105
movements of, 16, 48, 51–5, 76,
  97, 105
Prussian, 45, 108
Russian and Polish, 23–5, 71, 119
Wrocław, *see* Breslau

Yugoslavia, 131

Zabern (Saverne), 112
Zakrzewska, Maria, 51
Zamość, 16–18
Zamoyski, Jan, 17
Zasulich, Vera, 31
Zemlia i Volia, 31
Zentrum, 49
Zetkin, Clara (née Eissner), 11, 12,
  46, 54–5, 66–7, 76, 81, 83–7, 95,
  102, 104–5, 116, 127, 131, 139–40
Zetkin, Konstantin ('Kostja'), 83–6,
  88, 95, 115, 123, 135
Zetkin, Maxim, 115
Zetkin, Ossip, 54
Zietz, Luise, 105
Zimmerwald Conference (1915), 133
Zionism, 2, 19
Zundel, F., 84–5
Zurich, 22, 25–9, 35–8, 40–1, 46,
  122
Żyrardów, 18

178